D1265047

CHILDREN IN
ENGLISH SOCIETY

STUDIES IN SOCIAL HISTORY

Editor

HAROLD PERKIN

Professor of Social History, University of Lancaster

Assistant Editor

ERIC J. EVANS

Lecturer in History, University of Lancaster

For a list of books in the series see back endpaper

CHILDREN IN ENGLISH SOCIETY VOLUME II

*From the Eighteenth Century
to the Children Act 1948*

by

Ivy Pinchbeck and Margaret Hewitt

LONDON: Routledge & Kegan Paul
TORONTO: University of Toronto Press

First published in 1973
in Great Britain by
Routledge & Kegan Paul Ltd
and in Canada and the United States of America by
University of Toronto Press
Toronto & Buffalo
Printed in Great Britain by
C. Tinling & Co Ltd, London & Prescot
© Ivy Pinchbeck and Margaret Hewitt 1973

RKP ISBN 0 7100 7580 4
UTP ISBN 0 8020 2103 4

Contents

Illustrations

XII

◇◇◇

Childhood without Rights
or Protection

◇◇◇

OF all the vast changes which have taken place in the last two centuries, in our mode of life and in our sense of values, not least is the change in attitude to children. Today there is general recognition of the fact that children are the most valuable asset of the State. Indeed it is claimed that 'the progress of a State may be measured by the extent to which it safeguards the rights of its children'. Today the rights of the child – to adequate food, clothing, medical care, to appropriate education and relevant training; protection against exploitation, cruelty and neglect, against exposure to any kind of moral or physical danger or unnecessary suffering of any kind – are recognised and safeguarded by statute. But for hundreds of years children lacked such statutory protection, and the resulting abuses to which children were submitted, both by parents and employers, only became a subject of serious concern and debate in the nineteenth and twentieth centuries. Even then, the struggle to make such protection legally effective was long and bitter, and required a revolution in contemporary attitudes to social responsibility; to family and parental responsibility; and in the understanding of human nature itself.

In the 1936 Halley Stuart Lecture, Sir Percy Alden argued that there could be no solution to the many problems connected with social and community welfare unless one began with the child: 'the child is the foundation of the State and the first line of defence. We cannot lay too much stress upon the importance of the child if the State is to endure.' Such a view, both familiar and acceptable to Tudor spokesmen, had become discounted by the eighteenth century. Its reacceptance in the twentieth is reflected in legislation, social policy, and in the numerous national and international conferences annually devoted to various aspects of child welfare.

Why were our forebears so slow to recognise the independent rights of the child? Even to begin to answer this question one needs to remember the profound differences in the quality and character of parent – child relationships in pre-industrial England. Since these have been extensively examined in the first volume of this study, it is not proposed to indulge in repetition here, but merely to draw attention to some of the more striking of the traditional attitudes of parents towards their children which necessarily affected contemporary attitudes to children's rights. Of course, the great majority of parents have always loved their children, but the interpretation of affection has varied from one generation to another. In the past, when life in general was rough and hard for all classes, little attempt was made to soften it for children. Children were expected to accept the hardships of life at a very tender age and, at the earliest opportunity, to accept the responsibilities of the adult. They were, indeed, looked upon as little adults and therein lies the essence of the explanation of much otherwise inexplicable to us today. Until modern times, children dressed as their parents and, like their parents', their dress reflected their social status. In industry the children of the poor worked the same long hours as their parents, hours which were matched by the eleven- or twelve-hour day spent at school by the children of more prosperous parents. The official whippings of the vagrant and delinquent child were matched by the 'belastings' of upper-class children both by their schoolmasters and their parents. Few protested. For parental cruelty of any kind the law provided no remedy until the nineteenth century. Children were legally the property of their parents and were used by them as personal or family assets. Thus among the poor, the labour of children was exploited; among the rich their marriages were contrived; all to the economic or social advantage of the parents. Attempts to raise the legal age of marriage in the early seventeenth century failed, since this would have involved interference with parental rights. Not until 1929 was the age of consent raised to sixteen. As the years passed, however, easier conditions and more humanitarian attitudes began to soften conditions of life for at least some children even though many parents – perhaps the majority – still clung to the harsh and stern discipline of earlier times. In the eighteenth century, these two contrasting, parental attitudes are perhaps most dramatically illustrated by reference to the upbringing of Charles James Fox and of John Wesley; the one so spoiled that he was reputed to have been allowed to enter his father's dining-room riding on a saddle of mutton, the other long fed only spoon meats as a child – lest he become too obstreperous. Indulgence and understanding do not, of course, always necessarily go together. The young Southey, pampered almost beyond even present day belief by an indulgent mother, was not allowed to go out of doors lest his beautiful clothes should get wet or dirty. Yet he was allowed to drink to inebriation – as children commonly were allowed to do until the beginning of this century.

The extraordinary equanimity with which our ancestors viewed the illness and early deaths of their children was almost inevitable, lacking as they did sufficient medical knowledge to understand, still less to cure, the diseases which ravaged successive generations of under- and ill-fed children and adults. For many years, because of the deficiencies both in the laws concerning the registration of births and deaths and in the machinery provided to ensure such registration, precise infant death-rates in the nineteenth century are impossible to calculate. It is, however, more than clear that thousands of infant lives were then lost which today could well be preserved. Sir James Kay-Shuttleworth wrote that: 'Owing in a great degree to neglect and mismanagement, half of the children born in 1831 died in five years. The chief part of this mortality occurred in the first two years.'[1] Some thirty years later, public attention was being drawn to the fact that: 'In England and Wales, it is shown by the returns of the Registrar General, that of 1,000 children born alive, 737 attain the age of 5 years'; whereas, 'from a life table . . . based on the living and dying in 1851, it was found that of

---

[1] *Four Periods of Public Education*, p. 121.

1,000 children born alive, only 522 attained the age of 5 years.'[1] The infant mortality rate was thus declining, but was still spectacularly higher than that of our own day. Moreover, in a society where, for as long as memory could recall, life had not merely been short, but for the majority nasty and brutish as well, that neglect – even downright cruelty – should excite little comment still less public intervention, may appal but should not surprise us today. The earlier part of this study traced the efforts of Henry Fielding in the mid-eighteenth century to help both 'the vast numbers of wretched boys, ragged as colts, abandoned, strangers to beds who were to be found in London, and the young girls, sold by their parents to brothel keepers in the same city'.[2] Unknown numbers of boys were being sold to chimney-sweepers as 'climbing boys' whilst other children were traded to beggars to help them excite the generous pity of passers-by. The law offered them little protection against abuse. In the account of a trial in 1761 we read that 'The Court of Hick's Hall lately committed Anne Martin, *alias* Chepbury, to Newgate, where she is to be imprisoned two years persuant to her sentence. She is accused of putting out the eyes of children with whom she went begging about the country.'[3] This trial, it should be noted, took place at a time when a man might be hanged for petty larceny, but a then lesser offence, such as putting out the eyes of young children, was only punished by two years' imprisonment. Had it been the eyes of her own children possibly no notice would have been taken of the matter, for parents commonly treated their unhappy offspring as they chose.

In some measure, indifference to what we should now see as cruelty to children sprang from ignorance: ignorance of the necessary conditions of infant and child welfare; ignorance of the consequences of maltreatment in youth on the physique and character of the grown man; ignorance, indeed, of whole areas of knowledge which today make life both physically and psychologically a good deal more tolerable. But in some measure also, it was an indifference positively sanctioned by some contem-

---

[1] Robert Baker, in *Parliamentary Papers* (*PP*), 1864, XXII, p. 699.
[2] Quoted G. S. Cadbury, *Young Offenders*, pp. 18–19. Cf. our vol. I, pp. 110–24 passim.
[3] R. Bayne-Powell, *The English Child in the Eighteenth Century*, p. 149.

porary religious views, not least those of Wesley, who revived the belief of early Calvinism that all children were by nature evil and that, while they had none but natural evil to guide them, pious and prudent parents must check their naughty passions in any way they had in their power. Wesley himself would not suffer any of the children of the school at Kingswood to play any games, saying that a child who played when he was young would also play when he was a man. Extreme Calvinist views on the nature of the child, revived by Wesley, and inherited by nineteenth-century Evangelicals, all contributed to the repression of children of parents influenced by this religious tradition. Thus 'much that was harmless was forbidden, and much that was pleasant, frowned upon'.[1] This stern religious attitude found expression both in sermon and in story. Mrs Sherwood, author of *The History of the Fairchild Family*, described an ordinary, well-to-do, early nineteenth-century family in her pages. Mr Fairchild, with his pious quotations, prayers and sermons, beating his children and taking them, as a warning, to see the body of a murderer hanging in chains, is held up to her readers for admiration, not horrified condemnation. In real life, Mr Fairchild was to have his counterpart in Mr Brontë who burnt his children's coloured shoes rather than have them wear such vanities, though the alternative was to let them come in from a long walk with wet feet and have no shoes into which they could change. Charlotte Brontë's recollection of her own schooldays, which she portrays in *Jane Eyre*, is perhaps the perfect commentary on the mingled piety and cruelty shown towards many children in her own time.

The harshness of the parent was paralleled by the harshness of the State. The apparent cruelty of the law in the eighteenth century today fills us with horror. On none did it press so hard as on the child who, according to law and custom, was held to be adult, if above the age of seven, and therefore responsible for his crimes. Up to 1780, the penalty for over two hundred offences was death by hanging, and many a child, like the little girl of seven hanged in the market place at Norwich for stealing a petticoat, was hanged for a trivial offence which in our own day would normally entail a probation order. Children were amongst those publicly hanged after the Gordon Riots. 'I never saw boys

[1] ibid., p. 9.

cry so much', commented George Selwyn, who witnessed the execution of some of these miserable children. There are, in fact, instances recorded of children younger than seven being executed, as, for example, the pitiable case of a child of six who cried for his mother on the scaffold.[1] On one day alone, in February 1814, at the Old Bailey Sessions, five children were condemned to death; Fowler, aged twelve, and Wolfe, aged twelve, for burglary in a dwelling; Morris, aged eight, Solomons, aged nine, and Burrell, aged eleven, for burglary and stealing a pair of shoes. Cases such as these were to prompt Peter Bedford, a Spitalfields Quaker, to form a society 'for investigating the causes of the alarming increase of juvenile delinquency in the Metropolis'.

Meanwhile, however, the courts not only continued to hang children but, alternatively, transported them overseas if convicted of crimes then considered 'serious'. Extracts from the Registers of Stafford Prison illustrate the sort of 'crimes' which led to transportation. In 1834 and the following year, the records show 'William Biglen: Age 14, for stealing one silk handkerchief – sentenced to transportation for seven years . . . Matilda Seymour: Age 10, for stealing one shawl and one petticoat – sentenced to transportation for seven years . . . Thomas Bell: Age 11, for stealing two silk handkerchiefs – also sentenced to transportation for seven years'.[2] Transportation as a method of dealing with the juvenile delinquent had been authorised by Act of Parliament in 1718 and used intermittently ever since, sometimes for very young offenders indeed. In the course of a Parliamentary enquiry into the state of Newgate Prison, in 1814, one of the witnesses stated that he had an order for the 'removal of fifty-two who are under sentence of transportation, many of whom are seven or eight years old, one nine years old, and others not above twelve or thirteen . . . They are for transportation but they go to the hulks in the first instance.'[3] The hulks – old ships lying in the Thames, the Medway, at Portsmouth – had been pressed into service as overflows for the prisons after the American Wars of Independence. The peace had brought in its train unemployment and so large an increase

[1] ibid., p. 143.
[2] Cadbury, op. cit., pp. 38–9.
[3] ibid., p. 36.

in crime that the ordinary prisons were unable to house the many convicted. John Howard writes of the hulk at Gosport: 'Here were several to be transported for life and some whose sentences were for a short term; among them were boys of only ten years of age.'[1] As the hulks too became more and more over-crowded, conditions in them deteriorated and eventually, 'of all places of confinement that British history records, they were apparently the most brutalising, the most demoralising, and the most horrible. The death-rate was appallingly high, even for the prisons of the period.' Of the state of contemporary prisons Howard had himself written in 1776: 'I make no scruple to affirm that if it were the wish and aim of magistrates to effect the destruction present and future of young delinquents, they could not devise a more effectual method than to confine them so long in our prisons.'[2] Men, women and children were herded together, half-naked, half-starving in prisons stinking and disease-ridden owing to the complete lack of any sanitary arrangements in many of them, and infected each other both morally and physically. These conditions, and the consequent demoralisation and deprivation of the children subjected to them, continued into the nineteenth century, alleviated some-what by sanitary reforms and, here and there, by the attempts of voluntary societies to establish experimental industrial schools for young delinquents as a substitute for imprison-ment.

The organisation and methods of these industrial schools will be fully discussed later, but it is worth noticing that they con-tinued a tradition established in the previous century of volun-tary effort to shelter the young delinquent from the full rigours of contemporary English justice. In their emphasis on work and the necessity for young people to support themselves, they are also a particular indication that child labour, a characteristic feature of domestic industry, still continued as an accepted and acceptable ideal of the industrialist phase of English social development. In French's *Life of Crompton*, the inventor of the mule, we are given the following description of his childhood in the mid-eighteenth century.[3]

[1] ibid., p. 35.
[2] ibid., p. 21.
[3] op. cit., pp. 56–7.

I recollect that soon after I was able to walk I was employed in the cotton manufacture. My mother used to bat the cotton wool in a wire riddle. It was then put into a deep brown mug with a strong ley of soap and suds. My mother then tucked up my petticoat about my waist and put me into the tub to tread upon the cotton at the bottom. When a second riddleful was batted I was lifted out, it was placed in the mug and I again trod it down. This process was continued till the mug became so full that I could no longer safely stand in it, when a chair was placed beside it and I held on by the back . . .

When, due to later inventions, the textile industry moved from the home to the factory, the children went with it. Small children of only three or four years of age were employed to pick up cotton waste, creeping under unguarded machines where bigger people could not go. The older children worked for fifteen hours a day, and on night work too, under conditions which were often enforced by fear and brutality.

Worse even than the lives of children in the cotton factories were the lives of children employed until well into the nineteenth century in the mines of Staffordshire, Lancashire and the West Riding. The First Report of the Commission on the Employment of Children and Young Persons in Mines, presented to Parliament in 1842, described the children as being wholly in the power of their 'butties'. Employed down the mines for twelve hours a day, they worked as trappers, opening and shutting the doors which controlled the ventilation of the mine, filling the skips and carriages with the coal, and pushing or drawing the trucks along the coal-face to the foot of the shaft. The children who suffered most were those from the workhouses: 'these lads are made to go where other men will not let their children go. If they will not do it, they are taken to the magistrates who commit them to prison.' An eight-year-old girl, Sarah Gooder, in the West Riding described her day: 'I'm a trapper in the Gauber Pit, I have to trap without a light, and I'm scared. I go at four and sometimes half-past three in the morning and come out at five and half past. I never go to sleep. Sometimes I sing when I've light, but not in the dark: I dare not sing then.' Girls who drew the trucks along in the West Riding mines were vividly depicted by the Commissioners.[1]

[1] *PP*, 1842, XVII, p. 75

The immediate result of revelations such as these was the pro-hibition of the employment of children under ten in the mines.

Similar restrictions on the employment of very young children in the cotton mills had already been imposed and were to be extended and further strengthened by legislation. Nevertheless, it was still necessary, in 1866, to press for further legislation to protect children in various industries, not least from exploitation by their parents:[1]

> more especially would such legislation be a protection and benefit to the great numbers of very young children who in many branches of manufacture are kept at protracted and injurious labour in small, crowded, dirty and ill-ventilated places of work by their parents. It is unhappily to a painful degree apparent . . . that amongst no persons do the children of both sexes need so much protection as against their parents.

The combined indifference both of parents and of the com-munity to the suffering and exploitation of children, bred of long familiarity with both, was one of the greatest obstacles to be overcome by those seeking to establish their legal right to pro-tection. Of all those involved in the struggles of the nineteenth century to restrict the hours and improve the conditions of work of young children employed in factories and mines, Lord Shaftes-bury without doubt was the most successful and is the most affectionately remembered today. He was also anxious to assist another group of children whose conditions of work were no less in need of legislative control and had been so long before factory employment for children had become common. These children were the 'climbing boys' or chimney-sweeps of whom, in 1863, Charles Kingsley was to write in *The Water Babies*. Long before then, however, Jonas Hanway had protested against the employment of young boys and girls to sweep chimneys which, even in 1773, could equally well have been cleaned by 'machin-ery'. It was Hanway who publicised the accidents which occurred every year of children, overcome by fumes, being suffocated in the chimney flues: who described how the inevitable bleeding knees and elbows acquired in the course of their travels up and down the chimneys were treated with salt brine, to harden the raw flesh. Hanway it was who also tried to jolt the public

---

[1] Quoted R. Fletcher, *The Family and Marriage in Britain*, pp. 86–7.

conscience by retelling the 'reluctance' of the boys to make their first ventures into the sooty labyrinth, a reluctance which was soon overcome by their masters covering their heads and shoulders with 'stripes and bruises', and by the lighting of fires in the grates beneath the children, to force them to climb out of the smoke and away from the leaping flames. In his own day, Hanway's was a lone and ineffective protest, and indeed it was more than a hundred years before the employment of climbing boys was prohibited. In 1873 Lord Shaftesbury was producing the same sort of evidence, but to rather more effect, since in 1875 the use of boys for sweeping chimneys was prohibited by Act of Parliament. That it should have taken more than a hundred years to protect these children from the abuse of avaricious parents and masters is some indication of the complacency with which our forebears viewed the exploitation of children.

Although Hanway's had been a lone voice in 1773, during the next hundred years Commission after Commission, reporting on the appalling facts regarding the employment of the chimney-sweeps, had given them publicity on a scale impossible to Hanway. Indeed, law after law had been passed, purporting to alleviate the worst abuses of the children, but no serious attempt had been made to put the law into effect. In the 1860s, the employment of climbing boys was actually increasing although it was well known that it could have been entirely stopped by making it compulsory to put trapdoors on the sides of flues to enable the chimney to be cleaned by brushes inserted from outside. Partly because these might have had to be made in bedrooms or in other visible places, and partly because of activities of the more unscrupulous masters, who scattered soot on the furniture and claimed that the new 'machines' made more dirt in the client's house than their climbing boys, nothing was done. 'Never have I seen such a display of selfishness, frigidity to every human instinct, such ready and happy self delusion,'[1] Shaftesbury once declared in the course of a debate on a Bill to protect the factory child: it was a sentiment that could just as easily have applied to the plight of the chimney-sweeps.

The degree to which such self-delusion was possible in the

[1] Quoted S. Lynd, *English Children*, p. 40.

eighteenth and nineteenth centuries emerges from contemporary literature. Blake, for example, wrote a well-known and moving poem about a chimney-sweep:[1]

When my mother died I was very young
And my father sold me while yet my tongue
Could scarcely cry "'weep!, 'weep!, 'weep!'
So your chimneys I sweep, and in soot I sleep.

There's little Tom Dacre, who cried when his head,
That curled like a lamb's back, was shav'd; so I said
'Hush Tom! never mind it, for when your head's bare
You know that the soot cannot spoil your white hair.'

. . .

And so Tom awoke; and we rose in the dark,
And got with our bags and our brushes to work.
Though the morning was cold, Tom was happy and warm;
So if all do their duty they need fear no harm.

For Blake, the chimney-sweep's salvation lay in resignation, not legislative reform. To similar effect, a generation later, Charles Lamb wrote sentimentally of 'those almost clergy imps, who sport their cloth without assumption; and from their little pulpits, the tops of chimneys, in the nipping air of a December morning, preach a lesson of patience to mankind'.[2]

A good deal of this sort of complacency regarding the exploitation of children sprang from the notion, supported by religious sanctions, that in society there was a place for everyone, and everyone should remain in his place. Hence the knowledge that for some that place could be unpleasant was merely confirmation that they belonged to the lesser and lower orders of creation. But it was also linked with contemporary views of parental responsibility to which the governing classes clung tenaciously and which inhibited them from restricting the rights of parents by legislating against exploitation, cruelty and corruption of which they were well aware. In the minds of many – including Lord Shaftesbury himself – to undermine parental responsibility was to undermine family stability and thus the stability of society

---

[1] Cf. ibid, p. 37.
[2] 'The Praise of Chimney-Sweeps', *Essays of Elia*, Macmillan, 1931, p. 153.

itself. Hence Shaftesbury, though anxious that children should be safeguarded from the exploitation of the factory owners, was opposed to any proposals for the compulsory education of children. Although this would have been the most effective safeguard against the economic exploitation of young children, he argued that such proposals were a direct infringement of the right of a parent to bring up his child as he saw fit and could only encourage a dependence on the State instead of a robust development of the virtues of personal initiative and responsibility. This widely held philosophy made it appear perfectly reasonable to our forebears that, in 1830, Parliament should vote £30,000 to voluntary societies labouring to educate the children of the masses, and more than twice that sum (£70,000) towards the building of the Royal stables. That the stability of the family should be preserved at all costs was a recurring theme even amongst those most directly concerned for the welfare of the poorer classes in the nineteenth century. The Charity Organisation Society, one of the most active and effective welfare agencies of the later nineteenth century, strenuously opposed the introduction of school meals for the hopelessly undernourished children of the poor on the grounds that 'it is better, in the interests of the community, to allow in such cases [of children inadequately fed by their parents] the sins of the parents to be visited on the children than to impair the principle of the solidarity of the family and run the risk of permanently demoralising large numbers of the population by the offer of free meals to their children.'[1] The background of the Infant Life Protection Movement, discussed later, illustrates to what extremes this line of reasoning was sometimes taken. By the early 1860s, it had become quite clear that there was a direct association between the employment from home of mothers of children under one year old and a high local infant mortality rate.[2]

It scarcely needs to observe [wrote John Simon, Medical Officer of the Privy Council] that against this state of things there is no resource in any present provision of the law. At the root of this evil is an influence with which the English Law has never professed to

[1] Quoted E. Cohen, *English Social Services*, p. 20.
[2] Fourth Report of the Medical Officer of the Privy Council, *PP*, 1862, XXII, p. 111.

deal. Domestic obligation is outbidden in the labour market; and the poor factory woman, who meant only to sell that honest industry of hers, gradually finds that she has sold almost everything which other women understand as happiness.

It was significant that until late in the century only a minority even of the most enthusiastic reformers in this particular field called for legislative action. The current notion of the family as a unit whose peculiar sanctity should not be invaded by the State in any guise restrained all the rest from associating themselves with this radical group.[1]

> I desire to place it on record [proclaimed Whately Cooke Taylor in 1874], that I would far rather see even a higher rate of infant mortality prevailing than has ever yet been proved against the factory districts or elsewhere . . . than intrude one iota farther on the sanctity of the domestic hearth and the decent seclusion of private life . . . That unit, the family, is the unit upon which a constitutional Government has been raised which is the admiration and envy of mankind. Hitherto, whatever the laws have touched, they have not invaded this sacred precinct . . .

Of course, as Cooke Taylor well knew, it was not entirely correct to imply that the State had never made any attempt to interfere with 'the sanctity' of family life. From the time of the Tudors the Poor Laws, in conjunction with apprenticeship regulations, had operated at a primitive level to prevent the poor child from starving. Moreover, the operation of forced apprenticeship and the rigorous interpretation of the laws of settlement had resulted in many a child of poor parents being separated from home and family. Nevertheless it was certainly true that the State had largely refrained from interposing in the life and organisation of the many families who were able to support themselves and their children. Traditionally both the legal and the social structure of the family in England expressed the principle of paternal domination which religious sanctions had long supported. To propose that the State should restrict the exercise of parental authority was thus not merely to propose a restriction of parental rights which had long been established

---

[1] 'What influence has the Employment of Mothers . . . on Infant Mortality?', *Transactions of the National Association for the Promotion of Social Science*, 1874, pp. 574–5.

at law, but to propose a modification of a family pattern which had been held to be the will of God. Together, traditional interpretations of the significance of both the laws of man and the laws of God for the maintenance of social order proved powerful obstacles in the path of those who wished to legislate for the independent rights of the child.

In the early nineteenth century, however, there was some slight indication that views on these matters were beginning to change when, in 1814, legislation was introduced to prevent child stealing by making it an indictable offence in English law for the first time. In the course of his speech moving for leave to bring a Bill to punish the crime of child stealing, Mr W. Smith observed to the House of Commons[1] that

> it was singular that this offence, though there was none of greater enormity, was not at all punished by the existing law, unless in those cases where the person stealing a child could be convicted of stealing its clothes. It was surely a great blot on the statute book [Mr Smith continued] that a man might steal a child with impunity, though he could not, without punishment, take the shoes from that child. And . . . so far was the system carried, that the judge, in cases of this kind, if any doubt was entertained as to the person accused intending merely to steal the child, and not the clothes (that is, intending to commit the greater and not the lesser offence), that then they must acquit him.

According to Mr Smith, there were at this time three principal reasons why children were in fact stolen: for the value of their clothes; so that they could be brought up as the children of another; to be sold, some to beggars to excite charity in the observer, and some to unscrupulous employers in the less attractive trades in which children were employed – such as chimney-sweeping and prostitution. Under the existing law, only those against whom it could be proved that they had stolen a child for its clothes could be punished. Supporting the introduction of the Bill, Mr Serjeant Onslow asserted that: 'With respect to the directions given by the judges to acquit culprits of this description, they had merely done it in strict conformity with the letter of the law; at the same time that they did violence to their feelings – and deeply lamented the defective state of the

[1] Hansard, 3rd series, 1814, vol. XXVII, col. 929.

criminal code.'[1] In the event, child stealing was in fact made a felony and subject to all the penalties of grand larceny, the effect of which was to offer the protection of the State within this limited sphere to the child whose parent either would not or could not protect him himself. The ways and means by which statutory protection was extended to the child in England in many other spheres will be the major preoccupation of this second half of our study. Since this extension necessarily involved a re-interpretation of the rights of parents over their children, it will be worth while to examine contemporary understanding and legal definition of these rights in some detail.

[1] ibid., col. 931.

XIII

⟡⟡⟡⟡⟡⟡⟡⟡⟡⟡⟡⟡⟡⟡⟡⟡⟡⟡⟡⟡⟡⟡⟡⟡⟡⟡⟡⟡⟡⟡⟡⟡⟡⟡⟡⟡⟡⟡⟡

The Rights and Duties
of Parents

⟡⟡⟡⟡⟡⟡⟡⟡⟡⟡⟡⟡⟡⟡⟡⟡⟡⟡⟡⟡⟡⟡⟡⟡⟡⟡⟡⟡⟡⟡⟡⟡⟡⟡⟡⟡⟡⟡⟡

'CHILDREN are of two sorts,' wrote Blackstone in the mid-eighteenth century, 'legitimate and spurious or bastards; each of them we shall consider in their order; and first of legitimate children'.[1] We too shall begin by considering the rights of the lawfully wedded over their legitimate offspring; leaving the detailed consideration of the rights and responsibilities of the parents of illegitimate children to a later chapter. Blackstone also wrote that 'in marriage, husband and wife are one person, and that person is the husband.'[2] It is with this understanding of the nature of marriage itself, and of the relative authority of husband and wife, father and mother, that we must turn to the character of parental rights in the nineteenth century.

In the early nineteenth century, a father's rights over the custody of his children were paramount. At common law, a mother had no rights over her children during the lifetime of the father, nor was her position necessarily improved by his death, since, by a statute of Charles II, a father had the right to appoint a testamentary guardian who, at the father's death, took priority over the mother, who had no right to interfere with his powers. Even in deeds of legal separation, if the father voluntarily gave up his rights to his children, the courts held that such deeds were void in so far as they deprived the father of his

---

[1] *Commentaries on the Laws of England*, 5th ed., Oxford, 1765, p. 446.
[2] ibid., p. 442.

powers over his children, or provided that the mother should have possession of them in exclusion of him. Indeed, the rights of the father as against the mother were so absolute that the courts did not in fact have the power to grant a right of access to her children to a mother whose husband had not granted it himself.

The children were, at common law, in much worse position than the mother. Parents were under a moral duty to support and educate them; they might be held guilty of manslaughter if they allowed their children to starve or perish for lack of proper medical attention. But in practice, this was a very imperfect obligation, since there was no power of enforcing these duties except through the Poor Law, which laid down the duties of parents and grandparents to maintain poor children, and allowed that overseers might take action if a child were left to the charge of the parish. Similarly, the Poor Laws gave the overseers the right to apprentice poor children, so that they might learn some trade by which to support themselves. But 'the rich', as Blackstone says, 'are left at their own option, whether they will breed up their children to be ornaments or disgraces to their family'. Thus, in effect, children had little right against their parents at common law either as to maintenance or to education, or, indeed, to protection against cruel treatment from their parents.

Only for one group of children, the Wards of Court or Wards in Chancery, did the law attempt to intervene between parent and child. This very restricted group were the beneficiaries of the rise of equitable jurisdiction in this country and of the development of the Court of Chancery's wide jurisdiction over minors who were heirs to property, a jurisdiction which the court alone exercised on behalf of the Crown as *Parens Patriae* – the protector of those unable to protect themselves. Gradually, the Court of Chancery had acquired powers to enquire into the way in which any parent or guardian of such children was fulfilling his trust. Hence it became possible for children to be made Wards of Court or Wards in Chancery, as a result of which paternal rights in certain exceptional circumstances might be restricted, and the court itself acquired the power to supervise their education, religious instruction and marriage. In contrast to common law, at which the father's rights were paramount, the Court of Chancery proceeded on the principle that its primary consideration was the benefit of the child; hence the several grounds on which, if petitioned, the court could and would deprive the father of the custody of his child to which otherwise, *prima facie*, he was entitled. But it is important to remember not merely that, for the Court of Chancery to be petitioned on behalf of a child, some question as to the use and management of his property had to be in issue but, more importantly, the father's right was never, in theory, completely abrogated. This object was attained by appointing some other person to act as guardian. Until the later modification in the laws of guardianship in the nineteenth century, which we shall examine in some detail, no court in England ever regarded itself as entitled entirely to extinguish a father's right to custody. Moreover, the principle of 'benefit of child' was much more narrowly interpreted than it would be today, and whenever this principle came into direct conflict with the 'sacred right of the father over his own children', the Court of Chancery came down heavily on the side of the father. For example *in re Fynn*, a Chancery case of 1848, the Lord Chancellor stated that, had he been able to act in a private capacity for the benefit of the infants in the case: 'I should have no doubt whatever upon the question of interfering with the father's power. Without any hesitation I should do so.' As it was, the Lord Chancellor was not at liberty to act as if he was out of court and the court must be satisfied 'that the father has so conducted himself . . . as to render it not merely better for the children but essential to their safety or to their welfare, in some very serious and important respect, that his *rights* should be treated as lost or suspended, should be superseded or interfered with'.[1]

In actual fact, therefore, the court would only intervene and deprive a father of the custody of his child in very extreme circumstances. They would intervene, for example, where a father was openly profligate and adulterous, where his behaviour might contaminate or corrupt the morals of his child; or where the child was likely to be inculcated with irreligious or atheistic beliefs which both law and society regarded as immoral, and dangerous; or where a father had deserted or refused to support the child.

One occasion when the court actually did deprive a father of

[1] R. H. Graveson and F. R. Crane, *A Century of Family Law*, p. 64.

the custody of his children was when, in 1827, Lord Chancellor Eldon declined to restore the Wellesley children to their father who had issued a writ of *habeas corpus* for their possession against the maternal aunts with whom they were living. The children had come into the care of their aunts on the death of their mother who had left Wellesley and applied for a divorce on the grounds of his illicit association with a Mrs Bligh. Enjoined by Mrs Wellesley, shortly before her death, to resist any attempt on the part of her husband to regain custody of the children, the aunts sought the protection of the Court of Chancery. As an illustration of contemporary attitudes to sexual irregularities the Lord Chancellor's judgment makes interesting reading:

> Now, I own I never will let that girl go into the custody of Mr. Wellesley, so long as he has any connection with Mrs. Bligh . . . Under the existing conditions, is it proper that the girl should be placed under the care of Mr. Wellesley, while he has any connection with this woman, Mrs. Bligh? Certainly not . . . Under the circumstances I can never suffer the daughter to go under the care and custody of Mr. Wellesley, so long as there is any connection between him and a woman so abandoned as Mrs. Bligh appears to be. I cannot consent to separate the boys from the daughter, and, upon this point, I have the authority of Mr. Wellesley himself to say that that is a thing which ought not to be done. When I look at the whole conduct of Mr. Wellesley towards Mrs. Bligh, towards his children, and with reference to other points, which show the tenor and bent of his mind upon certain subjects, and the nature of his sentiments, I say that, if the House of Lords think proper to restore those children to Mr. Wellesley, let them do so; it shall not be done by my act.

After which resounding condemnation of Mr Wellesley's moral character, His Lordship was nevertheless moved to add: 'Into whatsoever hands these children may fall, it will be their duty to consult the interest and happiness of the children, by allowing filial affection and duty towards their father to operate to the utmost.'[1]

Ten years earlier, the Lord Chancellor had refused to restore the poet Shelley's children to him on the grounds that he was a declared atheist and 'he had written and published a work in

[1] Quoted G. Abbott, *The State and the Child*, vol. I, pp. 26–7.

which he blasphemously denied the truth of Christian revelation, and denied the existence of God as Creator of the universe'.[1] The belief, long established in English tradition, that sound child-training was fundamentally associated with sound religious principles, found expression in the Lord Chancellor's judgment. Pronouncing an order restraining the father and his agents from taking possession of the person of his children or 'intermedelling' with them till further order the Lord Chancellor observed:[2]

> This is a case, as the matter appears to me, in which the father's principles cannot be misunderstood, in which his conduct, which I cannot but consider as highly immoral, has been established in proof, and established as the effect of those principles: conduct nevertheless, which he represents to himself and others, not as conduct to be considered as immoral, but to be recommended and observed in practice, and as worthy of approbation.
>
> I consider this, therefore, as a case in which a father has demonstrated that he must and does deem it to be a matter of duty which his principles impose upon him, to recommend to those whose opinions and habits he may take upon himself to form, that conduct in some of the most important relations of life, as moral and virtuous which the law calls upon me to consider as immoral and vicious – conduct which the law animadverts upon as inconsistent with the duties of persons in such relations of life, and which it considers as injuriously affecting both the interests of such persons and those of the community. I cannot therefore think that I should be justified in delivering over the children for their education exclusively, to what is called the care to which Mr. S[helley] wishes it to be intrusted . . .
>
> I add that the attention which I have been called upon to give to the consideration, how far the pecuniary interests of these children may be affected, has not been called in vain. But to such interests I cannot sacrifice what I deem to be interests of greater value and higher importance.

In 1758, according to Blackstone, 'the power of the parent over the child is derived from . . . their duty; this authority being given them partly to enable the parent the more effectively to perform his duty, and partly as a recompense for his care and trouble in the faithful discharge of it.' These duties, three in all, he characterised as the duty of maintenance, a principle of natural law, since they had brought the children

[1] ibid., pp. 13–14.
[2] ibid., p. 14.

into the world; the duty of protection, also a natural duty, but rather permitted than enjoined by law; and the duty of providing an education suitable to the child's station in life, a duty pointed out by reason and of by far the greatest importance.[1] In his elaboration of these duties, however, Blackstone himself noted that existing legislation was defective in securing their fulfilment. Maintenance was only statutorily enforced on the poorer sections of the community (by the Poor Law); the only legislative provision for the education of children in England was contained in the Poor Law and the laws relating to the apprenticeship of poor children; and the only general statutory restriction on the rights of parents to educate their children related to their instruction in religion.

In 1827, Lord Chancellor Eldon drew attention to the practical difficulty of enforcing the duties of the father:[2]

The law makes the father the guardian of his children by nature and by nurture. An Act of Parliament has given the father the power of appointing a testamentary guardian for them; one would think that the guardian so appointed must have all the authority that Parliament could give him; and his authority is, perhaps, as strong as any authority that any law could give . . .

The important consideration is – is it necessary that the Court should thus interpose? If the Court has not the power to interpose, what is the provision of law that is made for the children? You may go to the Court of King's Bench for a *habeas corpus* to restore the child to its father; but when you have restored the child to its father, can you go to the Court of King's Bench to compel that father to subscribe even to the amount of five shillings a year for the maintenance of that child? A magistrate may compel a trifling allowance, but I do not believe there was ever a *mandamus* from the Court of King's Bench upon such a subject. Wherever the power of the law rests with respect to the protection of children, it is clear that it ought to exist somewhere: if it be not in this Court, where does it exist? Is it an eligible thing that children of all ranks should be placed in this situation – that they shall be in the custody of the father; although, looking at the *quantum* of allowance which the law can compel the father to provide for them, they may be in a state little better than starvation? The courts of law can enforce the rights of the father, but they are not equal to enforcing the duties of the father . . .

[1] op. cit., pp. 449–51.
[2] Abbott, op. cit., p. 22.

The fundamental reason why the courts were not equal to the task was that it had never been thought necessary to provide the essential condition which would have made such action possible, namely the reciprocal, legal rights of children. Children had never been of much account in England. All too many died before they reached maturity. Those who survived were hurried early into the ranks of adult society. Useful, in so far as they could be exploited; valued, perhaps, where their marriage might add to family fortune; but not the focus of attention when the family was thought more important than the individual, and when the urgent business of maintaining and advancing family fortune absorbed the energies and interests of adults.

Prompted by the circumstances of a particular case before the Court of Chancery, Lord Eldon's opinion reflected a growing concern in the early nineteenth century that, even where a court had considerable inherent powers in the matter of the guardianship of at least one group of children, powers which that court was increasingly disposed to use to modify the rights of the father in the interests of the welfare of the child, the contemporary laws of domestic relations operated in such a way as seriously to restrict the effectiveness of the court's jurisdiction. Nevertheless, the publicity given to cases involving the welfare of children, not least those heard in the Court of Chancery, where paternal rights were superseded and the children became Wards of the Court, was itself an effective contribution to the awakening of the public conscience on the question of the legal abuse by parents, which the law at that time had little or no power to remedy effectively. With this recognition of abuse came the necessity for considering radical changes in the laws of domestic relations themselves, so as to curtail the rights of the father, enlarge those of the mother, and make both subservient to the welfare of the child. But this was only fully achieved in the twentieth century, by granting all children both legal rights and legal status. The mental climate of the early nineteenth century inhibited any very sweeping changes in the law; hence such changes as there were came in the characteristic manner of English reform – by the gradual development of statute law to remedy the deficiencies of common law. But the ultimate result of this piecemeal legislation was a new structure of domestic relations. The principle developed in the Court of Chancery, that the welfare of the child should be the first and paramount consideration, has been extended by statute so that this is now the guiding principle of all modern legislation dealing with children and is constantly applied by the courts where 'the welfare of the child' has a far wider connotation than was the case in the time of Lord Eldon. The father's absolute right over his children has, since 1925, been replaced by the equal rights of both parents with respect to 'guardianship and rights and responsibilities conferred thereby', the law now subordinating both to the welfare of the child. Various statutes of the nineteenth and twentieth centuries have established the legal rights of the child to maintenance, education, and protection against cruelty and neglect and have given the court powers to deprive irresponsible parents of their rights over their children and to transfer those rights to the community.

The first statutory attempt to limit the exclusive powers of the father in the interest of the child was the Infants Custody Act of 1839,[1] Serjeant Talfourd's Act, which conferred on the Court of Chancery an absolute discretionary power with regard to the custody of a young child of up to seven years of age on the application of the mother. Contrary to much popular opinion, the irretrievable breakdown of marriage is no new phenomenon. In early nineteenth-century England, the effect of war on society was probably proportionately as great as in our own time. The notorious moral laxity of the Regency period resulted in the frequent breakdown of marriage, with the consequent and inevitable dispute between the separating parents as to the custody of their children. In innumerable cases, hardship to both mothers and children resulted from the enforcement of the absolute legal rights of the father. Mothers separated from their husbands on grounds of persistent adultery and cruelty were frequently deprived of their children, often denied access to them, sometimes even unable to discover their whereabouts, whilst the children themselves might be handed over to the care of complete strangers or to the father's mistress. Even in a society long accustomed to accept and uphold the primacy of the father's rights in his family and not over-

[1] 2 & 3 Vict., c. 54.

scrupulous concerning the happiness and welfare of its individual members, some of these cases aroused a good deal of public indignation and criticism in the early nineteenth century. In the case of *Rex* v. *de Manneville* in 1804, the wife and mother had been forced to leave her husband and had taken her eight-month-old baby with her. Although it was still being breast-fed, de Manneville forcibly removed the child from its mother's new home, with the result that she took proceedings first in the Court of King's Bench and subsequently in Chancery for the recovery of her baby; not least so that she could continue to feed it herself. In both courts the judges upheld the father's right to custody and the mother's deprivation of her child. Twenty years later, another case which gave cause for equal scandal, was the Skinner case, where the wife had separated from her husband on grounds of his extreme cruelty, and had taken her six-year-old child with her. Skinner recovered the child by fraud and when later confined to a debtors' prison, he left it in the care of his mistress, who subsequently went to live with him in prison, together with the child. But on the application of the mother, although the father was in gaol, the Court of King's Bench declined to interfere with the legal rights of the father. Yet a third case was that concerned with the custody of the McLellan children. Here, on the separation of the parents, the father had placed his daughter in a boarding-school, where she was taken ill. Her mother, anxious for the welfare of her one remaining daughter, the other having already died, removed her, whereupon McLellan applied to the High Court for restoration of custody. In giving judgment, the judge expressed his opinion that because the child was ill she should be in the care of her mother but, because the law was as it was, he had no option but to order that the girl be returned to the custody of her father. Another case which prompted perhaps even wider expression of public concern regarding the existing laws of domestic relations was the Greenhill case of 1836, in which the Court of King's Bench ordered Mrs Greenhill to hand over three small daughters, all under six years of age, to their father. Greenhill, who had committed every conceivable cruelty towards his wife and children, wished to hand the children over to the care of his mistress on the grounds that 'the legal custody is that of the father'. On her refusal to comply with the court's order, Mrs Greenhill was sentenced to imprisonment for contempt of court.[1]

These and similar cases which received great publicity at the time, not least because of the high rank of some of the parents involved, aroused widespread indignation and demands for changes in the law. The judges had no option but to administer the existing law, but as we have already seen in Lord Eldon's comments in a case in Chancery, they themselves are not always convinced that the existing laws were adequate. In 1839, Lord Durham, one of the High Court judges before whom the Greenhill case was heard, speaking in a House of Lords debate on a Bill which proposed to modify the law, declared: 'I believe there was not one judge who did not feel ashamed of the state of the law, and that it was such as to render it odious in the eyes of the country.'[2] Referring to a case in which he could find no legal ground on which he could deprive the father of the custody of his child, the Lord Chancellor of England had already stated twelve years earlier that: 'If any [alternative] could be found, I would most gladly adopt it; for, in a moral point of view, I know of no act more harsh or cruel than depriving the mother of proper intercourse with her child.'[3]

The Bill, in the debate on which Lord Durham had intervened, was an attempt to provide the judges with such an alternative. It had been introduced into the Commons by Mr Serjeant Talfourd who had himself twice successfully acted as counsel for husbands, one of them Greenhill, resisting the applications of wives, but to the violation of his own conscience. Hence his determination to attempt to reform the existing law which gave all control over children to their father, 'exclusive of the wife, whatever might have been his misconduct, or whatever might have been the claim of the innocent mother'. A law, he pointed out, as Lord Eldon had done before him, that could uphold the father's rights, but which had no power to compel him to perform his duty.

Serjeant Talfourd's campaign within Parliament was greatly assisted by the impassioned campaign outside it by Caroline Norton, a well-known society hostess and a close friend of Lord

---

[1] Cf. Graveson and Crane, op. cit., pp. 55–7.
[2] ibid., p. 57.
[3] ibid.

Melbourne. At the age of nineteen, Caroline had married the Honourable Richard Norton, and became at once one of the most successful hostesses of fashionable London. Her marriage, however, did not prove an equal success and, together with her three young children, she left her husband. Soon after, in the absence of his wife, Mr Norton seized the children and refused to allow her access to them. Only then did Mrs Norton realise her position in law – that she had absolutely no rights in her children and might never see them again until they were of age, unless her husband so decreed. Once, she contrived to meet them as they walked in St James's Park, in retaliation for which her husband promptly sent them to Scotland where for a long time she was unable to trace them. Long negotiations followed an attempt to secure Norton's agreement to allowing his wife access to her children, all to no avail. Sir John Bayley, Norton's legal adviser, was later to affirm[1] that he

> found Mrs. Norton anxious only on one point, and nearly heart broken about it, namely, the restoration of her children. She treated her pecuniary affairs as a matter of perfect indifference, and left me to arrange them with Mr. Norton as I thought fit. I found her husband, on the other hand, anxious only about the pecuniary part of the arrangement, and so obviously making the love of the mother for her offspring a means of barter and bargain that I wrote to him to say that I could be no part to any arrangement which made money the price of Mrs. Norton's fair and honourable access to her children.

Mrs Norton herself wrote:[2]

> What I suffered respecting those children, God Knows and He only. What I endured and lived past – of pain, exasperation, helplessness and despair . . . I shall not even try to explain. I believe men have no more notion of what that anguish is than the blind have of colours . . . I REALLY lost my young children – craved for them, struggled for them, was barred from them – and came too late to see one that that died . . . except in his coffin.

Desperate, Mrs Norton determined on the last, indeed the only way left open to her: she determined on a public campaign for the reform of the law. Even today, such a project would be

[1] Ray Strachey, *The Cause*, p. 36.
[2] ibid., p. 39.

no small matter; in Caroline Norton's day, since as a married woman she had no legal personality independent of her husband, it was a formidable undertaking. Fortunately, she had three major advantages. She was already known in her own right as a successful journalist and author. She had an established position in society, thus her passionately worded pamphlets readily found their way into influential circles where they were read and understood, even if the views they contained were not always readily accepted. Two of the most famous of the many pamphlets she wrote and printed for private circulation were *The Natural Claim of a Mother to the Custody of her Child as Affected by the Common Law Rights of the Father and Illustrated by Cases of Peculiar Hardship*, (1837) and *Separation of the Mother and Child by the Law of Custody of Infants Considered*, published in the same year. Her third, and very substantial, advantage was that she found a Parliamentary champion in Mr Serjeant Talfourd, who himself had already resolved to introduce an Infant Custody Bill before ever he met Mrs Norton.

In 1838 Serjeant Talfourd made his first attempt to introduce reforming legislation in the House of Commons. In his draft Bill he intended to allow any mother, whether guilty or innocent in a case of separation, to demand access to, but not custody of, her children. This particular provision was deleted on opposition, and the amended Bill then passed in the Commons, only to be thrown out by the Lords, where Lord Brougham criticised it adversely on grounds of administrative difficulty. Talfourd then introduced a second Bill, the following year, emphasising certain changes in its provisions which, he argued, 'assures the House that no charge of immorality is possible since if the mother is proved to be the adulterous partner, she would not be able in any circumstances to have the control of the child.'[1] The provisions of the Bill were in fact very cautious indeed. It proposed that, at the discretion of the court, a judge in Equity might make an order allowing mothers against whom adultery was not proved to have the custody of their children under seven, with right of access to their older children at stated times. Where the court chose to rule in favour of the mother, the effect, Talfourd argued, would be that of 'simply putting the mother

[1] Hansard, 3rd series, 1839, vol. XLVIII, col. 549.

of legitimate children in the same situation as a mother of bastard children was placed'.

The passions roused by what must seem today to be the most timid attempt to recognise at law the claims inherent in the natural relationship of mother and child, and the arguments advanced both in the debates in Parliament and in pamphlets circulated outside, are an interesting reflection of the state of contemporary public opinion on the proper structure of family relationships in the 1830s. *A Brief Exposure of the Most Immoral and Dangerous Tendency of a Bill affecting the Rights of Parents now under Consideration of Parliament, or, Summary of Reasons why this Bill, entitled 'Custody of Infants Bill', should not be allowed to become the Law of the Land,* written in 1838, urged that the Bill must inevitably undermine the institution of marriage itself, claiming that the children of a marriage were often the chief factor in maintaining its stability. The main argument against the Bill was therefore that 'it tends directly to favour separations between husband and wife', an argument, it should be observed, which clearly depended on assent to the view that children might properly be regarded as pawns in parental disputes. 'Now,' the pamphlet continued, 'it is notorious that one of the strongest hindrances in all cases . . . to prevent wives from lightly separating from their husbands, is the knowledge that they will thereby lose their maternal rights. This at all times has been a safeguard to preserve the institution of marriage, most important and indispensable.' Only as a subsidiary argument were its possible harmful effects on the children themselves introduced: 'It is true that it is by no means certain that wives who live with their husbands do fulfil all their duties to their children; but it is quite certain that those who are living apart from them do not and cannot fulfil *any* of them.' Moreover, the pamphlet asserted, separation of husband and wife 'tends to demoralise the children and destroy their education'.

The necessity of sacrificing the rights of the mother on the altar of the family was re-echoed time and again in the Commons debate on the Bill. Sir Edward Sugden, for example, declared that[1]

the objection he had to the clauses rested upon principle. He

---

[1] ibid., col. 159.

believed the operation of the Bill, if passed in its present shape, would reduce the obligations of marriage, and would thereby prove detrimental to the best interests of marriage of married women and their offspring . . . The law of England wisely was that the right of the custody of the children was vested in the father and that law was consonant with the laws of a higher authority. Why then should the legislature interfere? There might be, and he would not deny it, numerous cases in which the law operated with hardship upon mothers, but the legislature was bound to look to the welfare of married women as a class, and not to have regard to individual cases . . . though the evils of the present system were to a certain extent pressing, still these evils would be better corrected by the tone and morals of society, than by any law that could be devised.

Others ostensibly opposed the Bill on the grounds that it took too little care of the true interests of the child. On closer inspection, however, their real concern was to uphold the stability of marriage. Thus Mr Langdale thought that[1]

the greatest misfortune that could befall any woman was to be separated from her husband . . . Opposed as he was to the principle of divorce altogether, he could not become a party to any legislative measure for separating man and wife. The greatest evil of all was the condition in which poor children were placed, who were innocent parties. The primary object of a Bill of this sort ought to be the care of the children whom the parents were separated from. Now, the present Bill did not make a proper provision of this nature. Seven years was not a sufficiently long time for the mother to have care of her children, particularly if they were females. It would be much better to leave them with the father altogether, than place them under the mother's care for so short a time.

Those in favour of the Bill argued on the grounds of injustice to the mother, under the existing law. Since the law already allowed mothers of bastards to retain the possession of their children, *a fortiori*, must the law also allow the care of legitimate children to be vested in the mother. In the event, it was this argument which won the day in the House of Commons, and the Bill was sent on to the House of Lords, where again it came under heavy criticism. Lord Wynford, supporting an earlier speech by the Lord Chancellor, averred that,[2]

[1] ibid, col. 161.
[2] Hansard, 3rd series, 1839, vol. XLIX, col. 492.

His noble and learned friend had truly said that the custody of the children belonged by law to the father. That was a wise law, for the father was responsible for the rearing of the child; but when unhappy differences separated the father and mother, to give the custody to the father, and to allow access to it by the mother, was to injure the child, for it was natural to expect that the mother would not instil into the child any respect for the husband who she might hate or despise. The effects of such a system would be most mischievous to the child, and would prevent its being properly brought up.

The best that can be said of such an argument is that it appears to stem from a regard for the welfare of the child, even if its welfare might seem to require the inculcation of respect for an entirely worthless father.

Be this as it may, the Bill was eventually carried in both Houses, and became the law of the land in 1839. It could be said that the Act was not so much concerned with the welfare of the child as with the punishment of the mother proved 'guilty' in separation or divorce proceedings. It might be added that it was, by twentieth-century standards, a timid and hesitant measure. But in 1839, the Custody of Infants Act constituted an immense and startling innovation: the absolute right of the father was now subject to the discretionary power of the judge. It is important to notice, however, that although Talfourd had argued that his Bill 'placed the mother of legitimate children in the same situation as a mother of bastard children', this was in fact not the case. Whereas the mother of illegitimate children, irrespective of her character and behaviour, had absolute right in her children, the 'guilty' married mother was even denied any right of petition. Under the Act the practice of the courts was to decide if possible in favour of paternal right rather than against it, and to exercise discretion against the mother even as to young children. Nevertheless, despite its limitations, this piece of legislation has a special importance since it was the first statutory intervention in the common law rights of a father in this country. It was also the first of a series of nineteenth- and twentieth-century Acts of Parliament which gradually improved the rights of the mother as to the guardianship of her legitimate offspring until, in the twentieth century, the principle of equal guardianship was conceded in the Equal Rights of Guardianship Act of 1925.

Subsequent nineteenth-century modifications in the law of matrimonial causes were to exert a considerable influence on the way in which, in the future, the courts would uphold the rights of the mother as regards her children. The Matrimonial Causes Act of 1857 gave the Divorce Court very large discretionary powers as to the custody, maintenance and education of children involved in divorce or separation proceedings. For example, the courts might place such children under the protection of the Court of Chancery, a power which constituted a further curtailment of a father's rights, and which substantially prepared the way for the Custody of Infants Act of 1873. This extended the rights of the mother in a number of ways. First, the Court of Chancery was empowered to allow a mother access, custody or control of her children up to sixteen, as compared to seven years of age. Second, the Act removed the bar to any petition for access to, or custody of, her children by any mother against whom adultery had been established. Third, the Act legalised agreements between parents in deeds of separation which gave custody of the children to the mother 'except where the Court might deem it contrary to the benefit of the child to enforce it'. In support of this last, and substantial, proposal to modify the existing law, Mr Fowler urged in the House of Commons that:[1]

> At present, unless it can be shown that the husband has been guilty of such misconduct as would induce the Court to deprive him of the custody of his children where there is no agreement, the Court will refuse to enforce any agreement that would have that effect – nothing short of actual injury to the children, moral or physical, will induce the Court to deprive him of his right – and this was done in the 'interest of public policy'. The Bill before the House, however, would put an end to this cruel injustice, and the Court would enforce the agreement 'unless it should deem it contrary to the interests of the children to do so'.

In the Lords, Lord Chelmsford reinforced the necessity for this amending legislation to allow the courts more readily to act in the interests of the child rather than the maintenance of paternal rights. Referring to current practice, he claimed:[2]

---

[1] Hansard, 3rd series, 1873, CCXIV, col. 884.
[2] Hansard, 3rd series, 1873, vol. CCXV, col. 41.

The position of a wife separated from her husband was rendered even more distressing in consequence of the manner in which the Court dealt with separation deeds ... This deed might contain a certain clause giving the children to the mother; but if so, the deed was not in the slightest degree binding, because if the husband did not choose to be bound by it, and refused to give her the children, and if she appealed to the Court of Chancery for its interpretation, the Court must refuse its aid on the ground that it was contrary to public policy for the husband to relinquish his duty – the care and management of his children ... No cruelty to the wife, and no adultery, except it were committed in the home of the children, would induce the Court of Chancery to enforce a separation deed of that kind.

Within a very few years, however, the Act of 1873 was demonstrated as capable of such interpretation as to allow the court to restore the children to the father, despite a legal deed of separation giving custody to the mother. The *cause célèbre* which made this very clear was the legal dispute between Mrs Besant and her husband, the Rev. Frank Besant, a Church of England clergyman, which took place in 1879. It was a case very similar to that of the poet Shelley, whom the Court of Chancery deprived of his right of custody on the specific grounds of his publicly professed atheistical and immoral principles. In Mrs Besant's case, there was no doubt that a deed of separation between herself and her husband, in which it had been agreed that she should have the custody of their daughter, had been properly executed. Subsequently, however, she had both published an atheistical book and delivered atheistical lectures. Further, she had also written and published *Fruits of Philosophy*, which a jury had found to be calculated to deprave public morals, as well as other similar books which the Court of Appeal considered 'disgusting to decent English men and women, a violation of morality, decency and womanly propriety'. In ruling that the daughter be restored to the custody of her father, the court noted first the atheistical beliefs of Mrs Besant which, it held, was sufficient ground for removing the child from her mother's care, otherwise she would not be brought up in her father's beliefs, which he had a right to demand. Second, the court maintained that it was its clear duty to the ward to prevent her from being exposed to the risk of being brought up 'in

378

opposition to the views of mankind generally as to what is moral, decent, womanly and proper'. Thus, notwithstanding the separation deed, custody was restored to the father. Even today, in a far more secularised society, the pros and cons of this particular decision might well be challenged. In the moral climate of the 1870s the outcome was well-nigh inevitable. Nevertheless, it was not universally agreed, even then, that the courts should in practice generally uphold the father's rights of custody to the exclusion of the mother's. Hence the renewed activity in the 1880s to further amend the laws of England relating to the custody of the children.

In 1884, introducing what transpired to be an unsuccessful attempt at reform, Mr Bryce advanced three arguments in support of his Private Member's Infants Bill:

The law had remained on the same footing since 1873, subject to the extensive and beneficial provisions of the Act of 1857 (the Matrimonial Causes Act) – the Act which established the Court of Divorce and Matrimonial Causes. That Act gave a very large discretion indeed to that Court, on providing for the custody of children whenever it pronounced a decree, and he did not propose in the Bill to interfere in any way with its jurisdiction, since it did not seem to him to require amendment or enlargement. But even after the passing of the Acts of 1837 and 1873, there still remained very serious hardships in the law. It still failed to recognise the claims of mothers, and in constantly preferring the father, often produced injury to the child. In the first place, the mother, under the construction which the Courts had placed upon the Act of 1873, was usually excluded from the custody of her child, except where such grave misconduct could be made out against the father as might affect the child injuriously. Secondly, a guardian appointed by the father was the guardian of the child to the exclusion of the mother, and there was no provision for making the mother the guardian of her child on the death of the father. Even if the father had omitted to appoint a guardian, the mother did not hold that position, and the father could, out of spite, appoint a guardian who was hostile to the mother, although he might have neglected the child and she be wholly without blame. Thirdly, she could not appoint a guardian to take care of her child after her death even when no guardian had been appointed by the father.

Mr Bryce then continued that he 'need not remind the House of the hardships which had occurred under this law, in which grave injustice and much mental suffering had been inflicted on mothers. Even judges had remarked upon it as being partial and cruel, when mothers had appealed to them, whom they found themselves unable to help.'[1]

A particularly interesting feature of Mr Bryce's speech was that he regarded the reforms he proposed as a natural – perhaps even an inevitable – corollary of the Married Women's Property Act which had secured to married women, for the first time, the right of legal ownership of at least some portion of their own earnings and of property directly willed to them. At least in this respect the rights of married women in England had already been significantly extended.

Very wide interest was taken in this Bill largely because of the radical changes proposed and also because of a press campaign, on the whole favourable to the suggested reform, which stimulated discussion and educated opinion, and contributed to the growing public debate, started forty years earlier by the Norton case, on the status and role of the married woman, both in her home and in society.

On 5 March 1884, a contributor to the *Scotsman* supported Mr Bryce's Bill on the grounds of the indefensible anomalies of the existing laws relating to the custody of infants. He referred in particular to the curious and unsatisfactory situation which had arisen after the Matrimonial Causes Act of 1878, which had allowed justices discretionary powers to award custody to women in certain circumstances, but had failed to allow the Lord Ordinary similar powers of discretion:

> It is a somewhat remarkable thing, to find a Judge acknowledging, as the Lord Ordinary acknowledged last week, that 'it is with some regret' that he administers the law of the land. To the woman who had been subjected to sufficient cruelty to entitle her to claim a decree of separation, who had been beaten by her husband and refused admittance to the house, and who stood by while the child was handed over to the man who had ill-used her, it must have been a profound consolation to hear that the Judge who made the order which deprived her of her child did so 'with some regret'. Translating this euphemism into extra judicial language, we shall not be far wrong if we read, 'The Court is, unhappily, aware that it is doing injustices; but, as the law stands, it is powerless to do otherwise'.

[1] Hansard, 3rd series, 1884, vol. CCLXXXVI, col. 813.

On 29 March, reporting on the progress of the Bill through the Commons, the Parliamentary Correspondent of the *Sussex Daily News* commented tartly on the nature of the opposition to it:

> Mr. Bryce's Infants Bill has been read in record time by a large majority, in spite of the protests of some lawyers who are strongly opposed to change of any kind in legal procedure and of Mr. Warton, who denounced the Bill as impious. All that Mr. Bryce proposes is that mothers shall have greater control than they have at present over the guardianship of their children ... The whole course of legislation in these matters is directed to increase the powers and privileges of married women. This is very terrible to Mr. Warton, who solemnly informed the House that it was laid down in Holy Scripture as the law of God, that the husband should be supreme over the wife. Mr. Warton further announced that the best wives always acknowledged the supremacy of their husbands. So for a wife to have a will of her own where her children or her property are concerned is a sign of depravity. There was a time, no doubt, when this idea was accepted as a Divine Institution; but civilisation has made some progress since then, though Mr. Warton is still stranded among the fossils.

So much for Thomas Becon!

The following day the *Weekly Despatch* carried a less astringent, though no less pertinent, article on the need for such a Bill:

> With the large majority of people, the promoters of a Bill like that of Mr. Bryce's find their principal difficulty in explaining how bad the existing law is. A just-minded man finds it very hard to believe that in a free country and in the nineteenth century a widowed mother may be robbed of her young children, even if they are babes in arms, by some stranger appointed guardian by her late husband against her desire or by her late husband's distant relative whom she has never seen before ...

Although this particular Bill failed, a second Bill, introduced by the Attorney General, eventually passed both Houses in 1886. Once more in the course of debate there was apparent growing sensitivity to the contemporary discussions of the rights of women and of the legal claims of married women. Thus the Lord Chancellor, Lord Herschell, said that he

> would not argue on the justice of such a measure, except to say that, in a matter in which many of the women of this country took the

deepest interest, a Parliament of men returned entirely by men electors should take care that no injustice was done to women. Even if they introduced a modification of the franchise, men would still form the vast majority of the electorate, and so long as they had the power in their hands they were bound to try to look at the question as women looked at it.

Lord Ashbourne, however, took exception to at least one of the Bill's clauses since, as it stood,[1]

it would be quite competent when the father and the mother were living together for the mother, having different views from her husband as to how the children should be brought up, to ask the opinion of the Court whether she or her husband was right. That was a very dangerous power to give the wife, and might lead to litigation, confusion and unhappiness in families. It was a great change in English domestic life.

In this last Lord Ashbourne was certainly correct and, despite opposition, when the Bill was finally passed in 1886[2] it did in fact incorporate three very radical provisions. First, it provided that, on the death of the father, the mother, if she survived him, should be the guardian of her children either alone, when no guardian had been appointed by the father, or jointly with any guardian appointed by him. Thus the widowed mother could no longer be legally robbed of her young children. Second, the mother was given power, by will or deed, to appoint guardians for her children after the death of herself and their father. Third, and most important of all, on application of the mother of any child, the court might make such an order as it might think fit regarding the custody of the child and the right of access to it of either parent, 'having regard to the welfare of the child' – the principle operating in the Court of Chancery – and the conduct of the parents, and to the wishes of the mother as well as of the father. Thus at last the courts in England were given full jurisdiction to override completely the old common law rights of the father in relation to the custody of his infant children. No longer had the judges to regard the father's rights as paramount because they were powerless to do otherwise. They could now give the mother 'guilty' of misconduct the

[1] Hansard, 3rd series, 1886, vol. CCCVI, col. 3.
[2] 49 & 50 Vict., c. 27.

custody of her children if they thought it was in the interest of the children so to do.

For the further protection of the interests of the children, the High Court was also given discretionary powers to remove any guardian appointed under the Act and, if it thought fit, to appoint another.

Far-reaching though these changes were, however, they fell short of recognising the legal equality of parents as regards their rights of guardianship over their children. The shifts in public opinion regarding the status of women in English society, partly a response to the 'Women's Movement' and partly a consequence of the profound social upheaval of the First World War, were ultimately to find expression in a re-statement of the laws of guardianship in which this particular principle was embodied. The Guardianship of Infants Act, 1925,[1] repealed and re-enacted the provisions of the 1886 Act and, in addition, gave statutory force to the principle of the equal right of parents to guardianship, making the welfare of the child the paramount consideration in cases where guardianship had to be awarded to one parent alone. 'Whereas Parliament, by the Sex Disqualification (Removal) Act, 1919, and various enactments has sought to establish equality in law between the sexes,' runs the preamble to the Act, 'it is expedient that this principle should obtain with respect to the guardianship of infants and the rights and responsibilities conferred thereby'. The principle was given statutory force in Sections I and II of the Act itself,

> Where in any proceeding before any court . . . the custody or upbringing of an infant . . . is in question, the court, in deciding that question, shall regard the welfare of the infant as the first and paramount consideration, and shall not take into consideration whether from any other point of view the claim of the father, or any right at common law possessed by the father, in the fact of such upbringing . . . is superior to that of the mother, or the claim of the mother is superior to that of the father . . . The mother of an infant shall have the powers to apply to the court in respect of any matter affecting the infant as are possessed by the father.

Two important amendments to the 1886 Act were made by

[1] 9 & 10 Geo. V, c. 71.

the new legislation. First, subject to certain restrictions, jurisdiction concerning guardianship was extended to courts of summary jurisdiction, instead of being limited to the High Court. Poorer parents were thus enabled to seek the aid of the law in matters of guardianship, and the principle of the welfare of the child in the adjudication of cases of dispute was now made relevant to all children in English society, instead of being effectively limited to the rich and propertied. Second, fathers and mothers were put on the same footing as regards power to appoint guardians after the death of either parent, and such guardians were to act jointly with the surviving parent.

By this and preceding statutes, the father's common law rights were so diminished that, by statutory law, the Administration of Justice Act of 1928 definitely conferred on the father the right to apply for the custody of a child, thereby maintaining the balance between the rights of the parents. It nevertheless remains a fact that English courts will not interfere with the rights of a father in the exercise of his parental authority except where he forfeits these rights by gross moral turpitude. It is also important to note that these various Guardianship of Infants Acts did not apply to illegitimate children of whom the mother remained the sole legal guardian.

By any standards the achievements of the nineteenth century in the reform and development of guardianship rights had been considerable both for what was immediately achieved and for what was made ultimately possible. There were, in addition, numbers of other statutes which also bore on the custody of infants, some concerned with the consequences of breakdown of marriage, such as the Matrimonial Causes Act, 1878, and the Summary Jurisdiction (Separation and Maintenance) Act, 1895.[1] Here, the law gave magistrates discretionary powers regarding the maintenance and the custody of children, and power to deprive the father of the custody of his children if by neglect or cruelty he had forced his wife to live apart from him or if he had been committed for aggravated assault.

Nevertheless, although the new laws of domestic relations had clearly defined the rights of parents, as yet the duties of parents towards the real welfare of their children were left undefined. The experiences of the numerous voluntary and

---

[1] 41 & 42 Vict., c. 19; 58 & 59 Vict., c. 39.

philanthropic societies which sprang up during the second half of the nineteenth century showed all too clearly how many children were in fact still neglected and maltreated by irresponsible and malicious parents. Their annual reports, drawing attention to the fact that many parents conspicuously failed in their duties, helped develop a new social conscience both as to the role and the duties of parents and the rights of children themselves. This resulted in further legislation to confer rights on the child as against his parents, thus giving him an independent status.

Prominent amongst such legislation were the Prevention of Cruelty Act, 1889,[1] and also the so-called Poor Law Adoption Act[2] of the same year, which deprived the irresponsible of their parental rights, and transferred them to the overseers to ensure the children's welfare. A third Act was the Custody of Children Act, 1891.[3] This last refused to allow parents who had earlier abandoned and neglected their children to reclaim them later, when they were old enough to earn money, from the workhouse, the foster parents, the religious or charitable organisation under whose supervision they had actually been brought up. Arguing in support of this in the House of Lords, Lord Thring maintained that: 'It gives the poorer child the same protection given by the Court of Chancery to wealthier children who have property bestowed upon them',[4] the necessity for which had been brought home to him by the revelations of General Booth's recently published *Darkest England*. It would, he pointed out, especially apply to waifs and strays and deserted children found in workhouses, the parents of whom wait until they can earn their living and then demand their custody. It would also provide some protection against parents who sought to claim money as a kind of 'loss of earnings' allowance, from religious and charitable organisations which were caring for their children and did not wish to return them to their parents.

Later in the same debate, Lord Herschell underlined the desirability of giving such statutory protection to a child against his parents:[5]

[1] 52 & 53 Vict., c. 44.
[2] 52 & 53 Vict., c. 56.
[3] 54 & 55 Vict., c. 3.
[4] Hansard, 3rd series, 1891, vol. CCCXLIX, cols 1508–10.
[5] ibid., col. 1511.

When a parent has abandoned or deserted his child, has cared nothing for it, and has left it to be cared for by others, it is outrageous that he should be allowed to go before a Court and say, 'Although I have neglected every duty which I owed my child, and although to deliver him up to me now will be most disastrous to the child, still I have a legal right to the custody of the child, that custody I will have, and you must give it to me.' Can anyone maintain such a proposition thus barely stated? All that this legislation proposes to do is that where the Court is satisfied that a parent has so behaved as to disentitle him to the custody of the child, it shall have power to refuse its writ to procure the delivery of that child back to the parent.

It is interesting to notice, however, that even though Lord Herschell and others were supporting statutory intervention in the exercise of parental rights, they did not seek authority to set aside the existing rights entirely. Thus special provision was made in the Act to enable the court, whilst denying the parents custody, to order that the child be brought up in the religion in which the parent retained the legal right to demand he should be brought up. In this respect the Act deliberately sustained what was, by long tradition, both the right and the duty of parents in England. In every other respect, it was a contribution to a growing body of statute law, the effect of which was to give legal authority to a system of domestic relations radically different from that previously upheld by the courts of this country, and one which reflected the inherent differences in the character and the context of family life in a society increasingly dominated by the town rather than the village, the factory rather than the farm.

XIV

◇◇

Children as Wage Earners
in Early Industrialism

◇◇

THE increase of the population in nineteenth-century Britain is one of the most startling facts of our history. From an estimated 7,250,000, in 1751, and a possible 9,250,000 in 1781, the people of Great Britain had increased to a measured 10,943,000 in 1801, the date of the first census, to 12,597,000 in 1811 and to 14,392,000 in 1821. In 1831, the return was to be 16,539,000. Even when one allows for the extremely speculative nature of any eighteenth-century population statistics and for the admitted deficiencies of the early nineteenth-century censuses, it is clear that a community of a very different order from any that had previously existed in Britain was being created. From the point of view of the sociologist, however, it is equally clear that there are good reasons for underlining the significance of continuing and traditional features of English society. For example, it appears to be the case that, contrary to the beliefs of a previous generation of scholars, these decennial increases in our population are to be accounted for by an increase in the birth-rate, as well as by a decrease in the prevailing death-rate, the consequence of which was to maintain one of the most conspicuous features of pre-industrial society, its overwhelming youthfulness.

Gregory King had calculated in the late seventeenth century that above 45 % of all people alive in his day were children, with some variation between town and country. There were, he reckoned, 33 % in London, 40 % in other urban areas, and 47 %

in the villages. The study of historical demography is not yet so far advanced as to enable us to confirm or criticise these figures from a wide sample of Stuart population, but the following table, constructed by Peter Laslett, shows that King's estimates of age composition of England and Wales were about right for three communities of which he himself has relevant statistics. It also demonstrated that the age composition of England and Wales in 1821, when economic transformation was in full spate, was almost exactly the same as it had been in Gregory King's time and radically different from what it was to become in the present century.[1]

Comparative Age Table

Age group	Ealing (pop. 403) 1599 (%)	Lichfield (pop. 2801) 1695 (%)	Stoke-on-Trent (pop. 1629) 1701 (%)	England and Wales (from Gregory King) 1695 (%)	England and Wales 1821 (%)	England and Wales 1958 (%)
0–9	20·2	20·9	28·1	27·6	27·9	14·8
10–19	25·6	28·3	19·8	20·2	21·1	14·2
20–29	17·5	13·5	14·3	15·5	15·7	13·8
30–39	13·6	12·5	13·9	11·7	11·8	14·1
40–49	7·7	6·9	8·7	8·4	9·3	13·9
50–59	6·6	10·4	6·9	5·8	6·6	13·2
60 and above	6·1	7·0	8·4	10·7	7·3	16·9

The previous chapter outlined the authoritarian character of the traditional legal structure of the family in England, and in the first volume of this study a good deal of space was devoted to the authoritarianism of traditional social life and educational practice. Such authoritarianism becomes a little easier to understand when the youthfulness of so much of the community is borne in mind. In examining the social attitudes towards children in the early period of industrialisation in this country, it is well to remember that, relatively, children had less of a 'scarcity' value then than they have now.

[1] Peter Laslett, *The World We have Lost*, 1965, p. 103.

Again, it is easy to fall into the error of believing that the distribution as well as the structure of our population was rapidly influenced by the dramatic increase in the gross population, since a good many studies have been published to illustrate the growth in population of particular towns in the early nineteenth century.

	1801	1831	1851
Manchester and Salford	95,000	238,000	401,000
Leeds	53,000	123,000	172,000
Bradford	13,000	44,000	104,000
Bolton	18,000	42,000	61,000

That certain towns should develop so rapidly is not, however, a clear indication that, by the time Victoria ascended the throne, England was a typically, or even predominantly, urban society. The point is well made by Clapham:[1]

The man of the crowded countryside was still the typical Englishman. The census of 1831 showed that 961,000 families were employed in agriculture, or 28% of all families in Great Britain. If to these are added the fishing and waterside families outside the towns, the workers on the country roads and canals, and all those rural handicraftsmen who are essential to the most purely agricultural life under civilised conditions . . . there can be very little doubt that some 50% of the families of Great Britain lived under conditions which may properly be classed as rural. . . . The fact that, after twenty more years of rapid urbanisation, nearly 50% of the English population was still enumerated in rural districts in 1851 is favourable to the view that at least an equal percentage may well have been economically rural in 1831. The town statistics for 1831 point in the same way. . . . At that time about 25% of the population of England and Wales and 23% of that of Scotland lived in towns of 20,000 inhabitants and upwards. It is most unlikely that more than another 25% lived in what could properly be called towns, if the smaller country market town be grouped as rural.

The basic structure of the society which both Clapham and Laslett delineate so clearly had a good deal more in common with that of seventeenth- and eighteenth-century England than that of the England of the mid-twentieth century, or even of the late nineteenth century, and it is scarcely surprising to find that

[1] J. H. Clapham, *An Economic History of Modern Britain. The Early Railway Age* (2nd ed.), 1930, p. 66.

the role of children in such a society continued to be largely traditional. The dawn of the nineteenth century did not dispel the oppressive shadows in which the majority of English children lived and died. For children, as for their parents, the beneficial effects of large-scale organisations, of urban industrialism, were a long time coming. Too many of the old ways of life and work survived to be carried forward into the age of the great cities, amongst which not the least significant were the old ways of viewing children as a source of family income and the practice of putting them to work as soon as they were able to earn a few pence.

The old social ideal of child labour died hard in England. Even when all relevant experience had proved such schemes unprofitable, Pitt, supporting Whitbread's Bill For the Better Support and Maintenance of the Poor (1796), in which a modest scheme for family allowances for the poor was being proposed, argued strongly in favour of the linked proposal that parents in receipt of such allowances should be compelled to send their children to a school of industry.[1]

> Experience had already shown how much could be done by the industry of children and the advantage of early employing them in such branches of manufactures as they were capable to execute. The extension of schools of industry was also of material importance. If anyone would take the trouble to compute the amount of all the earnings of the children who are already educated in this manner, he would be surprised, when he came to consider the weight which their support by their own labourers took off the country, and the addition which, by the fruits of their toil, and the habits to which they were formed, was made to its internal opulence. . . . Such a plan would convert the relief granted the poor into an encouragement to industry, instead of being, as it is by the present poor-laws, a premium to idleness, and a school for sloth.

In fact, of course, if one does take the trouble to compute the earnings of children in schools of industry, the economic 'fruits of their toil' were miserably poor, as indeed they were for children employed elsewhere. Poor though they were, however, the rewards of child labour were at least of some assistance in swelling the equally miserable wages of their parents. The replies to a questionnaire circulated among 'farmers of capital'

[1] *Parliamentary History*, vol. XXXII (printed by Hansard, 1810), cols 710–11.

in Suffolk and Norfolk in 1843, showed the average earnings of wives to be £2 12s. 7d. a year. The man's average earnings in these families worked out at £18 19s. 8d. a year, or 7s. 3d. a week. Neither of these figures included harvest earnings and gleanings. The average value of corn gleaned varied from 17s. 10¼d. for the wife's work only, to £1 6s. 9½d. where there were four children. The full importance of the earnings of women and children was shown by the difference between the family income of the married man and that of the single man. The average annual wage of the latter including harvest and task work was £25 0s. 0d.; the average income of a married man with no children was £30 12s. 10¼d., and of a man with a wife and four children above ten years of age, £50 18s. 6d. In this last group of families, only half the family income was earned by the man.[1]

In the absence of modern farm machinery, the hours the children worked for so little reward in the early nineteenth century were exactly the same as those worked by their counterparts of three hundred years before: from dawn to dusk in winter, from eight until six in the spring; and in harvest time often from five in the morning until nine at night. In the eastern counties, however, where the development of new, scientific, agricultural techniques was associated with a reluctance to allow settlement and a resulting dearth of labourers' cottages, the gang system of labour had been developed, which added to the hours actually worked the extra fatigue of considerable journeys to and from work itself.

The first appearance of the system seems to have been in the 'open' parish of Castle Acre (Norfolk) about 1826, and from there it spread to a much wider area. The village was surrounded by large farms of up to 1,200 acres situated in 'closed' parishes where settlement was not allowed and where there was, therefore, a deficiency of labourers, while in Castle Acre there were many anxious for employment. A farmer wanting a piece of work done would apply to a gang master at Castle Acre who would contract to complete the work and furnish the labour for a specific sum. He then selected from the people in his employment as many men, women and children as he thought necessary for the task, and sent them to the farm under an overseer whose

[1] Ivy Pinchbeck, *Women Workers and the Industrial Revolution, 1750–1850*, p. 96.

business it was to accompany them and supervise their work. One of the worst features of the system was the physical hardship imposed on both young and old on their journeys to and from work in all seasons and all weathers. In the winter, if the task was fairly near, a two-journey day was worked; the gang set out at 7 a.m., returned at mid-day, and went again from 1 p.m. until dark. But in the summer, the gang sometimes had to walk seven or eight miles each way, and work from 8.30 a.m. to 5.30 p.m. making a day of intolerable length and hardship even for adults. For children of seven years of age – and some were still younger – such conditions must have involved indescribable suffering. On longer journeys the gang was driven to its destination and generally remained there while work lasted, sleeping in barns, stables and any available shelter.[1]

The children were paid 3d. or 4d. a day, and for these rates were compelled to work as hard as though working for themselves at task work. By threats, and not infrequently by blows, they were urged beyond their strength. In bad weather long walks were taken for nothing. If rain came on after five or six miles, the gang returned without earning anything since the day was divided into four quarters and unless at least one had been worked the gang received nothing.

Some of the children in the gangs were very young indeed, beginning work at four, five or six years of age. Not only had they no opportunity of education, but they were physically injured by the long walks and the very laborious work to which they were constantly put. The father of a child of eleven who had been working in a gang for two years gave evidence before the 1843 Commission:[2]

> I'm forced to let my daughter go, else I'm very much against it . . . She has complained of pain in her side very often; they drive them along – force them along – they make them work hard. Gathering stones has hurt my girl's back at times. Pulling turnips is the hardest work; they get such a hold of the ground with their roots; when the land's strong it's as much as we can do to get 'em out, pull as hard as we can pull. It blisters their hands so that they can hardly touch anything . . . My girl went 5 miles yesterday to her work, turniping; she set off between seven and eight; she walked; had a piece of bread before she went; she did not stop work in the middle of the

[1] ibid., p. 87.
[2] Quoted ibid., p. 89.

day; ate nothing till she left off; she came home between 3 and 4 o'clock. Their walks are worse than their work; she is sometimes so tired, she can't eat no victuals when she comes home.

Morally, the results were still more injurious. The possibility of employment drew young men and women from all districts to the overcrowded open parishes. 'All sorts of characters are employed in the gangs,' said one of the overseers, 'some of all sorts. This is the coop of all the scrapings of the country. If a man or woman do anything wrong they come here, and they think that by getting among them here, they're safe.'[1] Some parents, well aware of the deplorable influence such company could exert on the young, tried to see that their children came home each night, instead of sleeping out in the barns. It was not so easy to protect their daughters from the lascivious attentions of some of the gang masters themselves.

In 1843, the commissioners enquiring into the employment of women and children in agriculture paid particular attention to the gang system, and found it almost universally criticised in consequence of its injurious influence, both physical and moral. Despite the fact that their Report condemned the gangs on these very grounds, gang work not only continued but actually increased, since, economically, it had proved workable and satisfactory, and because it was believed that 'the work could not be done without it, especially in the Fen'. Many of these later gangs, usually of between twelve and twenty people, had been formed by the farmers themselves, and were kept entirely in their own employment. They thus became known as 'private gangs' to distinguish them from the much larger gangs of the old gang masters, who undertook work for numbers of local farmers, and thereby freed them from all supervision. The private gangs, however, were much cheaper from the farmer's point of view, since he saved the gang master's profit and, by employing more children and fewer adults in his own gang, he also made a considerable saving in wages. Moreover, children could usually be worked for longer hours. Women with household duties to attend to could often not leave home before eight o'clock in the morning, whereas the children often worked from six in the morning until six o'clock at night.

Constant and public criticism of the gang system, which

[1] ibid.

aroused opinion against it, eventually led to the Gangs Act of 1867, which allowed no child under eight years of age to be employed in them, and empowered local justices to regulate the distances which the older children were to be permitted to travel on foot. More effective a protection against the exploitation of children in agriculture, however, was the Education Act of 1876 which, by making it illegal to employ any child under ten years of age in agricultural work, proved the death blow of the gang system for children.

The employment of children in gangs had made manifest in a particularly conspicuous way the degree to which child labour could and would be exploited in a society which as yet saw little wrong in putting children to work for their own support at an early age. Such had been the traditional experience of parents and employers continued to see hard work as a necessary social discipline. Thus schools of industry were still canvassed as 'the most powerful instruments in the hands of those who manage the concerns of the Poor, in order to reform the habits of the lower class of people and to give a proper turn to the disposition and manners of the rising generation'.[1] Furthermore, although the 1843 commissioners censured landowners and gang masters for their part in creating and operating a system of employment so injurious to the health and welfare of those employed, there is little to show that, in the many other industries in which children were employed in the early nineteenth century, conditions were conspicuously better. Whilst a father might inveigh against the effects of employment in a gang on his daughter's health, there is overwhelming evidence that, in areas where there were alternative employments for children, not least employments in which the father was the 'gang master' of his family, the children worked equally long hours under conditions which some today might consider even worse. J. H. Plumb, for example, writes: 'The worst conditions, long hours . . . gross exploitation of female and child labour, were to be found in small-scale and domestic industry.'[2] L. C. A. Knowles claimed that:[3]

---

[1] W. H. Saunders, *Observations on the Present State and Influence of the Poor Laws*, 1821, p. 84.

[2] J. H. Plumb, *England in the Eighteenth Century*, p. 88.

[3] Quoted R. Fletcher, *The Family and Marriage in Britain*, p. 80.

it must be remembered that family work and the family wage often meant that the members of the family were sweated by their parents ... Much of the success of the domestic worker depended on the fact that he could control the cheap labour supply in his wife and children or apprentices. This laid the work of wife and children open to considerable sweating and very long hours were worked.

Contemporary evidence reveals how justified both these comments are.

A weaver's cottage in the West Riding, described in 1842, consisted of two rooms and a pantry for a family of man, wife and nine children. In the room above where the weaving was carried on, in a space of about twelve feet square were three looms, three old oak stump bedsteads, three chests, 'one oak chest used as a child's bedstead', and a quantity of lumber. Five of the children worked as weavers in this restricted space and yet this was not the home of a weaver in poor circumstances. As for the weavers in the towns, many of them lived and worked in a single room amidst horribly insanitary surroundings. It was to the Lancashire hand-loom cotton weavers' working conditions that one witness to the 1840 Hand-loom Weavers Commission was referring when he testified:[1]

I have seen them working in cellars dug out of an undrained swamp; the streets formed by their houses without sewers and flooded with rain; the water therefore running down the bare walls of the cellars and rendering them unfit for the abode of dogs or cats. The descent to these cellars is usually by a broken step ladder. The floor is but seldom boarded or paved ...

The widespread diseases of the eye, through working long hours in candlelight; of the lungs, through working with tightly closed windows lest the fresh air affect the colour of their work; consumption, and diseases of the stomach, the result of the constant pressure against the beam of the loom, were inevitable, and children suffered equally with adults.

Other domestic industries offered no better conditions. In the pillow lace industry, children were taught to handle the bobbins when they were only three or four years old, and were often working regular hours at a cottage lace school at the age of five. In the machine lace industry, children commonly started work

[1] Quoted ibid., p. 81.

at home at four or five years of age. In one extreme instance brought to light by the investigators of the 1843 Children's Employment Commission, a child of four years of age had already been drawing lace for two years, and was then working a twelve-hour day and never going out to play. Two other children in the same family, aged six and eight, were working a regular fifteen-hour day.[1]

The majority of children employed in these industries worked in cottage schools owned either by the mistress herself, or by a dealer who provided materials and employed a teacher or overlooker to supervise the children for him. In some schools, reading was taught once a day – usually verses from the Bible – but in actual practice the schools were nothing but workshops in which children were commonly tasked beyond their strength either by parents or mistresses . . . While learning, children generally worked from five to eight hours a day, and afterwards, a twelve- or fourteen-hour day with two hours for meals was the rule. Some idea of the conditions and pressures under which children worked may be obtained from the following description of an early nineteenth-century Northamptonshire lace school:

'Here the hours were from 6 a.m. to 6 p.m., in the summer, and from 8 a.m. to 8 p.m. in the winter. Half an hour was allowed for breakfast and tea, and one hour for dinner, so that there were ten hours for actual work. The girls had to stick ten pins a minute, or six hundred an hour; and if at the end of the day they were five pins behind, they had to work for another hour . . . They counted to themselves every pin they stuck, and at every fiftieth pin they called out the time, and the girls used to race each other as to who would call out first.

'They paid 2d. a week (or 3d. in winter) for lights, and in return they received the money realised from the sale of the lace they made, and they could earn about 6d. a day . . . In the evenings 18 girls worked by one tallow candle, value one penny; the "candle-stool" stood about as high as an ordinary table with four legs. In the middle of this was what was known as the "poke-board", with six holes in a circle and one in the centre. In the centre hole was a long stick with a socket for the candle at one end and pegholes through the sides, so that it could be raised or lowered at will. In the other six holes were placed pieces of wood hollowed out like a cup, and into each of these was placed a bottle

[1] Cf. Pinchbeck, op. cit., pp. 233–4.

of very thin glass and filled with water. These bottles acted as strong condensers, or lenses, and the eighteen girls sat round the table, three to each bottle, their stools being on different levels, the highest nearest the bottle, which threw light down upon the work like a burning glass. In the daytime as many as thirty girls, and sometimes boys, would work in a room about twelve feet square, with two windows, and in winter they would have no fire for lack of room.'

In the lace schools monotony was sometimes relieved by the singing of 'lace tells' which assisted in counting and stimulated the workers to a regular pace. Many of the patterns consisted of nine-teen rows: hence the counting frequently began with that number:

'Nineteen miles to the Isle of Wight,
Shall I get there by candle light?
Yes, if your fingers go lissom and light,
You'll get there by candle light.
Nineteen long lines being over my dour,
The faster I work it'll shorten my score,
But if I do play, it'll stick to a stay,
So high ho! little fingers, and twank it away.'

It was as well for the children if they did 'twank away'. In the lace schools and among embroiderers where the mistress often sat with a cane, any 'looking off' was considered as 'losing a stitch', and for that the children were well beaten.

A description of the life of an embroiderer and of the effects of long employment in this trade is contained in the evidence given by Elizabeth Sweeting to the Children's Employment Commission, in 1843:[1]

Has worked at the trade twenty-one years; when she first began it was a very good business; begins at 7 a.m. and leaves off about 10 p.m. but oftener later than earlier; often works till between 11 and 12, has done so all the winter round; in the summer generally begins between 5 and 6, and works as long as it is light, often till 9 p.m.; often does not go to the bottom of the yard for a week; can earn by working hard 7d. a day ... Finds her sight very much affected, so much so that she cannot see what o'clock it is across her room; the work affects the stomach and causes pain in the side, often makes her light-headed; generally the lace runners are crooked, so that the right shoulder is higher than the other ... Her candles cost her about 8d. a week.'

[1] Quoted Fletcher, op. cit., p. 83.

Elizabeth's comment that, 'when she first began it was a very good business', should not, incidentally, be taken to mean that her conditions of work were necessarily better. True, the lace runners, the embroiderers and the hand-loom weavers were, by 1843, suffering disastrously from the introduction of power driven machinery and factory organisation in the textile industries, but there is little to show that the hours worked in these trades were significantly longer than they had been in various domestic industries a hundred years before. It has been said [writes Mrs George][1]

that the domestic worker produced what he liked and worked when he liked. Of course he was more of a free agent in many ways than the factory worker. When he worked at home his hours were his own concern, but if he was to earn a living wage they were certainly long. Arthur Young remarked in 1767 that the Witney blanket weavers could make from 10s. to 12s. a week – high wages for weaving which was a badly paid occupation – but their hours were from four in the morning to eight at night, and in the winter they worked by candlelight. This working by candlelight must have had disastrous effects on the eyesight of the workers. Hutton notes that stocking weavers all go to the workhouse 'when they cannot see to work.'

Mrs George also has some astringent comments to make regarding what one might term the 'romantic interpretation' of the life of the hand-loom weaver in a system of domestic industry:

Many people seem to assume that the hand-loom weavers of the old days were in the position of the modern hand-loom weaver. It would be as reasonable to suppose that an Elizabethan ale-house resembled the modern inn or tea-shop which calls itself 'Ye Olde Englyshe Hostelrye'. The weaver as a rule was achieving mass-production by dint of unremitting bodily effort. He worked to a standard, often the warps given out by his employer. The element of design did not even come into the work of the Spitalfields brocade weavers, though these were highly skilled men. The employers, who were usually the mercers, gave out the patterns, sometimes copied from French materials, sometimes supplied by the professional pattern-drawers of Spitalfields.

The theory that the domestic weaver felt a creator's pride in his

---

[1] Quoted ibid., p. 82.

work started, I think, in the days of Ruskin and William Morris. Doubtless some did – pride in work, mercifully, is not uncommon – but it seems unlikely that the average weaver, toiling hour after hour, throwing the shuttle backwards and forwards on work which was monotonous and exhausting, had the reactions which would satisfy a modern enthusiast for peasant arts.

Nor was it possible, in a system of industry which demanded unremitting toil of all members of a family from extreme youth to premature old age, that children should have anything even approximating to what we now think of as a minimal education:[1]

Attempts to establish ordinary schools in districts where domestic industries were carried on frequently ended in failure, and most children depended entirely on Sunday Schools for such education as they received. The result was that for the most part they grew up in complete ignorance of everything but their own particular industry. The popular cry against the factory system, that it prevented girls acquiring any knowledge of domestic duties, was a mere repetition of an argument that had long been used against all domestic industries in turn. The girl who had been perpetually spinning from infancy knew nothing, it was asserted, but how to turn her wheel; in straw districts girls were 'ignorant of everything but straw plaiting'; buttonmakers were 'so ignorant as scarcely to know how to wash and mend their own clothes', and lace makers were helpless and 'good for nothing else'.

When asked to find a nurse girl for a friend, the poet Cowper could only reply, 'Girls fit to be nurses . . . are . . . especially scarce in this country, where the lace pillow is the only thing they "dandle".'[2]

The effects of child labour in agriculture with regard to education were very similar. School attendance was often limited to occasional days or weeks, fitted in to the irregular rhythm of the farming year.[3]

The knowledge gained by many was so imperfect that it was quickly forgotten, and even those who were able to read and write a little were generally in a state of ignorance with regard to needlework, cooking and domestic economy. Their homes for the most part were too poor to give any training in these matters, and the result was

[1] Pinchbeck, op. cit., p. 235.
[2] Quoted ibid.
[3] ibid., p. 108.

that only field work and the poorest kind of domestic service were open to them. Prevented by ignorance and lack of training from improving their position, the lives of too many children in the agricultural classes proved to be a mere repetition of those of their parents. More than anything else the lack of education was responsible for the continued exploitation of the lack of women and children.

The conditions of children's employment in agriculture and the domestic textile industries differed hardly at all from those of the other domestic industries in which they were employed. A sub-commissioner, reporting on the nail makers in 1840, gave the following description of the conditions which prevailed in their industry:[1]

The best kind of these forges are little brick shops of about fifteen feet long and twelve feet wide, in which seven or eight individuals constantly work together, with no ventilation except the doors and two slits, or loop-holes, in the wall; but the great majority of these places are very much smaller (about ten feet long by nine feet wide), filthily dirty, and on looking in upon one of them when the fire is not lighted presents the appearance of a dilapidated coal-hole or little black den. They are usually ten or twelve inches below the level of the ground outside, which of course adds to their slushy condition, since they can never be cleaned out except by a shovel, and this is very seldom, if ever, done. In this dirty den there are commonly at work a man and his wife and daughter, with a boy and girl hired by the year. Sometimes there is an elder son with his sister, and two girls hired; sometimes the wife (the husband being a collier or too old to work, has taken to drinking, or is perhaps dead) carries on the forge with the aid of her children. These little work places have the forge placed in the centre generally, round which they each have barely standing-room at an anvil; and in some instances there are two forges erected in one of these shops . . . The effluvia of these little work dens from the filth on the ground, from the ragged, half-naked, unwashed persons at work, and from the hot smoke, ashes, water, and clouds of dust . . . are really dreadful.

No more dreadful, however, than the poisonous atmosphere breathed by children who were employed in the mines. Ayton, describing a visit to the Whitehaven mines in 1813, wrote that he saw a horse drawing a line of baskets,[2]

---

[1] Quoted Fletcher, op. cit., p. 88.
[2] R. Ayton, *A Voyage Round Great Britain*, quoted Pinchbeck, op. cit., p. 243.

driven by a young girl covered with filth, debased and profligate, and uttering some low obscenity as she passed by us. We were frequently interrupted in our march by the horses proceeding in this manner . . . and always driven by girls, all of the same description ragged and beastly in their appearance, and with a shameless indecency in their behaviour which awe-struck as one was by the gloom and loneliness around one, had something quite frightful in it, and gave the place the character of hell. All the people we met with were distinguished by an extraordinary wretchedness; immoderate labour and a noxious atmosphere had marked their countenance with signs of disease and decay.

The workers, commented Ayton, were regarded as mere machinery,

of no worth or importance beyond their *horse* power. The strength of a man is required in excavating the workings, women can drive the horses, and children can open the doors; and a child or a woman is sacrificed, where a man is not required, as a matter of economy, that makes not the smallest account of human life in its calculations.

The later report of the Royal Commission appointed to investigate the employment of children in mines and colleries revealed the conditions of children's employment in all their horrifying detail in 1842. At the age of five or six many girls spent the entire day in darkness as 'trappers' attending to ventilation doors. Young boys, girls, and women dragged heavy loads of coal along passages to the bottom of the pit shaft. 'Chained, belted and harnessed like dogs in a go-cart, black, saturated with wet, and more than half naked, crawling upon their hands and feet, and dragging their loads behind them – they present an appearance indescribably disgusting and unnatural,'[1] wrote one commissioner in describing this work. He claimed that, in Lancashire, workers pulled their loads – often in passages no higher than 20 to 30 inches – for a distance of four to six miles a day. In East Scotland girls and women between the ages of six and sixty or more carried to the surfaces of the pit, on their backs, burdens of coal varying in weight between $\frac{3}{4}$ cwt and 3 cwt. A woman witness to the Commission, who had been employed in the mines for some thirty-three years, explained that one of the reasons for very young children

---

[1] Quoted Pinchbeck, op. cit., p. 249.

being employed in the pits was to assist their mothers whose health had been ruined by too early a return to work after child-birth. 'Women so soon get weak that they are forced to take the little ones down to relieve them; and even children of six years of age do much to relieve the burden.'[1]

Deplorable as were the physical effects of underground employment on the health of the children, the brutalising conditions and vicious depravity with which they came into daily contact were said to be even worse. A variety of witnesses bore 'the strongest testimony to the immoral effects of their employment', especially on the girls. The tragedy was that 'the savage rudeness' of the upbringing of girls in the pits was not counteracted by any system of education. Introduced into the pit in early childhood, they gradually 'grew accustomed to obscene language, vice, debauchery, and knew no impropriety in them.'[2]

In many cases, parents appear to have been unmoved and indifferent to the effects of mine work on their children which so appalled middle-class investigators. For the most part, they were reconciled by use to children's early introduction to the pit, hardened by similar experiences in their own youth. 'I went to pit myself when I was five years old,' [said one Yorkshire mother], 'and two of my daughters go. It does them no harm. It never did me none.' Many declared that they could not exist without the wages of their children, yet it was often in the best paid districts that the worst abuses in this respect were found. In the West Riding, the sub-commissioners found that the work of children was almost in every instance 'compelled either by the avarice or improvidence of their parents'.[3]

Against the evidence of the widespread exploitation of child labour from an early age under conditions that today would be considered intolerable for an adult man, those under which some children were employed in factories in the early nineteenth century appear less singular. Indeed, it is worth remembering that in the report of the Commission which enquired into the conditions of employment of children in factories in 1833, it was said:[4]

[1] ibid., p. 261.
[2] ibid., p. 262.
[3] ibid., p. 265.
[4] Quoted Fletcher, op. cit., p. 86.

1. The Spitalfields 'Market for Children' at which, in the mid-nineteenth century, children of nine or ten years of age were hired for a shilling or fourteen pence a week to clean and cook for weavers' families in the district (The Mansell Collection)

2. Drouet's infant pauper establishment (Radio Times Hulton Picture Library)

It appears that, of all employments to which children are subjected, those carried on in the factories are among the least laborious and of all departments of indoor labour amongst the least unwholesome. Hand-loom weavers, frame work knitters, lace runners, and work people engaged in other lines of domestic manufacture are in most cases worked at an earlier age for longer hours and for less wages than the body of children employed in factories.

Nevertheless, to some nineteenth-century writers, who described them in vivid terms, conditions of employment for children remained deplorable:[1]

in stench, in heated rooms, amid the constant whirling of a thousand wheels, little fingers and little feet were kept in ceaseless action, forced into unnatural activity by blows from the heavy hands and feet of the merciless over-looker, and the infliction of bodily pain by instruments of punishment invented by the sharpened ingenuity of insatiable selfishness.

Many years later, in 1873, Lord Shaftesbury was to recall in a speech in the House of Lords the plight of factory children in the days when he first assumed championship of their cause:[2]

Well I can recollect in the earlier periods of the factory movement, waiting at the factory gate to see the children come out, and a set of sad, dejected, cadaverous creatures they were. In Bradford especially, the proofs of long and cruel toil were most remarkable . . . A friend of mine collected a vast number together for me; the sight was most piteous, the deformities incredible. They seemed to me, such were their crooked shapes, like a mass of crooked alphabets.

Perhaps there could be no more tragic example of the maxim 'nobody knows what nobody sees' than the impact of these misshapen 'alphabets', which spelled out to a hitherto illiterate public the consequences of the premature employment of the young. By concentrating children in employment, the urban factories, like the rural 'gangs', forced the consequences of unregulated child labour on the attention of the public and gradually sensitised them to the need for some statutory intervention.

Generations of twentieth-century schoolchildren, themselves

---

[1] 'Alfred' (Samuel Kydd), *The History of the Factory Movement*, quoted Fletcher, op. cit., p. 101.
[2] Quoted ibid., p. 101.

withheld from the labour market until they are three or four times the age at which the majority of their forebears began to work, have all too often been given to understand that it was largely if not exclusively the factory owners, anxious to employ the cheapest labour the better to increase their own profits, who were responsible for the presence of large numbers of of children among factory populations. This very naïve view over-simplifies a much more complicated situation in which low adult wage rates played a very considerable part, and explained a good deal of the anxiety of parents in the mill towns as in rural areas that their children should contribute to their own support, sometimes going to considerable lengths to ensure that they did so.

Less easily overlooked in the factories than in the fields and cottages, the need to protect the welfare of children in the mills was urged by successive Commissions of enquiry appointed from the early nineteenth century onwards. After the Factory Act of 1819, no child was to be employed in cotton mills or factories under the age of nine, and in this and subsequent Factory Acts, penalties were imposed both on the employer for infringement, and on the parent or guardian of the child for misrepresentation of age. Years later, however, factory inspectors were reporting deliberate contravention of the law by parents. In 1860, twenty-three years after the compulsory registration of births, marrriages and deaths had become operative, Robert Baker, factory inspector in the north-west of England, wrote:[1]

> Much has been said, at various times, about the value of the Register of births as a proof of age for factory children, when it can be obtained. But I have reason to believe that many children are never registered at all. Sometimes the account which a child gives of its birth-place is incorrect, and therefore its register cannot be found; and even when obtained, it is often fraudulently ante-dated; there is so large a temptation for parents to falsify registers . . .

Under the Factory Act of 1833, which extended the exclusion of children under nine years of age to all textile mills and factories with the exception of silk mills, children between nine and thirteen years of age were required to have two hours'

[1] *PP*, 1860, XXXIV, p. 466.

schooling each day, besides their work. The four factory inspectors appointed under the Act to enforce this, as all other provisions of the Act, had to see that a register was kept of the children employed in the factory and a note of school attendance was to be made in it where appropriate. The effect of the educational clause was to discourage employers from accepting children under thirteen years of age. Mr Hickson, one of the inspectors, reported that:[1]

> Their parents first endeavour to get employment for them in other factories, or in collieries, which are not under the operation of the Acts and, if they fail in that, the children are seen running wild about the streets. To send a child to day-school rarely enters the minds of parents. The child not contributing now to its own support, the parents can less afford to pay school fees than before, and they know that at the age of fourteen the factory will be open and no questions asked whether the child has been to school or not.

Later in the nineteenth century, when women and children employed on the same process as men were used to undercut the men's wage-rates, and sometimes even deprived them of a livelihood altogether, working-class organisations were to oppose the employment of children in factories as strenuously as they might. But in 1833, witnesses before the commissioners on the employment of children in factories argued very differently. One of the objections made to the limitation of the labour of children in textile mills was that it would encourage married women to become employed. The commissioners in their Report commented: 'By many others it was stated that the restriction of the hours of infant labour would compel the mothers of families to work in mills; a consequence which is much deprecated as extremely mischievous.'[2] It would seem from this that where full-time employment meant a full day's absence from home, the men operatives were less concerned for the consequences of the employment of their children than they were for the consequences of the employment of their wives, one of which was held to be the distrastrous effects on the lives of their very young children.

Debate on this question has continued, in one guise or another, right up to our own day. There is no doubt, however,

[1] *PP*, 1840, XXIV, p. 686.
[2] Quoted Margaret Hewitt, *Wives and Mothers in Victorian Industry*, p. 12.

that in the nineteenth century, where mothers were much employed from home in mills, workshops and factories, the infant mortality rates were inflated by the deaths of babies ill-fed and often ill-used by those in whose care they were left by their mothers. Some starved to death; others died from being fed totally unsuitable food (patent baby foods did not appear in this country until 1867); many more were the victims of the reckless use of the narcotics – opium, laudanum, morphia – which were major ingredients of the Godfrey's Cordial, Atkinson's Royal Infant's Preservative and Mrs Wilkinson's Soothing Syrup, administered to calm children and which in many cases 'established a calm that was but a prelude to a deeper quiet'. There was nothing unusual in this. Whenever mothers of young children were fully employed, whether in the field, the cottage or the factory, the administration of drugs to keep children quiet was, and as far as we know always had been, a common phenomenon. Among embroiderers, for example:[1]

> The practice, which is most common, usually is begun when the child is three or four weeks old; but Mr. Brown, the coroner of Nottingham, states that he knows Godfrey's Cordial is given on the day of birth, and that it is even prepared in readiness for the event. The extent to which the system is carried may be judged of by the fact, expressly ascertained by this gentleman, that one druggist made up in one year 13 cwt. of treacle into Godfrey's Cordial – a preparation of opium exclusively consumed by infants. The result of this terrible practice is that a great number of infants perish, either suddenly from an overdose, or, as more commonly happens, slowly, painfully and insidiously. Those who escape with life become pale and sickly children, often half idiotic, and always with a ruined constitution.

Here, as in so many other respects, the experience of factory industry, far from being unique was in fact the experience of cottage and workshop industry writ large for all to see. More readily observed in the factory than in the obscurity of the cottage, the conditions and consequences of employment in the mills, especially of women and children, were increasingly made a matter for concern at a time when public support was being vigorously canvassed on behalf of the oppressed slaves of the sugar plantations overseas.

[1] Cf. ibid, chapter X.

Writing about factory labour, Southey remarked in 1833 that 'the slave trade is mercy compared to it'. And Gibbins commented: 'The spectacle of England buying the freedom of the black slave by riches drawn from the labour of her white ones, affords an interesting study for the cynical philosopher.'[1] In 1832, *A Memoir of Robert Blincoe* was published in Manchester, in the preface to which Wilberforce is strongly criticised for only pleading the black slave's cause, never that 'of that homely kind, as to embrace the region of the home-cotton-slave-trade'. The details of the experiences of Robert Blincoe, taken at seven years old as a parish apprentice from the St Pancras workhouse to Lowdham Mill, near Nottingham, and subsequently moved to Litton Mill, near Tideswell, Derbyshire, were intended to show that the comparison between the lot of the young factory worker and that of the slave on the sugar plantation was not without substance. At Lowdham Mill, 'from morning till night he was continually being beaten, pulled by the hair of his head, kicked or cursed' by overlookers who had to have so much work produced or be dismissed. His hours of work were fourteen a day for a six-day week, plus frequent overtime, despite Peel's Factory Act of 1802 which was then in 'operation', and laid down that no poor law apprentice was to work more than twelve hours a day. It was also required by the Act that two copies of its provisions were to be displayed prominently in every factory to which they applied. Blincoe never saw a copy until twelve years or so after its passing!

After four years, Lowdham Mill closed down and he was moved to Litton Mill, where he served the remaining ten years of his apprenticeship under incomparably worse conditions. Few children were provided with eating utensils. Many were verminous, ill-kempt and ill-clad. 'No soap was allowed – a small quantity of meal was given as a substitute; and this, from the effects of keen hunger, was generally eaten . . .' Half famished, the children would also try to steal the meal-balls fed to the pigs in their troughs, and 'picked new cabbage leaves and the potato and turnip parings thrown on the dunghill'. Children frequently died as a result of epidemics and 'so great has the mortality been, that Mr Needham [the owner of the mill] felt it advisable

[1] L. A. C. Knowles, *The Industrial and Commercial Revolution in Great Britain in the Nineteenth Century* (3rd ed.), 1924, pp. 90 and 96.

to divide the burials, and a part of the dead were buried in Tadington Church-yard, although the burial fees were double the charge of those in Tideswell'. In all this, the two 'Visitors' whom the Act required the local magistrates to appoint annually, and who had the right to inspect the factory and the duty to report back as to the observation of the Act's provisions entirely failed to intervene. Certainly the magistrates themselves did not do so. Blincoe's explanation that the magistrates, the mill surgeon and the mill owner were all close friends is all too likely. 'That such numerous draughts made from the mills, where there was no increase in building or of machinery, or apparent call for more infant labourers should not have caused parish officers to institute inquiry as to the fate of their predecessors, goes far toward confirming the worst imputations cast by the surviving sufferers, upon their parochial guardians,' he comments.

Overlookers were harsh, and the children were sometimes made to work a sixteen-hour day without rest or food. On Saturday nights, they had to work until midnight. Not surprisingly, Blincoe records that after this, they were too tired to profit from the 'lessons' given for an hour or two each Sunday by some semi-literate engaged for this purpose.

During his 'ten years hard servitude' in this mill, Blincoe's body was never free from bruises and from wounds resulting from the sadistic punishments of overlookers and managers, to all of which ill-treatment, he claims, the owner himself was privy. Indeed, the owner often beat the apprentices unmercifully himself.

Robert Blincoe, of course, is recalling his experiences of some twelve or so years before and describes some of the worst consequences that could follow from apprenticing the poor children of London far from their home parish, a practice made illegal in 1816, and which had ceased long before his *Memoir* was published. It is worth noticing, however, that Blincoe goes out of his way to show that not all parish apprentices were subjected to such vicious treatment, contrasting the conditions in Litton Mill with those of Samuel Oldknow's mill at Mellor where he worked after his apprenticeship was finished. The *Memoir of Kitty Wilkinson*, written three years after Robert Blincoe's own *Memoir* was published, illustrates how very different conditions in some mills were from the two in which Blincoe himself was apprenticed. Born in Ireland in 1786 and brought up in Lancashire, Kitty lived to the great age of ninety-four. She had been brought up by a widowed mother in very poor circumstances, and was sent to work in the cotton mill at Caton at the age of eleven, remaining there until she was eighteen years old.

> Over this mill and the apprentice house belonging to it where she had first lived, so kind and judicious a superintendence was exercised that she had frequently been heard to say, when relating the events of her life: 'If ever there was a Heaven upon Earth it was that apprentice house, where we were brought up in such ignorance of evil.' Mr. Hudson, the Manager of the Mill, was like a father to the children under his care; not only watching over their mental and moral progress, but frequently devoting his evenings to their amusement, by reading to them and playing with them a variety of games.

Unlike Robert Blincoe, Kitty Wilkinson was not a Poor Law apprentice. She had been sent to the mill by an old lady (a relative of Hudson) who had befriended and taken a special interest in her. Nevertheless, there is no evidence to show from her *Memoir* that she was in any way singled out for specially kind treatment, nor does it seem likely, on general grounds, that men like Mr Hudson were reserved by some special dispensation of Providence to be the managers of any mill save one in which parish apprentices served their indentures.

More to the point, however, is the fact that, by the time Robert Blincoe's *Memoir* was published, the number of children who were actually 'apprenticed' in the cotton mills was insignificant compared with those who accompanied their fathers and mothers as mill 'hands'. Much that has been written of the cruel treatment of children in the early days of the factory system – and a good deal has been made of the pictures of unrelieved gloom given as evidence to Sadler's Committee of 1832 – fails to distinguish between the various categories of children employed in the mills of the 1830s, just as it seizes on evidence of the worst possible treatment of children, some of which dates from many years before, and attributes it to the factory system in general. When the Factory Commissioners of 1833 checked some of the allegations made to Sadler's Committee, sometimes re-examining the same witnesses, they were forced to very different conclusions. It emerged that it was often the operatives themselves who were chiefly responsible for such ill-treatment as did occur, bringing into the factory the brutality which the standards of the time permitted them to practice on their wives and children at home. 'Much cruelty,' stated the Commission, 'is daily practised in many a cottage, which is not fit to rank even with the strap and the billy roller.'

The conflicting evidence relating to the effects of factory labour arose very largely from the great diversity of conditions. Whilst it is true that factory labour at its worse was indescribably bad, and that some of the masters were indifferent to the comfort and health of their employees, regarding them 'in no other light than as tools to let out to hire', nevertheless, in the opinion of the commissioners and inspectors alike, such accusations were far from being applicable to factories and masters generally. Inspector Horner, in 1836, emphatically denied[1]

> the truth of those general accusations against the masters so frequently indulged in . . . and of those pictures of oppression, debilitated health, and suffering, represented to be characteristic of factory employment . . . That instances of cruelty and oppression are common, or that there is among them [employers] a smaller proportion of benevolent good men, may be most confidently denied. Indeed I know of no description of persons of whom so many instances may be brought forward of active and benevolent exertions and large pecuniary sacrifices to promote the welfare of the people they employ. To this I bear the most willing testimony from very ample opportunities of observation.

Just as much of the alleged cruelty in the factories was but a reflection of the brutality of life outside them, so also were the moral standards which are often said to have debased the morals of factory children. One witness to the 1833 Factory Commission claimed that 'it would be no strain on his conscience to say that three-quarters of the girls between fourteen and twenty years of age were unchaste'.[2] Yet, as has already been seen, allegations of debasement of morals were a common feature of almost

---

[1] Quoted Pinchbeck, op. cit., pp. 197–8.
[2] Quoted Hewitt, op. cit., p. 49.

every account of occupations in which children were to be found, and seem more a product of overcrowded and unsavoury domestic conditions than of the actual occupations themselves. Cooke Taylor, who, unlike many of the severest critics of the factory workers, knew of their conditions of work at first hand, observed:[1]

> They speak as if men and women were herded together the whole day, subject to no superintendence, with opportunities and facilities for licentious conversation. Now conversation in a mill is all but physically impossible, the operatives are separated from each other by frames of working machinery which require their constant attendance, and the overseers would soon dismiss tenters who abandoned the care of their frames to indulge in idle gossip . . .

Many years later, in 1904, reviewing the evidence that had accumulated from numerous sources regarding the morality of the working classes in England, one witness to the Interdepartmental Committee on Physical Deterioration commented that 'the standard of morals in a factory very largely reflects the standard outside it'.[2] In the early nineteenth century, however, very little indeed was actually known of prevailing moral standards amongst the labouring classes; hence it was easy to imply the existence of a standard from which children were bound to be diverted when industry moved from the home to the factory. Eden's *The State of the Poor*, which appeared just before the new century began, contains a passage which very clearly illustrated this point:[3]

> Habits of industry and perseverance are undoubtedly of so much importance that they cannot be too early or too strongly inculcated. These, however, may be (and I am persuaded are) in general acquired at home, by the children of the labouring classes, full as effectually, and at less cost and less risque, than in working schools and manufactories. The objections which have been repeatedly urged against parochial work-houses, and houses of industry; that by removing the young from their parents, they destroy all domestic connections; that, under the lash of the task-master, the freedom of the British spirit is broken; and that, reared in crowds, the rising generation lose the spring of health in contagion and restraint;

[1] ibid., p. 54.
[2] ibid., p. 60.
[3] pp. 420–2.

seem to be no less applicable to those places in which great numbers of boys and girls are thronged together or, at the spinning wheels, the loom, or any other mechanical employment. It may, perhaps, be worthy the attention of the Public, to consider whether any manufacture, which in order to be carried on successfully, requires that cottages and workhouses should be ransacked for poor children; . . . and that numbers of both sexes of different ages and dispositions, should be collected together in such a manner, that the contagion of example cannot but lead to profligacy and debauchery; will add to the sum of individual or national felicity.

Six years later, in 1803, Lord Addington was to receive a letter expressing similar concern and urging legislation to protect children drawn from the cottages and workhouses into industry:[1]

In those manufactures, where numbers of children and other persons are collected and employed, without parental protection, and without any discrimination of age, or sex or character, it will appear from some of the reports how necessary it is become, that the Legislation should pay constant attention to their effects, . . .

While it continues our ruling object to undersell all the world, by the improvement of machinery, and by the extension of our factories, we may without care and attention on our part, reduce the scale of morality and happiness in this country to as low and cheap a rate as the price of our manufactures.

More than the hours the children worked; more than the deplorable conditions in which they worked; more than the effects of both on life and health; more even than the alleged cruelty with which they were treated in the factories; the belief that employment in the growing number of mills, factories and mines endangered the morals of children and young people, stirred men like Ashley to engage in a long struggle for the legislative control of working conditions and accounts for the recurring provision in the early Factory Acts for time to be set aside for 'education', which more often than not took the form of being enabled to read the Bible.

The association between industrial training and moral education had a long history in England and had been emphasised in the discipline imposed on apprentices in the sixteenth and seventeenth centuries. The insistence on sobriety of dress and

[1] *Reports of the Society for bettering the condition of the poor*, 1803, IV, p. 16.

manner; the fines imposed on loose talk and free behaviour; the exhortations to religious devotion, all testified to a profound belief that to be a good workman was also to be a virtuous and spiritual citizen. But in many areas, apprenticeship had already broken down during the eighteenth century. In the nineteenth, it was decreasingly observed, decreasingly enforced, and decreasingly useful in the new factory industries. As a consequence, increasing numbers of labourers' children received neither technical instruction nor moral discipline in a society which had yet to evolve its own methods of providing either. In some skilled trades, where apprenticeship did survive, a relatively small group of children continued to benefit from the early training and later security and protection the old system guaranteed. For the majority, urban industrialism offered employments requiring little skill and few prospects of advancement. In a rapidly increasing population, the number of children competing for such employment added to its inherent insecurity and perpetuated, where it did not actually produce, a serious problem of vagrancy and unemployment. Meanwhile, piecemeal attempts to regulate the conditions of those at work for many years often exacerbated local problems connected with the employment of children in the nineteenth century. Lack of training and employment forced many boys into blind-alley jobs, from which they were often dismissed at the age of sixteen, when they could no longer be used as cheap labour. Girls, who remained cheap labour after they had grown into womanhood, entered those almost inevitably unskilled employments where such labour was most used. For both, in town and country alike, the insecurity and frequent unavailability of employment was a serious problem in conditions of developing industrialism. Hence, long before the conditions of children's employment attracted widespread public attention, the consequences of their unemployment were becoming a matter of some anxiety. It was an anxiety prompted by a regard for the poor rates. It was also an anxiety that, without work, a child was without social and moral discipline. Such were the considerations which underlay a good deal of the effort to provide for the education and training of children in the early stages of industrialism.

XV

Early Experiments in Training and Reform

―――――――――――――――――――――――――――――

Prominent among organised schemes for the welfare of children in the late eighteenth and early nineteenth centuries were the industrial schools which Pitt so much admired, and which he unsuccessfully commended for statutory development. For many of their promoters, as for Pitt himself, the main attraction of industrial schools was that they were believed to be a self-supporting and thus a rate-saving form of provision for the children of the poor. It was, of course, possible to set up such institutions under the legislation of 1601,[1] which still operated, and an attempt to do so had been made by the magistrates of the southern division of Lindsey, in Lincolnshire, in 1783 as a result of the increasing unemployment due to the dislocation of industry at the end of the American War. The scheme was limited to the setting up of working schools for children only, to whom poor relief in money might be refused unless they performed the tasks allocated to them. Children under the age of six were to be taught to knit, and children between the ages of six and nine were to be taught to spin materials provided by the overseers in a place of work specially set apart for the purpose. Special premiums in the form of articles of clothing were to be awarded to the children producing the best work both in quantity and in quality. One very interesting feature of this scheme was that the magistrates did not apparently wish

[1] 43 Eliz., c. 2.

that the scheme should be operated entirely under the enabling
statute, but deliberately sought local support for their project
by co-operating with a Mr Bouyer in the founding of a voluntarily supported Society for the Promotion of Industry, in the
Southern District of the Parts of Lindsey, in the County of
Lincoln.[1] The Society sought to finance the school partly from
the parishes, who were each asked to contribute a sum equal to
one per cent of their previous year's poor rate and partly by
inviting voluntary subscriptions of five shillings a year from
individuals, and was thus an interesting mixture of voluntary
and state action organised along lines very familiar in the
sixteenth and seventeenth centuries.

Just as, almost a hundred years before, John Cary's attempt
to set the children of the Bristol poor to work for their own
support attracted a good many imitators, so the Lindsey scheme
towards the end of the eighteenth century was copied elsewhere.
In 1787, at Oakham, Rutland, a spinning school was founded on
the Lindsey model with the explicit instruction that: 'No persons
[were] to receive relief from the parish upon account of their
families who refuse to send their children to the school: unless
they can prove to the satisfaction of the overseers, that they can
employ them to more advantage elsewhere.' The school was to
provide instruction in spinning jersey and linen, knitting, sewing
and, 'for those who choose it', in reading. The hours of work,
as one would expect, were long: from eight o'clock until one
o'clock, and from two until seven o'clock every afternoon save
Saturday. Later, a dinner was provided for a charge of sixpence
a week and the children allowed 'as much as they choose to
eat . . .'[2] In November 1794, a Society for the Promotion of
Industry, in the Hundreds of Ongar and Harlow, and the Half
Hundred of Waltham, in the County of Essex,[3] was instituted
and within a month eleven parishes had voted to join the scheme.
Similar societies were said to be running successfully at Shrews-
bury and as far north as Glasgow. Two years later, Robert

---

[1] Cf. R. G. Bouyer, *An Account of the Origin, Proceedings, and Intentions of the Society for the Promotion of Industry, in the Southern District of the Parts of Lindsey, in the County of Lincoln* (3rd ed.) 1789.

[2] Cf. *Reports of the Society for bettering the condition of the poor*, 1802, I, pp. 40–2.

[3] Cf. *An Account of the Origin and Progress of the Society for the Promotion of Industry, in the Hundreds of Ongar and Harlow, and the Half Hundred of Waltham, in the County of Essex*, 1797.

Saunders, a local overseer and a friend of the Poor Law reformer, Gilbert, helped found a school of industry at Lewisham for children between five and twelve years of age, and in 1799, in Kendall, a local worthy, Dr Briggs, opened a school for children above the age of three.

The explicit intention of these schools to train children to contribute to their own support by the acquisition and practice of simple industrial skills and thereby not merely 'to relieve the indigent, but to prevent indigence itself', had always been the intention of the Tudor legislation to which some of their founders looked for statutory authorisation. Unlike Tudor experiments in statutory and voluntary co-operation to this end, however, the heavy emphasis on industrial training precluded any but a scant attention to the children's formal education and almost without exception excluded any attempt to educate children according to their individual abilities, such as had been made by the founders of Christ's Hospital. Dr Briggs' school seems to have been rare indeed in setting aside one hour each day for instruction in reading and writing, which he left confidently in the hands of a 'master' of eighteen years of age and an usher four years younger; in allowing for the teaching of 'practical geography' once a week; and in encouraging the children, when they left the industrial school, to go on to one of the local 'blue-coat' schools.[1]

Even within the narrow limits of training which the schemes actually provided, the schools of industry seem to have been far from successful judging from the brief life of many of them, including the Lindsey scheme, which itself collapsed after only eight years. Opinion seems to have been divided as to the reasons for their failure. According to Eden, some thought that the schools[2]

> were not only expensive to the parish, but detrimental to the children themselves; for, by being so long confined to a sedentary employment, at an early period of life, they were often rendered puny and weak; and at the age of twelve or thirteen when they ought to go out to service with the farmers, or become apprentices, they were extremely ignorant of everything except spinning, that it was

[1] Cf. *Reports of the Society for bettering the condition of the poor*, 1802, III, pp. 244–59.
[2] *The State of the Poor*, pp. 400–1.

a long time before they could be of any service to their masters; besides which, the great and sudden change of employment was often injurious to the children.

Others thought the schools had not been given a fair chance to prove their worth, but Eden himself thought their optimism unjustified, and he wrote:

> The experience . . . of eight years has proved that, although schools of industry may flourish for a while, under the active zeal of their first promoters, yet, when after a few years trial, they are left to the superintendence of less interested administrators, they dwindle into the ordinary state of the parish poor-houses.

It was certainly true that the schools had been more of a financial liability than a financial asset to the parishes. The profits of the Lewisham school, for example, which Saunders himself estimated to cost roughly two hundred pounds a year to run, amounted in the first ten months of its operation to forty pounds net. But there was a good deal more to their failure than an over-optimistic calculation of the earning power of unskilled child labour. Not least was the resistance of the poor themselves who, in a period of almost indiscriminate poor relief, had come to believe that they had an unqualified right to financial support for themselves and their families, without any obligation to send their children to the local industrial school. In any case, they preferred their children to work even as casual labourers in the normal employments of the locality rather than spend their time acquiring skills irrelevant to the needs of the local employers.

Nevertheless, the school of industry continued to have its enthusiastic supporters, the most famous perhaps being Sarah Trimmer, who founded her own school of industry at Old Brentford and, in her widely read *Oeconomy of Charity*, published in 1801, urged the setting up of similar schools in every parish in the land, financed from the poor rates. Mrs Trimmer's enthusiasm, however, did not spring from a disingenuous belief that the schools were financially profitable; on the contrary, she commented on the fact that hopes that this would be the case had very largely been disappointed due to the wasting of materials, and the bad work of the children and the bad management of many of the schools by those appointed to run them.[1]

[1] op. cit., pp. 306–12 passim.

For Mrs Trimmer, as for Robert Saunders, the motive for establishing schools of industry for the children of the poor was, above all else, the wish to rescue boys and girls from the demoralising influence of the factory and the workshop, of the workhouse and the street, and even of their own homes. Hence her approving interest in the work of Mrs Cappe and Mrs Gray who had successfully campaigned in York in 1784 for voluntary subscriptions for a spinning school, stimulated by the obvious need for such an institution in a city where many mothers went out to work washing and cleaning, leaving their children uncared for.[1] The nature of the difficulties these two ladies had to contend with were themselves an indication of the quality of life in the homes from which the children were drawn. It was difficult, for example, to devise suitable punishments for bad work or misbehaviour. Corporal punishment was useless as the children were inured to it in their own homes. Small privations and marks of disgrace were thus resorted to, not altogether successfully. In this particular school, the children were supposed to be paid a wage equal to that they could have earned in a local factory. In fact, when a child could spin four hanks of wool a day, he was given clothes *in lieu* of part of his wages: had all the wages been paid in money, many would have been sent ragged to school. In 1797, a special appeal was made for funds to enable the school to make a free distribution of milk to its pupils at breakfast-time, as it was found that at home they merely received tea without sugar or milk. Mrs Cappe, in her *Account* of this and another school which she and Mrs Gray had pioneered in York, laid particular stress on the inadequacy of the homes of many of the children of that city, and lamented the many still uncared for children on the streets of that city for whom the schools were unable to provide. 'Nothing less than the interference and protection of the Magistrates, would be effectual to complete its cure',[2] she claimed, and urged the setting up of sufficient schools of industry throughout the country to admit all needy children.

In effect, Mrs Cappe and Mrs Trimmer were appealing for some sort of preventive measures associated with statutory

[1] Cf. Catherine Cappe, *An Account of Two Charity Schools for the Education of Girls*, 1800.
[2] ibid., p. 14.

support to protect the large numbers of children in late eighteenth-century and early nineteenth-century society who, either through contemporary organisation of industry, or temporary dislocation of trade, or through parental neglect or inadequacy, were in some moral danger. They begged, roamed the streets in a neglected condition, and eventually appeared before the magistrates for offences for which, even at the age of eight and nine, they might be sentenced to death, imprisoned as felons, or transported across the great seas to the penal settlements of Canada and Australia.

Since such measures did not exist, however, any attempt to protect needy children in moral danger was either undertaken within the narrowly interpreted clauses of the Poor Law or devolved on the individually inspired and voluntarily supported philanthropical societies and institutions. Three of the most famous of these were the Marine Society and Jonas Hanway's Female Orphan Asylum and Magdalen Hospital, all of which had been founded in the mid-eighteenth century[1] and had been followed by numerous other rescue societies as the century wore on. The most remarkable of these was founded in 1788; the Philanthropic Society for the Prevention of Crimes, and the Reform of the Criminal Poor; by the Encouragement of Industry, and the Culture of Good Morals, among those Children who are now trained up to Vicious Courses, Public Plunder, Infamy and Ruin. Designed as an Introduction to a New System of National Police in all Civilised Countries, this Society, from small beginnings, was to exert a considerable influence on the care and treatment of delinquent children, an influence which has continued up to the present day. Its original aim was 'the protection of poor children and the offspring of convicted felons, and the reformation of children who have themselves been engaged in criminal practices, that they may learn the happiness and benefit of a home'. It had been founded on the initiative of Robert Young, who had been much impressed by the need for such a society from his observation of the large number of children who haunted the streets and alleys of London, without or beyond parental control and protection, drifting into a life of petty crime and violence. On 5 September 1788 Young called a meeting at his house to discuss their plight. Among those who

[1] Cf. vol. I, chapters VI and VIII.

attended were the Marquis of Carmarthen, the Duke of Leeds, Lord Cremorne, General Rainsford, Lord Aylesford, Lord Bulkley, the Hon. Philip Pusey, Sir James Sanderson and Dr James Sims, the president of the Medical Society of London. The kind of children this meeting was concerned with can best be illustrated by examples taken from the later Admission Register of the Society:[1]

Mary Grady. Mother transported for fourteen years.

George le Foy. Lived in a notorious resort of thieves, and was with his mother in a complete state of vagrancy.

John Fletcher. Father a convict, mother a vagrant.

Nicholas and Paddy Sweetman. Taken from a notorious resort of infamous people.

Mary Crawley. Cruelly treated, almost starved, and turned into the streets by a brutal father-in-law [step-father] who consumes his earnings in drunkenness; this girl was exposed to danger of seduction and ruin . . . but for the timely succour of this charity.

George and John Barrat. Father a drunken scoundrel, boys trained to beg and thieve.

Jane Windsor. Her father is a penny barber, a notorious drunkard, who with his wife and four children all sleep in one small bed.

James Stillwell. Was turned out of home by his father, came under the tuition of a gang of villains, and had committed a great number of thefts, for which he had been sent to prison.

James Smith. His father was a drunken, brutal fellow, who occasioned the death of one child, by turning him in his mother's arms out of doors in severe weather; the boy a vagrant in the streets, almost naked.

William Burrell. A vagrant boy, taken from a lodging-house of thieves in an infamous part of the town. Has no knowledge of his father or mother; was brought to town by his brother, who deserted him.

Henry London. Aged twelve, came out of Gloucestershire in a wagon to seek for work, had not a single acquaintance in town, and remained several days in the inn-yard and stables, with little to eat but horse beans; he was turned out by the Innkeeper. He appears to be a natural child; is remarkably tall for his age; was very ill from weakness, being nearly starved.

To offer help to such children, the meeting decided to establish a New Asylum for the Prevention of Vice and Misery

[1] *An Address to the Public from the Philanthropic Society*, 1790, pp. 17–19.

Among the Poor. Young was appointed Intendant, or Director, and the Marquis of Carmarthen elected President. The meeting also resolved that if any building were to be put up for the care of such children there should be no surrounding wall, in order to make a clear distinction between an 'asylum' and a 'prison'. An appeal for funds was to be made to the public.

As Intendant, the hard work of organising the Society's operations was thus left in the hands of Young, who had already made himself acquainted 'with many haunts of thieves; visited every prison and Bridewell in the Metropolis; solicited information and aid from the Bow Street and other magistrates . . . and had also engaged the constables, runners, and turn-keys' in his interest, and was very well aware both of the indifference and of the antagonism which the Society would have to face. 'Argument, ridicule, and even invective were employed to oppose the plan.' Nevertheless, an enthusiast for his chosen cause, Young persevered. 'The system of moral Reform was my own, and it was new; on it the success of all my hopes depended . . .'

The first children taken into care by the Society were boarded out with foster parents, but when the number reached twelve, the Society rented a small house at Cambridge Heath, Hackney, for £10 a year, put a matron in charge, and placed the children there to be taught to knit stockings and make lace. More cottages were soon acquired in the same district and tradesmen and their wives were made responsible for the care and training of the children, since it was the policy of the Society to keep all who were apprenticed under its immediate care, to prevent their exposure or return to corruption. Thus one house had a shoe-maker, another a tailor, and a third a carpenter.

By the time of the Society's first Report, in 1789, a fourth house had been acquired and it had been decided that the boys and girls, who at first had been accommodated together, should now be separated, and the numbers in each home, originally twelve, be raised to twenty. Despite these modifications, it was the hope and intention that each unit should resemble as far as possible a normal home. 'The mode of living is in distinct houses, as separate families,' states the Report. 'A manufacturer has a house for himself and his wife, if married, and a certain number of wards whom they are to regard as their own children. In these respects, the design is to approach as nearly as possible to common life.'[1] Later in the same year, a second Report showed that the Society had sixty children in its care and six shoemakers, six tailors and six carpenters in its employ as instructors. Some of the boys were being set to knit stockings or weave garters, whilst the girls, who were apparently all accommodated in one of the five houses the Society now rented, were taught needlework and knitting. 'By this constant and rapid increase,' the Report observed, 'the establishment already begins to give the semblance of a little village, which, in order and industry, and good morals, is a pattern to the poor . . .'[2]

Unfortunately, Young's own conduct about this time failed to provide an equally admirable pattern. Within two years of the Society's inception, allegations of irregularities in his accounts were being made, and the Committee called upon him to produce them, whereupon he resigned his treasurership. Subsequent enquiries led the Committee to dismiss him in 1790 from all offices in their Society. They then proceeded to appoint four 'visitors', predominantly clergy, to supervise the children's homes and to further the work of the Society by seeking out 'such objects as appear most likely to become obnoxious to the laws, or prejudicial to the community'.

The Address to the Public from the Philanthropic Society, issued shortly after Young's dismissal, recorded certain constitutional changes. In addition to the appointment of the four 'visitors', a steward and a chaplain-superintendent, who was to be in charge of the homes, had been appointed and were in residence. The Duke of Leeds had become the Society's President, supported by a large number of nobility and gentry as Vice-Presidents. But it also showed that the original objects of the Society were to continue unchanged: 'The Philanthropic Society aims at the prevention of crimes, by removing out of evil counsel and evil company those children who are in the present state of things, destined to ruin: in a word, to educate and instruct in some useful trade or occupation the children of convicts, or other infant poor who are likely to be engaged in a vagrant or profligate course of life.' Quite correctly, the *Address* claimed that the work of the Society did not overlap with poor relief – which many critics constantly alleged to be the case – since poor relief

[1] *First Report of the Philanthropic Society*, 1789, p. 34.
[2] *Second Report of the Philanthropic Society*, 1789, p. 57.

only dealt with those who actually applied for assistance: 'It is the part of the Society to inspect abodes of profligacy and dishonesty, to find out the proper objects, and to allure them from their evil habits and connections by peculiar advantages and peculiarly good treatment.'

It is illuminating to see the 'peculiar advantages' of life in the homes as reflected in the children's daily regime set out in their winter and summer time-tables:

Winter time-table		*Summer time-table*	
6.30	Rise	5.30	Rise
	Work		Work
8–9	Breakfast	7–8	Breakfast
	Work		Work
12–2	Dinner	12–2	Dinner
	Work		Work
4–5	Play	6–8	Play
5–7	Work	8 o'clock	Supper
7 o'clock	Supper	9 o'clock	Bed
8 o'clock	Bed		

Instruction given every Wednesday by the chaplain-superintendent 'in the principles of religion and morals' was supported by the daily practice of morning and evening prayer and two attendances at church each Sunday. It was the chaplain-superintendent's additional responsibility to instruct the children in reading in the interval between the two church services, 'and also at such hours of leisure in the evening as shall appear convenient'.[1] This represented a distinctly lower standard of formal education than that provided for children almost a century before in many of the early workhouses, both in the time allocated to reading and in the absence of instruction in writing. As has already been seen, however, sixteenth-century enthusiasm for better education facilities for the poor had long ago given way to the belief that some sort of industrial training, linked with such elementary instruction as would enable them to read the Bible and dimly comprehend the awful authority of God, was more than sufficient for the station to which Providence had chosen to call them. It was precisely this belief which dictated the régime devised for the children in the care of the

[1] *Address . . .*, 1790, pp. 13–14.

Society, so that it might fulfil its plan 'to restore [the children] to the civil community, to their proper condition as men, and to the right knowledge of their God'.

Of their success so far, the authors of the *Address* were in no doubt. Sixty-eight boys and girls were in the Society's homes. 'They are all of them cheerful and happy. They are scarcely ever found guilty of profaneness or any irregularity of conduct. Their diligence will be best estimated by the annexed statement of the profits of their labour.' Turning to which, one finds that it was calculated that the children had produced work worth £789, which was claimed to represent a profit of some £289, although, since the value of the stock-in-hand was included in the credit balance, and the goods themselves were actually bought by the Society itself, this was in fact a very notional figure indeed.

With renewed vigour and enthusiasm, the Society drew up plans for the extension of their work and premises. Through the good offices of the City of London, in 1792 they acquired some property in St George's Fields, Southwark, and an institution was opened there to which the children were transferred. Dormitories and workshops were set up for teaching tailoring, shoemaking, printing, bookbinding and ropemaking. A separate section was set aside for girls who were to be taught needlework and work in the laundry and kitchen. The new institution also had a section which was set aside as a 'prison' (this meant the introduction of cells which are later referred to as a means of punishment), and a special building for newly admitted boys who passed through a probationary period before moving into the general institution. Admission was restricted to two classes of children. First those who were 'offspring of felons', which usually meant that, with one or both parents executed, transported or imprisoned, the children were destitute, in addition to being presumed 'tainted' by their contact with criminal parents. The second category was of those children who had themselves been involved in crime. To begin with, convicted children were not separated from those who had not undergone the processes of the law.

Within four years, therefore, the Society had established a full-scale institution for delinquent and potentially delinquent children of both sexes. In the process, the early 'family system' of care had been discontinued and much larger groups of children were accommodated in the various 'houses' of the institution. As yet, very little attention had been given to the question of staffing, but by assembling large numbers of children in one institution, problems of order and discipline became inevitable. The Committee ordered conduct books to be kept and evening schools to be established for the children. The first chaplain-superintendent, the Rev. Dr Gregory, lasted less than a year, and his successor, the Rev. Durant, was dismissed soon after his appointment because, during his short reign, the girls as well as the boys were guilty of serious misconduct.

Meanwhile, the lack of experience of the managers led them to spend rather more on food and clothing for the children than they could properly afford. As a result, in 1793, a special committee was set up to investigate expenditure. Food was cut by buying milk diluted with water in a proportion of two quarts of water to one pint of milk, the cheese supper allowance was cut and free access to 'small beer' for the boys was stopped. At the same time, the original green uniforms were changed to a plain coarse canvas and the trimmings of the girls' hats were dispensed with.[1]

None of these difficulties appear to have much inhibited the Society nor diminished the obvious satisfaction of its members in the work they had set on foot. At their Annual Dinner in 1793,[2]

> the children under the Society's protection walked in procession round the room, first upwards of 30 girls presented by their mistress. After this, near on 100 boys, each department led by respective masters, the carpenter, printer, shoemaker and tailor. The decent appearance and orderly demeanour of the children filled the minds of the spectators with the most pleasant sensation; the natural result of contemplating the happy change which had been wrought in the institution of this numerous little group lately in the high road of vice.

The pattern of the houses in the institution had now been established. The basement of each was equipped with kitchens, pantry, wash-house and cells. Every house accommodated a master and mistress and forty-five boys or girls. If the boys who

---

[1] Cf. Carlebach, *Caring for Children in Trouble*, p. 7.
[2] Quoted ibid., p. 8.

were apprenticed to the masters absconded, they were taken before the magistrates as 'refractory apprentices'. The girls were sent out at a very young age as 'menial servants' although the Society was most careful to see that the mistresses of the girls were of the best character. Thus, in December 1794, they refused an application from a woman seeking a servant on the grounds that she kept a lodging-house. In the same year, the Society decided to appoint a matron who was 'to superintend and direct the conduct of the cook, take care of the boys' linen, mend their stockings, act as nurse whenever any of the children are ill, take the young boys under her particular care, and see that the children and their dormitories are kept perfectly clean and neat'.

The children in the Society's care were, not very surprisingly, a fairly rough lot and discipline was a constant problem. A Committee order dated 13 June 1794 stipulated that:

> the boys be not permitted to go into the country for a holiday unless the superintendent and masters see that they have no weapons as guns, pistols, etc., of any sort; and that they behave themselves with the greatest regularity and never get into any gardens, orchards, pleasure grounds, etc., by which they could give offence or do any mischief and that they be always present with some of the masters . . .

Otherwise this 'indulgence' was to be stopped. For reasons not hard to imagine, another 'indulgence', the Guy Fawkes bonfire, was definitely stopped that same year.[1] Corporal punishment is not mentioned in the early records of the Society, but the basement cells were used frequently 'with bread and water', although this punishment could only be awarded by one of the visitors. Deprivation was not the Society's sole instrument of discipline, however, since it had found a system of rewarding well- behaved boys to be effective.

Both in May 1794 and December 1795 the Society attempted to get government support for their work. On the first occasion, to enable them to extend it to 'such adult criminals whose crimes are not of such malignity as to subject them to transportation', and on the second, to relieve the financial distress in which the Society now found itself in continuing its work with

[1] ibid., p. 9.

children. Neither appeal was successful, but the petition of 1795 is of interest since it clearly described the function of the Society as it was then seen by the managers. It existed[1]

> for the purpose of receiving the destitute infant children of convicts, and to rescue them from vice and infamy to which the example and sentence of their parents exposed them and for the reform of such young criminals whose youth gave promise of amendment by impressing on their minds principles of morality and religion and instructing them in useful occupations to enable them to gain an honest livelihood and become beneficial members of society.

In the absence of parliamentary support, the Society's finances were seriously strained, and no children were admitted in 1795.

In 1796, a special sub-committee of the Philanthropic Society was appointed to report on its first seven years of work, and on the 176 boys and 60 girls whom it had taken into its care. Dealing with the boys first, the committee reported that of 176 boys, 51 had absconded, a figure which illustrates the difficulty experienced by the voluntary institutions in holding on to their charges without legal powers. Seventeen had gone to sea, five had been sent to the Marine Society, three were expelled, ten had returned to their families, seven were placed in employment and three had died; eighty boys were still in the institution. It was noted that, of the fifty-one absconders, thirty-one had been aged thirteen or more at the time they were admitted and the committee suggested that boys of thirteen and over should not in future be admitted, because at that age, 'they were so far advanced in years as to afford little chance of their being reclaimed'. The committee further suggested that boys who manifest vicious dispositions, should be kept separate from other boys, and where possible removed from the institution. No boy should be dismissed without fair trial, but once it had become clear that he would not mend his ways, the interests of the other boys, no less than of those who supported the institution financially, demanded that such youngsters should be removed.

The behaviour of the girls was said to be rather better than that of the boys. Be this as it may, it was apparently very difficult to find suitable places for them outside the institution. Some of the difficulty appears to have been the heavy demands

[1] ibid., p. 10.

made on even the youngest of them, which were often sufficient to make the girls return, although the committee pointed out with remarkable candour, that a girl would not return to 'a life which the girls live in their gloomy apartments' if they had an even moderately comfortable position. But some of the difficulty probably arose from the disposition of the girls themselves. An illustration given of this problem is contained in the Society's Register of Admissions. Mary Smith was admitted on 14 December 1792 at the age of nine years. She was 'an artful and depraved character. The person under whose protection she had been, having often found it necessary to correct her, died, and during the time he was in his coffin, she stole the opportunity, unseen, of getting into the room, uncovered the sheet and spoke to the corpse in these terms – "I don't mind you – you can't hurt me now".[1]

In the institution, the girls were employed 'in making and mending their own gowns, doing their own linen and that of the boys, washing the same, the stockings, the sheets and house linen and keeping the house clean', whilst the boys were employed as follows:

34 with the shoemaker
20 in the rope walk
10 with the tailor
 6 in the printing office
 3 with the cook
 2 at the gates
 1 with the steward
 4 too young for any employment

The diet of the children was:

Breakfast: bread, milk and water
Dinner:
Monday: broth and potatoes (no bread)
Tuesday: the meat of which Monday's broth was made and potatoes
Wednesday: puddings of potatoes and flour
Thursday: legs of beef stewed and potatoes
Friday: beef and mutton and potatoes stewed
Saturday: rice pudding
Sunday: boiled beef and potatoes
Lunch: bread with milk and water, bread and cheese

[1] ibid., p. 12.

428

The girls had the same as the boys except that they had milk and rice on Thursday instead of meat, but this appears to have disagreed with them and they were given rice pudding instead.[1]

This particular report highlights what were destined to become and to remain some of the dominant factors determining the success or failure of this and similar institutions: the nature of the admissions, the classification of inmates within the institution, the problem of discipline, the involvement of staff within the institution, and disposal after training. The subsequent history of the Society was to show that some of these problems could only be overcome by a radical delimitation of the scope of the work it had originally set itself. The age of admission, originally set at seven years, was raised to eight in 1797. In practice often a more difficult group to deal with than the boys, the only girls admitted after 1817 were those without a criminal record. Even then, the society found difficulty in containing them in the same institution, and ultimately, in 1845, decided not to admit girls at all. In the same year, the Society abandoned its practice of admitting non-delinquent boys and restricted future admissions to boys who had in fact been convicted of a criminal offence. Four years later, the Society was to open the farm school at Redhill, Surrey (still in existence), for boys 'who had entered on a life of crime'.[2]

In little more than half a century, therefore, the Philanthropic Society had gradually changed from a voluntary organisation with a rather diffuse conception of rescue and reform of the young to a specialised organisation bent on the rehabilitation of delinquent boys. This development had been foreshadowed early in the nineteenth century by the setting aside in 1802 of the Reform at Bermondsey for the reception of delinquent children only, so that they might be segregated from children not guilty of crime and thus make it possible for the Society to make special arrangements for their supervision. In effect, these were to make the Reform far more like a prison than any of the Society's other ventures. For example, the grounds were to be surrounded by a high wall, the boys were not allowed out, and visits by family or friends were only allowed by special permission. The boys' Manufactory continued in St George's

[1] ibid., pp. 12–13.
[2] ibid., pp. 22–3.

Fields, where the Society admitted the sons of convicts who were not themselves criminals. The profits of the workshops, 'which are considerable', went to the Society, but something was given to industrious boys as a reward and incentive, and some of the profits were kept back to enable the Society to give its wards some small sum on their discharge from their care. In the Manufactury, to which boys from the Reform might be admitted if and when the time was considered suitable, supervision was a good deal less strict than in the Reform, and it seems to have been run more like an industrial boarding-school.

Even though the work of the Society inexorably and inevitably narrowed in scope over the years, its contribution to the development of the public care for children in England was considerable. By the time of the Society's Incorporation in 1806, it had established the first institution in this country for delinquent and potentially delinquent children. The three sections of the Asylum: the Reform, as a prison school for young delinquents; the Manufactury, for the employment of destitute boys and partially reclaimed delinquents and the training school for girls, were to provide a basic pattern for the later Approved Schools. The Society's aim at the prevention, rather than the punishment of juvenile crime, and its rudimentary attempts at classification and rehabilitation of the children who came into its care, were influential in the moulding of public opinion and of other philanthropic ventures concerned with delinquency. Last, but by no means least, the Society's work gave special emphasis to juvenile delinquency as a particular social problem.

XVI

Vagrancy and Delinquency
in an Urban Setting

1. *The Reformatory Movement*

JUST as voluntary effort made the first institutional provision
for children who were either potentially or actually delinquent,
so also it was voluntary enterprise which, in 1815, set on foot
the first systematic investigation into the contemporary causes
of juvenile delinquency under the auspices of the Society for
Investigating the Causes of the Alarming Increase of Juvenile
Delinquency in the Metropolis. Whether or not the rate of
juvenile delinquency was in fact increasing at an 'alarming' rate
in the early years of the nineteenth century is an interesting but
statistically unanswerable problem. Certainly the Report eventually published by the Society contains no figures on which the
necessary calculations could be based. But it is clearly true that
it was the contemporary conviction that crime was rapidly increasing which prompted some to ask, 'Where do criminals
come from?' and 'What causes delinquency?', questions which
directed attention especially to young offenders and those in the
first stages of crime, and led naturally to the serious investigation of the causes of delinquency. Some members of the Society,
however, had additional reasons for being interested, reasons
which arose from their work amongst the poor and the deprived
of London, and had prompted Peter Bedford, together with his
friends William Crawford and Dr Lushington, to call together

a group of interested people to form a society for investigating and, as far as possible, removing the causes of 'the terrible amount of juvenile crime and degradation found to exist in London, and especially in the neighbourhood of Spitalfields'.

Peter Bedford, the tradesman's son who became known as the 'Spitalfields Philanthropist', was less in the public eye than his fellow Quakers, Elizabeth Fry and James and Samuel Gurney, partly, it was said, because of his lack of education and his comparatively low social position, but, like them, he devoted a considerable amount of his time and his money to assisting existing philanthropic societies and organising new ones. His particular interest was the welfare of the hand-loom weavers of the once prosperous silk industry of Spitalfields, where it was estimated that some 30,000 men, women and children were dependent for support on the notoriously irregular operation of 10,000 hand-looms. For these people, in 1797, the Spitalfields Soup Society, an early and unusual example of oecumenical enterprise of which Bedford became an active supporter, provided soup for some 7,000 people a day. Becoming increasingly aware of the 'fearful' amount of ignorance in the district, this same Society then started a school, on the monitorial system advocated by Joseph Lancaster, into which they proposed to take 1,000 boys and 500 girls.

Through his association with the Soup Society and the school, his work with the Spitalfields Association for the Relief of Special Cases of Distress among the Industrious Poor, and the Refuge for the Destitute (founded in 1804 at Cuper's Bridge, Lambeth, 'to help discharged prisoners, prostitutes and deserted females and others who, from loss of character, or extreme indigence, cannot procure an honest maintenance, though willing to work'), Bedford gained an immense amount of information regarding the lives of the London poor. He also developed a special interest in the operation of the criminal law as it affected the young among them. Horrified by its severity, Bedford laboured to change the penal code as it affected children. 'Amongst children and youths, the havoc of the gallows is awful',[1] he declared. Details of current sentencing practice at the Old Bailey, to which reference has already been made,[2] reveal

[1] Quoted William Beck, *Peter Bedford, the Spitalfields Philanthropist*, p. 20.
[2] Cf. chapter XII, p. 352.

just how true this was. The case which particularly aroused
Bedford and his friends, however, was tried in the following
year. This was the case of young John Knight, who was wrong-
fully arrested for pickpocketing a watch from a man in Hoxton,
tried, and sentenced to death. Asked by a fellow Quaker,
William Crawford, to interest himself on Knight's behalf,
Bedford collected irrefutable evidence of the boy's innocence,
which he forwarded to Lord Sidmouth, the Home Secretary,
who nevertheless refused a reprieve. Angered by Sidmouth's
decision, Bedford became all the more concerned with the
problem of the young delinquent and called together a group of
people whom he knew to be equally interested.

At the meeting £300 was offered to enable the Refuge, the
boys' part of which had now been moved to Hoxton, to admit
a larger proportion of juvenile delinquents, but the real enthusiasm of those present was for investigating the causes of delinquency itself. To this end, the meeting decided to establish the
Society for Investigating the Causes of the Alarming Increase
of Juvenile Delinquency in the Metropolis, the object of which
was 'to obtain every possible information respecting the nature
and causes of the evil in question, in order to ascertain the most
efficient means of removing it . . .'. Peter Bedford and William
Crawford acted as elected secretaries to the Committee amongst
whose fifty members were included Basil Montagu, David
Ricardo, Favell Buxton, James Mill, Dr Lushington and the
younger Samuel Hoare.

To accomplish its purpose, the Committee determined that
all the prisons of London should be regularly visited by specially
appointed sub-committees, 'the youths in confinement [to be]
separately examined and privately admonished, the evil consequences of their conduct represented to them, and every
persuasion used for their recovery which kindness could suggest'.
Anxious to have what would now be called a 'social background
report' on each of the delinquents, the Committee framed a
questionnaire, divided London up into districts, allocated yet
other sub-committees to each district, and set them the task of
completing the questionnaires with the help of friends whose
names had been given to the Committee by the boys in prison.
The accuracy of this information was clearly questionable, 'more
especially as a pecuniary inducement was deemed needful in the

first stage of the business'. On the whole, however, the Committee believed that the answers received were fairly accurate. 'The instances have not been many, in which the accounts received have, upon investigation, proved inaccurate.' Far more formidable a problem they feared was the reform of those boys who had already adopted a life of crime. 'The boys were doomed to mix with characters the most atrocious; in a society where the first risings of penitence would be repelled by mockery, and the name of religion treated as a jest.'[1]

Within twelve months the Committee collected a vast amount of information which it published in the form of a Report. 'The results of all these researches were truly awful to contemplate', wrote one of Bedford's friends, 'and presented a record of temptation, ignorance and destitution sufficient to account for almost any extent of vice and crime, indeed far more than was actually committed, though this was a frightful amount.'[2] More positively, the Committee themselves felt that enough material was collected to 'ascertain the causes in which evil originates'.

Four cases cited give some idea of what these causes were:[3]

A.B. aged 13 years. His parents are living. He was but a short time at school. His father was frequently intoxicated; and on these occasions, the son usually left home and associated with bad characters, who introduced him to houses of ill-fame, they gambled until they had lost all their money. This boy had been five years in the commission of crime, and had been imprisoned for three separate offences. Sentence of death has twice been passed upon him . . .

C.D. aged 10 years. He was committed to prison in the month of April, 1815, having been sentenced to seven years imprisonment for picking pockets. His mother only is living, but he does not know where she resides. He has a very good capacity but cannot read. When first visited, he discovered much anxiety about his condition; but every favourable impression was effaced shortly after his confinement to prison . . .

E.F. aged 8 years. His mother only is living and she is a very immoral character. This boy has been in the habit of stealing for upwards of two years. In Covent Garden Market there is a party of between thirty and forty boys, who sleep under the sheds and

---

[1] *Report of the Committee of the Society for Investigating the Causes of the Alarming Increase of Juvenile Delinquency in the Metropolis*, 1816, pp. 7–9.

[2] William Tallack, *Peter Bedford, the Spitalfields Philanthropist*, p. 53.

[3] Report, Appendix, pp. 29–31.

3. East End children waiting
for food, 1912 (Radio Times
Hulton Picture Library)

4. Peter Bedford, the 'Spitalfields Philanthropist' (Radio Times Hulton Picture Library)

baskets. These pitiable objects, when they arise in the morning, have no other means of procuring subsistence, but by the commission of crime. This child was one of the number; and it appears that he was brought up to the several police offices upon eighteen separate charges. He has been twice confined in the House of Correction, and three times in Bridewell. He is very ignorant but of good capacity . . .

Q.R. aged 12 years. He has had no education: has a mother who encourages the vices of her son. She turns him into the street every morning, and chastises him severely when he returns in the evening without some article of value.

Amongst the causes of such delinquency the Committee listed five as being the most significant:[1]

(1) The improper conduct of parents.
(2) The want of education.
(3) The want of suitable employment.
(4) The violation of the Sabbath and habits of gambling in the public streets.
(5) Other auxiliary causes, which aggravate and perpetuate the evil. These may be traced to and included under the following heads:
   (a) The severity of the criminal code.
   (b) The defective state of the police.
   (c) The existing state of police discipline.

The comments and recommendations which the Committee made in relation to each cause showed them to have been not merely more sympathetic to the predicament of those whose lot they had elected to investigate than the majority of their contemporaries, but to have acquired an understanding of the problem of juvenile delinquency at once more fundamental and far-reaching. The evil of parental neglect, they argued, cannot have a single or even immediate remedy. Unemployment was seen as an important cause of the weakening of parental care and affection: improvident marriages, the degrading tendencies of the Poor Laws and the increased facilities for the consumption of liquor among the poor they regarded as exacerbating influences. They urged the necessity of establishing schools organised and financed on the lines of the school with which several of the Committee had been associated in Spitalfields, so that children

[1] *Report*, p. 10.

might have the advantage of both a formal and a religious training to protect them from the temptation and the necessity to resort to a life of vice and crime as their only means of self-support. Realising all too well, however, that opportunities for reputable employment were no more readily available in London to the young than to their parents, the Committee recommended the setting up of 'Public Establishments' in the most populous districts of London to provide suitable employment, and thus prevent them from falling into bad company and even worse habits.[1]

> While waiting for a situation, their time is their own to idle away. He falls in with those gambling in the streets and becomes contaminated. In this manner has many a deluded youth been ruined, who was first incited to gamble in the streets from want of an industrious occupation; he graduates from petty pilfering to experienced thieving, until he is put in prison. Here he mixes with the most abandoned criminals and he acquires a *taste* for the commission of crime.

The belief that street-gambling exerted a pernicious influence on the young moved the Committee to urge not merely that the existing laws which forbade gambling in the streets on Sundays should be more rigorously enforced by the parochial officers assisted by local voluntary associations of reputable inhabitants, but that the laws should be extended to cover every day of the week.[2]

It was the Committee's comments on the auxiliary causes of juvenile delinquency, however, which were to prove the most important in influencing contemporary attitudes to the problem of juvenile delinquency. Together with similar statements from a variety of other sources, these were both to encourage more voluntary effort in providing institutions whose aim was to reform, not merely punish, delinquent youth, and also to inspire attempts radically to reform the law regarding juvenile crime. According to the Committee, the severity of the existing criminal code, with its two hundred offences liable to capital punishment, was itself a cause of juvenile crime, and 'acts very unfavourably on the mind of the delinquent, for while the

[1] ibid., pp. 16–17.
[2] ibid., pp. 21–2.

humanity of the present age forbids the execution of the greater part of these laws, the uncertainty of their operation encourages the offender to calculate, even if convicted, on a mitigated punishment'. Further, they claimed that 'the vicious inclinations of the delinquent' were directly facilitated by the consequence of the system of offering rewards to police officers on a sliding scale, which made it advantageous to overlook the minor depredations of the incipient thief, and thus fail to check him in the early stages of a criminal career, since 'it is in the officer's interest that the young criminal should attain to maturity in crime, when he will get more money for arresting him'. As the Report very clearly demonstrated, the consequences of the system of rewarding the police for actual conviction in addition to the practice of paying for information leading to conviction, not merely inhibited them from the uniform and full perform-ance of their duty, but led to some of them actually inciting young people into crime: 'Many a poor unsuspecting and even guileless youth was enticed into crime . . . by the police them-selves, who then gave information of, and received a bounty for, the very offences which they have conceived, planned, suggested, aided and secured the commission of.'[1]

Impressed by the failure of the law and its officers to restrain the young delinquent from a career of increasingly serious crime, the Committee were no less concerned with the disastrous effects of punishments meted out to those already embarked. Their frequent visits to the London prisons prompted them to quote from Howard's original *Report on the Condition of Prisons*: 'if it were the aim and wish of magistrates to effect the destruc-tion present and future, of young delinquents, they could not devise a more effectual method than to confine them so long in our prisons, those seats and seminaries, as they have been properly called, of idleness and vice.' Yet, of the many cases investigated by the Committee, they believed that they had met with few of whose amendment they would despair by the applica-tion of more enlightened treatment. Indeed, the Report stated that:[2]

The Society have in fact assisted and restored to credit and useful-ness many delinquents and . . . from the success which has hitherto

[1] ibid., p. 23.
[2] ibid., pp. 26–7.

attended the exertions of the Committee, they feel a decided and growing conviction that, if in the treatment of juvenile delinquents the degree of punishment were proportioned to the nature of the offence – if the operation of that punishment were uniform and certain – if during confinement, they were not exposed to the temptations of idle hours and corrupt society – if the infliction of bodily punishment were to give way to mildness of persuasion and gentleness of reproof – if appeals were oftener made to the moral sensibilities of these youths; and exertions made to raise rather than to degrade them in their own estimation – the number of juvenile depredators would materially diminish, and the conductors of public prisons would frequently enjoy the unspeakable felicity of turning the culprit from the error of his ways.

The belief that juvenile delinquency could be substantially reduced by establishing separate prisons for the young offender with 'a system adapted to the reformation of youth' which should combine all the advantages of education, classification and employment, prompted Peter Bedford and his friends to found in May 1818 the Society for the Improvement of Prison Discipline and for the Reformation of Juvenile Offenders. This was to continue and enlarge the work of their earlier society; to undertake more detailed study in this country of the effects of contemporary prison conditions on the young people committed to them; and also to make extensive visits to the special juvenile prisons and reformatories already established on the Continent. Convinced that independent, voluntary effort was insufficient to the task, and using the information they had collected, the Society then submitted to the Home Secretary a plan for a reformatory for boys, which they suggested should accommodate six hundred delinquent boys and combine in its organisation and structure all the advantages of regular inspection, classification, education and employment. Every class was to have its own dining-room, workshop and 'airing ground'. Each prisoner was to have his own cell. For many years, however, it proved impossible to convince successive parliaments of the desirability of state support for schemes such as this. Thus, the development of reformatory, as distinct from punitive, institutions for the juvenile delinquent was left to a number of enthusiasts such as Peter Bedford, and later Mary Carpenter, and the voluntary societies which helped them in their work.

The immediate impact of the work of Bedford's two societies on the public discussion of the problem of juvenile delinquency was nevertheless considerable. This was not so much because of the novelty of their views. Vagrancy, mendicity, parental neglect, ignorance and unemployment had been associated with delinquency in England for centuries and education and industrial training had been offered as the panacea since Tudor times. The need to separate the young criminal from the older and more hardened convicts had been appreciated by men like Fielding and underlined by Howard's investigation of English prisons in the eighteenth century. The possibility of 'reforming' the young delinquent had seized the minds and prompted the experiments of societies such as the Philanthropic Society. What made the Bedford societies' work so impressive to their contemporaries was that by their patient and systematic investigation of the causes and conditions of juvenile delinquency, they had not merely made explicit a good many of the implicit assumptions with regard to it, but had made possible rational and effective policies for its solution by isolating and evaluating the variable factors which precipitated large numbers of young people into a life of criminal activity. They had, in effect, made themselves 'experts', and as such were invited to give evidence before the several official enquiries sponsored by the State which followed the publication of the *Report of the Society for Investigating the Causes of the Alarming Increase of Juvenile Delinquency in the Metropolis*. James Miller, a member of the Committee of the Society, gave evidence before the Select Committee on the State of the Police of the Metropolis in 1817, as did the Society's secretary, William Crawford in the following year. The Committee on Prisons within the City of London and the Borough of Southwark, whose Report was also published in 1818, included extensive evidence on the conditions in these prisons from Bedford himself, and from Favel Buxton whose recently published essay *An Inquiry whether Crime and Misery are Produced or Prevented by our Present System of Prison Discipline* had 'powerfully operated upon the public mind'.[1]

Whilst the appeal for parliamentary support for the establishment of reformatories fell on deaf ears, the growing awareness

[1] *Report of the Committee of the Society for the Improvement of Prison Discipline and for the Reformation of Juvenile Offenders*, 1818, p. 28.

that prisons operated as 'nurseries of vice' prompted the first attempt in this country to frame legislation which would specifically deal with the young offender. A Bill for the Punishment, Correction, and Reform of Young Persons, charged with Privately Stealing from Houses, or the Person in Certain Cases, introduced in 1821, embodied the suggestion that instead of the existing practice of committing children to prison to await trial at Quarter Sessions or Assize for petty offences – such as stealing an apple or a baker's tart – summary powers of conviction might be given to two local justices. The preamble to the Bill drew attention to the increase of petty crime among young persons 'who in many instances have been before imprisoned for similar offences, and returned to their former associates and criminal pursuits', and suggested that 'a prompt and summary punishment might, in many instances, reform such Juvenile Offenders'. The Bill thus provided that two justices should be empowered to convict or imprison a young offender charged with theft, and commit him to a House of Correction or Penitentiary 'or other place of correction and reform'; instead of committing him for trial as a felon to some prison in which he almost certainly would become tainted by association with hardened criminals during the often prolonged delay before he could actually be tried. The effect of the Bill was to give magistrates powers of discretion not to account felonies as such in the case of 'young people', a term not defined in the Bill which was so roughly drafted that it proved impossible to find sufficient parliamentary support for its adoption. The rejection of this, and subsequent Bills, unfortunately meant that summary jurisdiction for juveniles was delayed for more than a quarter of a century until, in 1847, the statutory foundations of our present practice with regard to the trial of young offenders were effectively laid.

This attempted legislation, however, underlines the extent to which public opinion had gradually been educated with regard to the treatment of the young offender. Since the subject had been seriously considered, the dominant theme of reports had been that the juvenile offender must not be 'contaminated' by association with the adult criminal, because he 'was much further back on the road to crime and might yet be deterred if only he could be kept from the company of those more hardened than himself'. The juvenile offender was indeed thought of as a half-fledged adult offender, but a new consciousness was developing, to which Bedford's own work had made a substantial contribution, that the juvenile offender was also different in kind from the adult. His offences often arose from mischief, ignorance or bad upbringing, and, unlike the adult, the juvenile offender was malleable, and therefore different treatment was required, since it was desired to reform rather than deter him. Recognition of this attitude can be seen as early as 1828 in an official Report which pointed out that rich men's sons got beaten for offences for which poor men's sons were committed to prison, and was very much fostered and encouraged by the more enlightened voluntary institutions founded for the care of destitute and delinquent juveniles.

By the 1840s it is possible clearly to distinguish two schools of reformers regarding the nature of the institutions to which the juvenile offender might properly be committed; one advocating the establishment of separate juvenile prisons, the other educational and home-like reformatories. Before the position became clarified, however, the whole subject was again intensively investigated by two committees, sitting about the same time and covering very much the same ground: the Select Committee on Criminal Commitments and Convictions, which issued two Reports, the first in 1827 and the second in the following year; and the Select Committee on the Police of the Metropolis which reported in 1828.

Both these Committees were appointed to enquire into the increase in the number of criminal commitments and convictions, the former dealing with England and Wales and the latter, as its name suggests, restricting its investigations to the Metropolis. Both were at pains to point out that, to some degree, the 'increase' in juvenile delinquency was more apparent than real, the numerical increase in commitments being related to changes in criminal procedure which allowed prosecutors' expenses, and more especially to the replacement of the old night-watchman by a more efficient, regular and professional police force. As to the causes of juvenile delinquency, both were also in agreement in listing, among others, the low price of spirits which encouraged heavy drinking at an early age for both parents and their offspring; the general want of employment; the parental neglect of children, increasingly large numbers of whom were said to be abandoned at an early age. They also pointed to the change in the apprenticeship system which now allowed 'outdoor' apprentices; the maladministration of the Poor Law under which less and less attention had been paid to the law's continuing requirement that the young should be adequately trained and disciplined to fend for themselves; and the failure of the penal system to provide suitable methods of treatment.

On this last point, the Select Committee on Criminal Commitments and Convictions found that[1]

> they cannot doubt that the present system of long imprisonments for young offenders, besides the expense and inconvenience attending it, greatly promotes the growth of crime . . . a boy is committed to prison for trial, the degradation and the company he meets there prepare his mind for every vice; after long delay, he is sentenced to six months' or a year's imprisonment, he herds with felons, and comes out an accomplished thief, detesting the laws of his country, and prepared with means to evade them.

Very cautiously they commended the experiment of giving the justices powers of summary jurisdiction with regard to certain petty offences of juveniles under sixteen or seventeen years of age so as to avoid the moral dangers of detaining them in prison for long periods. The only effective alternative, they argued, was to hold the Sessions at much shorter intervals of three or, at the most, four weeks. This particular recommendation was accompanied with the affirmation that, for thefts 'under a certain . . . value', swift justice should be followed by short periods of imprisonment and whipping: 'Great advantage may be derived from the application of corporal punishment to boys.'[2] In fact, private whipping and short periods of solitary confinement seemed to be the only proper punishment for boys guilty of petty thefts for the first offence. One witness had gone so far as to state unreservedly: 'I think it [summary jurisdiction] would be imperfect, unless you give them powers of ordering whipping or solitary confinement; I think solitary confinement for a fortnight with a boy for his first offence is much the best possible punishment.' After which, he hastened to add: 'I do not mean to

[1] Report from the Select Committee on Criminal Commitments and Convictions, *PP*, 1828, VI p. 12.
[2] ibid., p. 13.

say solitary confinement in the dark, but that they should see no one but the chaplain and the officers of the prison during that time.'[1]

Their obvious attachment to certain old, 'well-tried' methods of punishment for the petty criminal did not, however, blind the Committee to certain advantages of more recent methods of dealing with the young offender which had been tried out with success on the Continent, particularly in France. Thus they enthusiastically endorsed the French principle of 'treating boys differently from men', and were deeply interested in their system of bringing together all those convicted under the age of twenty into one prison where methods of reform were adopted. It was this which influenced them to recommend the establishment of a House of Correction for Young Criminals with a system of management totally different to that operating in adult prisons.

This particular recommendation was reinforced by the Report of the Select Committee on the Police of the Metropolis, which advocated a separate prison for juvenile delinquents, specially built for the purpose or, if the cost of such a scheme be thought prohibitive, the stationing of a convict ship in the Thames, specially fitted up for the reception of boys.

In addition to advocating a special prison to which young offenders might be committed, this Committee was also concerned for the effective after-care of children released from prison, realising that without this many would inevitably return time and again. Like others before them, they believed that the solution to this particular problem was to send boys to sea, either on the men-of-war of the Royal Navy or on merchant vessels. 'If, on their discharge from prison, they could thus be separated from their former associates and weaned from their former habits, a better security against the repetition of offence would be provided than could be hoped for from any improvement of their morals that could be effected by the discipline of prison.'[2] Alternatively, they recommend that young offenders should be sent after their discharge from prison to some institution similar to the Refuge for the Destitute, at Hoxton, where

[1] ibid.

[2] Report from the Select Committee on the Police of the Metropolis, *PP*, 1828, VI, p. 8.

they could be trained in some employment and thus diverted from the necessity of returning to a life of crime.

Detailed evidence on the work of the Refuge had been presented to the Committee by James Ross, the Superintendent of the Boys' section, which not only gave some indication of the success of the institution as a reformatory, but also contained details of its organisation and finances which are of considerable interest. As regards the Refuge's success, Ross calculated that, out of 282 who, in the course of about four years, had stayed sufficient time to receive 'the benefits of the house', 117 were doing well; 10 were dead; there were 106 of whose conduct after leaving the Reformatory he was 'partly doubtful' and partly without information; and the remainder, about 50, he knew to have returned to crime again. Explaining his uncertainty as to the fate of the 106, the Superintendent remarked that, candidly, he 'was not surprised that there were many of them of whom I could not hear anything, because they are rather shy of us, and they feel ashamed of being in the house when they do well after leaving it'.[1] Perhaps this was a rather sanguine view yet, even if the Refuge could claim only the 117 as 'doing well' on their discharge, this represented no small success for their work, and undoubtedly impressed the Committee. By 1828, it seems that the Refuge was only accepting boys of between twelve and twenty years of age whom they liked to keep in the institution itself for at least two years, during which time an attempt was made to give them basic training in some skill – tailoring, shoe-making, basket-making – after which they were usually apprenticed to the various trades in which they had had preliminary instruction. Some, however, were sent to sea, some emigrated to South Africa. To each boy the Refuge gave £5 and a suit of clothes on his discharge. When the Superintendent gave evidence, fifteen of the eighty boys in the house had been sent there by judges under what was called 'respited sentence', a legal device by which delinquents found guilty could be fined one shilling and discharged with the condition that they were to be sent to the Refuge.[2] Within the house, discipline was maintained by curtailment of diet; reprimand by the Committee; suspension from training and a return to the 'hard labour' of woodcutting

[1] ibid., p. 182.
[2] ibid.

444

(on which all boys were employed when they first entered the Refuge); solitary confinement in the dark; and, for those who failed to respond to any of these punishments, expulsion. Ross's evidence on the financing of the Refuge is also worth noting since, whilst some of the boys were paid for by private philanthropists and voluntary reform associations, some money had been contributed by the Government itself.[1] According to Ross, 'at one time' this had amounted to £5,000, but in 1827 this sum had been reduced to £4,000, and in 1828 '£3,000 is recommended'. Naturally, the Committee were interested to learn whether or not these grants gave the agents of the Government the automatic right to send a number of boys to the institution. To this question, the Superintendent gave the guarded reply: 'I do not know what the claim is, but I never knew an instance when the Secretary of State sent a boy, when he was not taken on the permanent establishment, and the same with the judges.'[2] From this evidence, it also emerged that the Government was not entirely satisfied that the grants it had made in previous years had been altogether well managed, and the outcome of a good deal of correspondence between the Secretary of State and the Committee of the Refuge conducted during the previous year had resulted in a reduction of costs in the Refuge – and also a reduction in the Government aid.[3]

The Select Committee had been pressing Ross for details of the Refuge as an institution to which boys could be sent for effective aftercare on their discharge from prison, although it is clear that the Refuge was also being used to a limited extent as an alternative to imprisonment. At least one other witness was also anxious to urge them to consider the merits of an establishment to which boys might be sent before they were fully embarked on a criminal career. This was Sir Richard Birnie, the Chief Bow Street Magistrate, and a successor to Fielding not merely in respect of his office but in his deep concern that boys should be protected and, if need be, removed from a way of life which was none of their choosing and which was almost inevitably bound to corrupt them:[4]

[1] ibid., p. 184.
[2] ibid.
[3] ibid., p. 185.
[4] ibid., p. 39.

There were last night and it will be the same tonight, perhaps from ten to fifteen or eighteen boys sleeping under the green stalls in Covent Garden, who dare not go home without money, sent out by their parents, to beg ostensibly, but to steal if they cannot get it; and I have reason to believe . . . that it is the same in Fleet Market and other markets, little urchins that I have taken out at night, with no home to go to or, if they have, they dare not go home under sixpence, and then those boys become the prey to older boys, and so organised gangs are established; to get away those boys before they are completely contaminated . . . would be a great national object. I am talking of those children of eight to twelve; that if they could be taken from their parents when they are found in the streets, and put into some asylum, where they could be trained up to industry, it would be an immense thing, and then the gangs would want recruits, and would fall to decay.

It was just this determination 'to begin at the root of the problem' of delinquency which had moved Fielding in the middle of the previous century to associate himself with the Marine Society, and it was to precisely the same legislation as had empowered the Society to act with regard to children in moral danger that Sir Richard Birnie appealed as the sanction for his own proposal. 'How would you compel them [the children] to enter into an institution . . . without having some evidence of their having committed a crime?' he was asked. 'There is an unrepealed Act of Anne', he replied, 'which authorises a Magistrate, with the consent of the churchwardens of the parish where the delinquent is found, who either begs, or his parents beg, who cannot give a proper account of himself, to bind that boy to the sea service.' The great difficulty in operating this particular scheme in the nineteenth century, as Birnie himself was the first to point out, was that masters of merchant vessels had become increasingly reluctant to accept the boys as apprentices, although 'in time of war, they were glad of them'. For this reason, Sir Richard proposed a modification on the original idea.[1]

Now my plan would be this, and it would not be expensive, neither would the Government have much to do with it, to get a good old roomy Indiaman, and moor her off Woolwich, and to put in her a master and a superintendent governor and carpenter, whom government must otherwise provide for, and to bind those boys to

[1] ibid.

those men; and if after they have been three years under the discipline of such men as those, every merchantman would be glad to
take them.

The Committee, however, remained more concerned with
reform than prevention. 'Do you not think that there would be
a great advantage in having a hulk for the reception of young
boys that had committed thefts?', they asked Birnie, who still
pressed his original point: 'Perhaps it might; But I want to
provide for those who have never committed crimes.' The
Committee then asked: 'Do you think it would be advisable to
separate those boys from the boys that have committed crimes?'
A question to which Birnie inevitably replied: 'Most assuredly
. . . I would have another hulk, or another depot of the same
sort, so that they were taken from the streets of London.'[1]

There was, in fact, nothing novel in the idea of setting aside
one hulk to which only children were to be sent. This had been
suggested ten years earlier and, in 1823, the *Bellerophon* at
Sheerness had been set aside for juvenile use and about 320 boys
put on board. Two years later, the *Bellerophon* was broken up,
and the boys were transferred to the much smaller frigate, the
Euryalus stationed at Chatham. It was concerning the *Euryalus*
that J. H. Capper, clerk for the criminal department of the
Secretary of State's Office and Inspector of the Hulk Establishment, gave evidence before the Committee. Since the *Euryalus*
constituted the first government-sponsored scheme to separate
boys under the age of sixteen from the older convicts, description
of the daily régime on the hulk is of considerable interest:[2]

Monday, at half-past five in the morning, all hands called, ports
opened, hammocks lowered and rolled up, boys washed and hammocks got on deck and stowed; at six, boys sent into chapel, the
morning hymn sung, and a prayer read by the schoolmaster [an
adult convict], the officers and guards being present; after prayers,
breakfast is served, under the inspection of the first mate and
officers, consisting of one half of the daily allowance of oatmeal,
boiled, and one third of the daily allowance of bread; after breakfast,
the boys confined on one deck, are sent to the main deck for air and
exercise; those on the other decks after the mess-tables . . . are
cleared away, are set to their respective trades [nearly all of them

[1] ibid.
[2] ibid., pp. 103–4.

were in fact employed in making clothes for the Convict Establishment, taught either by a guard or by an older convict]; . . . at half-past nine, the surgeon generally attends; one division of the boys go on deck; their hammocks, bedding and clothes inspected, hair trimmed and persons washed in a cistern of salt-water . . . at half-past eleven, boys leave their work, clean their wards, wash themselves; dinner served, consisting of one-third of the daily allowance of bread, and one-half of the daily allowance of oatmeal boiled; at half-past five, the boys of one deck sent to school, and those of another sent on the main deck for air and exercise; and hammocks sent below; at half-past seven, the school over, previous to the boys being dismissed, they sing the evening hymn, and prayer is read by the schoolmaster. Boys mustered into their respective wards, and secured for the night. At half-past eight, the watch set . . .

Each succeeding day is the same, with the exception of Saturday, when one-third of the allowance of bread, and three ounces of cheese only are served for dinner, and the day is devoted to general washing and cleaning of the ship; packing and sending to the store the articles made by the boys during the week. No school is held at noon, but in the evening all the boys are sent to chapel, and those who committed hymns to memory recite them, which closes the evening with hymn and prayer as on the other nights. At seven, boys mustered into their wards, clean shirts, handkerchiefs, etc. served to them, and secured for the night.

Sunday morning commences as on other days; at eight o'clock, boys let on deck by divisions, and inspected; at a quarter before eleven, they are sent into chapel, at which time the chaplain attends, and reads a part of the morning service, and delivers an extemporaneous discourse, which generally occupies about fifty minutes to an hour; dinner is served when the service is over, . . . after dinner, the boys of one deck sent on to the main deck for air and exercise; at half-past two sent below, and the boys at each ward assembled at their tables to hear the Scriptures read by boys selected for that purpose; at half-past three another division of the boys sent on deck for air; at five, supper service; at six, all hands on deck for air, evening service read by the schoolmaster, and the boys catechized; at eight, mustered and secured for the night, and the watch set.

Not surprisingly, Capper was unable to conclude his evidence with an assurance to the Committee that the regime of the *Euryalus* produced encouraging results. Asked: 'Have you any means of knowing what has been the conduct of the boys who have been confined on board this separate ship, after they have been set at large?', he was obliged to reply: 'I am sorry to say it had been very indifferent; for eight out of ten that have been liberated, have returned to their old careers.'[1]

The respective merits of committing young offenders either to reformatory institutions or to hulks were to be reconsidered seven years later. For the moment, the recommendations of both the Select Committee on Criminal Commitments and Convictions and of the Select Committee on the Police of the Metropolis as regards the desirability of either setting up a special prison for young offenders or of maintaining a separate hulk for them appear to have had little effective influence on the development of public policy. As far as a separate prison was concerned, neither Committee could disguise the considerable cost of such a venture, and as regards the separate hulk, the evidence of the *Euryalus*, the only one of its kind in operation, scarcely encouraged its duplication.

The only recommendation of either Committee to be incorporated even in draft legislation was that of giving powers of summary jurisdiction to justices of the peace so as to expedite the trial of young petty offenders, a proposal submitted to Parliament in the ill-fated Bill to extend the Power of Summary Convictions of Juvenile Offenders (1829). This Bill, which was intended only as a temporary experiment for a period of two years, proposed that two or more justices might try and summarily convict any boy under the age of fifteen charged for the first time with simple larceny, where the value of the stolen goods was not above ten shillings. If he was acquitted, the justices were to be empowered to discharge the boy forthwith, but if he was convicted, they were to be allowed to sentence him to imprisonment with or without hard labour, or in solitary confinement, provided that they did not order more than ten days' solitary confinement without a break, during which fresh air and exercise could be allowed. The Bill further stipulated that, at the next Quarter Sessions after the Bill received the Royal Assent, the justices were to set aside part of a gaol or House of Correction (or, if need be, build a separate gaol) for the exclusive use of boys thus sentenced. The stipulation was purely academic, however, as the Bill failed to receive adequate support in Parliament and the Royal Assent was thus never sought.

[1] ibid., p. 105.

The Select Committee on Criminal Commitments and Convictions, which had been particularly interested in the idea of granting summary powers to justices with regard to juvenile offenders, had been fully aware of the strength and nature of the opposition to such a proposal:[1]

> It could not appear otherwise than strange to see a country gentleman with no legal education, deciding summarily upon an offence which cannot be punished by the most learned judges of the land without the verdict of a jury. [Yet, they argued], an answer has been made . . . to these objections, which merits attention. It is not necessary, it is said, to consider the offences for which juvenile offenders would be thus punished, as crimes amounting to felony. A petty theft committed by a boy of ten or eleven years old has not that grave character, which by our laws has hitherto belonged to it. By the Acts introduced by Mr. Secretary Peel, there are many petty trespasses against property, such as stealing wood above the value of 1s. and others, which are viewed rather as offences against order than serious crimes, and are punished summarily by a single Magistrate.

In reality, however, the Committee's proposals assumed assent not merely to the view that certain offences could now be regarded as less serious than before, but that the age of the miscreant was in some measure to be regarded as a mitigating circumstance, and one which could make less serious any possible misdirection of justice stemming from the alleged inadequacies of the magistrates, inadequacies on which the Committee itself declined to comment. Moreover, the dual interest of reformers in both modifying the trial of young offenders and in providing separate institutions to which they might be committed on conviction all too often served to confuse the evidence of their supporters and thus strengthen the criticisms of their opponents. In evidence quoted in a further *Report of the Select Committee on the Police of the Metropolis* published in August 1834 W. A. A. White, himself a magistrate, drew the Committee's attention to the difficulties caused by the refusal to extend the summary powers of justices. 'Robbery had taken place, but they were petty things, such as a boy taking gingerbread, and the magistrate cannot avoid saying that it is a felony.' It would, he believed,

[1] Report from the Select Committee on Criminal Commitments and Convictions, p. 13.

be of 'great advantage' if only the magistrate could deal with such offences summarily. 'We have had parents requesting their children to be punished, and we have had a poor widow coming and requesting her son to be punished, wishing that we should give him summary punishment; we can only say, if he goes into prison, he will be worse than before he went.'[1] The following year, however, a Select Committee of the House of Lords was appointed whose specific terms of reference 'to inquire into the present State of the several Gaols and Houses of Correction in England and Wales' enabled them more easily to concentrate their attention effectively on the one issue of the character of the institutions to which offenders were or should be committed. In the course of the five Reports presented by the Committee, reference was inevitably made time and again to the large numbers of children inflating the annual criminal statistics.

According to Capper, the number of boys and girls under the age of twenty-one who had been committed in 1834 was 9,077, of whom 400 were aged twelve and under; 2,204 aged between thirteen and sixteen years of age; and the remainder, 6,437 between seventeen and twenty-one.[2] Another witness, W. A. Miles, the recently appointed schoolmaster to the children in Newgate Prison, produced figures (the source of which he did not divulge) which showed not merely that the rate of delinquency in general was higher in the counties of Middlesex and Surrey than in England and Wales as a whole, but that the proportion of young offenders was significantly greater, thereby strengthening the view that crime and density of population were integrally related.[3]

In company with several other witnesses from other parts of the country who appeared before the Committee, one of whom declared that 'the Houses of Correction now throughout the country are not Houses of Correction, but Houses of Contamination', Miles was quite clear that prevailing conditions of imprisonment were such that, for the young offender, 'the longer he remains in Gaol the more perfect he becomes in Crime'.[4] The results of confinement in the one place specially

---

[1] op. cit., p. 52.
[2] House of Lords Sessional Papers, 1835, no. 42, p. 220.
[3] ibid., p. 510.
[4] ibid., p. 511.

designated for the reception of children, the hulk *Euryalus*, were no better. This had already been admitted by the Inspector of the Hulk Establishment, in evidence to the 1828 Committee and was now dramatically underlined by the evidence of Thomas Dexter, an ex-convict who had been a male nurse in the Juvenile Convict Hospital to which many of the boys from the *Euryalus* were sent. Dexter had seen no signs of reformation in these boys as a result of their imprisonment; quite the contrary, they appeared to deteriorate and seldom showed any signs of contrition at their crimes. 'Frequently when I have seen it in a newspaper that a Judge has sentenced a Boy out of Mercy to him to the Hulks, I have made the observation that was it a Child of mine, I would rather see him dead at my feet than see him sent to that place.'[1]

In the light of Capper's earlier description of the daily routine on the *Euryalus* with all its crushing monotony, rigid discipline and cynical religiosity, it would indeed be difficult to entertain any great hope of the hulk as a fundamentally 'reforming' establishment. Overcrowded from the beginning, the number of boys on the *Euryalus* had risen to some 400, of whom 250 were under fifteen years of age. No classification was attempted and all the evils of the larger hulks and prisons were reproduced in miniature between her decks. Bullying appears to have been incessant. According to Dexter, the boys dreaded not so much the imprisonment itself as the ill-treatment they received from their fellow prisoners, one set of whom were known as the 'Nobs'. He had, he said, seen Nobs 'take a broomstick and strike a boy over the arm almost to break his arm, and the other dare not say a word to him'. Again,[2]

I have known it when three or four have been obliged to be locked up in a cell by themselves, in order to shelter them from murder – those who they call Noseys, that is, those whom they considered had been to the officers to tell them anything that was going on . . . I have known patients come into the hospital who have declared that they have not tasted meat for three weeks together, but that they have been obliged to give their portions to those Nobs, and that they have fed themselves upon gruel and parings of potatoes.

[1] ibid., p. 321.
[2] ibid., pp. 323–4.

Such food as was spared to the boys by the Nobs was frequently withdrawn by the officers since cutting off rations was more resorted to than any other mode of punishment. 'Stopping their meat and lowering their diet', Capper himself informed the Committee, 'has a great effect'.[1] Little wonder, perhaps, that the Nobs were eager to seize any food from their less hardy shipmates, some of whom were but nine years old and so young 'that they can barely put on their clothes'. Nor is it surprising that some practised the art of self-mutilation so as to escape to the hospital ship where, according to Dexter, their treatment was 'remarkably correct'. In hospital they did at least receive regular food and better accommodation, were free alike from the Nobs and the guards, and might even be treated with sympathy and humanity by such a man as Dexter himself appears to have been. They resorted to all sorts of expedients to gain admission. One was to apply a red-hot copper button to their skin, rub the wound with soap, and then wrap it up until it turned septic and 'piteous to behold'. A much more drastic method was also described by Dexter:

'I have known several cases in which they have broken their arms to get into hospital; they held their arms upon a form and let the edge of the table drop upon them and break them in two. They would get some other boys to do it for them, and then the excuse was that they had tumbled down a ladder.'[2]

Recognising the significance of the evidence before them which illuminated the conditions under which boys aged between nine and sixteen years might be held for as long as seven years, the more 'fortunate' no doubt looking forward to transportation when they were fourteen, the Committee condemned the commitment of boys to the hulks in the strongest possible terms: 'their unavoidable Intercourse with one another must give them innumerable Opportunities of contaminating each other's minds, and thus rendering their Confinement, not a salutory Preparation for an ultimate Change of Country, but a Hotbed of Vice destined to expand in all its Maturity in a new and congenial Soil.'[3] The abandonment of the use of hulks for boys was urged as soon as conceivably possible and the use of unoccupied

[1] ibid., p. 280.
[2] ibid., p. 324.
[3] ibid., p. v.

barracks or forts near to the ports from which those sentenced to transportation would ultimately sail was suggested as a possible alternative. Despite this, the *Euryalus* was not abandoned till twelve years later, in 1846.

The hulks were subjected to the scrutiny of the Committee because they were part of a system of statutorily organised and publicly financed provision for the criminal population. The voluntary reformatory schools attracted their attention partly because they were already being used as an alternative place of commitment for juvenile offenders, and were specially organised to meet their needs, but largely because of the vigorously canvassed claims of their superiority as a method of solving the problem of delinquency among the young. Among the reformatories which particularly interested the Committee were those run by the Children's Friend Society under the guidance and chairmanship of its founder, Edward Pelham Brenton, a retired Royal Navy captain. Captain Brenton had already conducted a spirited campaign against the inherent and inevitable consequences of imprisoning together the young and the old offender, the 'apprentice' and the master criminal. He had written to Lord Grey, the Duke of Richmond and Lord Melbourne canvassing their support for his scheme for a 'floating asylum' for the reception of delinquent boys on board which 'the system pursued towards these unfortunate children should be one of kindness, conciliation, and firmness, restraint, privation for faults, but very rarely punishment . . .' In 1823, he had sent a petition to Parliament on this subject which was presented and read in the House of Lords by the Bishop of Rochester and in the House of Commons by Dr Lushington, Bedford's friend. In the course of his petition, Brenton claimed:[1]

> That your Petitioner has examined most of the prisons of the Metropolis, where he has found many children of a tender age confined as felons and criminals, to their great detriment and certain ruin; and further, that your Petitioner has discovered among the poor of the Metropolis an immense number of children who have no means of gaining a livelihood; that they are constantly brought forward before the civil power for very trivial offences against the laws; . . . Your Petitioner therefore prays, that your Right Honourable House will take the case of these unhappy children into your

[1] E. P. Brenton, *The Bible and the Spade*, p. 13.

serious consideration, and apply such remedies as in your wisdom you shall deem fit; and your Petitioner humbly prays that children of either sex under the age of sixteen years may no longer be committed to the common prisons of the land, but be carefully guarded and educated and kindly disposed of, either at home or in the colonies of His Majesty . . . .

The following year, Brenton published his much discussed *Observations on the Training and Education of the Children of Great Britain* in which he made a virulent attack on the *Euryalus*.[1]

Who would have believed in the existence of such a ship, and for such a purpose, as the *Euryalus* at Chatham:– 417 boys, between the ages of nine and sixteen, confined as convicts for seven years, each to cost from £70 to £100. – A floating Bastille; – children in iron cages, who should have been in a nursery garden; – children pining in misery, where the stench was intolerable . . . And while unfortunate girls are starving for want of needlework, these boys are confined in dungeons, making shirts for convicts . . . I denounce this system as atrociously extravagant, cruel and vindictive, and I challenge any man to come forward and justify it . . .

If there is no record of any man accepting Brenton's challenge, it is certainly clear that his activities had created a good deal of public sympathy for his efforts to improve the lot of criminal and semi-criminal children. Indeed, the same year that he published his *Observations*, he was successful in gaining 'high patronage' for his Society which enabled him to add to the Brenton Asylum for boys at Hackney Wick, the Royal Victoria Asylum for girls at Chiswick. Small wonder that the Select Committee were particularly interested in his work.

Like the Refuge with which Peter Bedford was associated, the Brenton Asylum had been opened in 1830 not merely for the benefit of convicted juvenile delinquents but for the vagrant and the poor children who haunted the streets of London, without employment, without education, often, though by no means invariably, without parents to care for them. Brenton himself described the objects of his Society thus:

I   To collect the most destitute and forlorn of the Vagrant Boys, who are wandering about the streets of the Metropolis, without a home or any means of subsistence, but from begging and thieving.

[1] p. xx.

II   To assist parishes to manage and to dispose of their refractory boys, who are alternately the inmates of goals and workhouses.

III   To afford aid to industrious small tradesmen, artisans and labourers, to reclaim and dispose of such of their children as have been entrapped by the receivers of stolen goods, and seduced by some of the numerous gangs of young depredators of which there are frequent examples at the different police offices in the Metropolis.

The Asylum at Hackney Wick had been equipped to house fifty boys, 'or as many as funds permit', and was under the supreme authority of the Master to whom was 'the first duty of every boy'. The Master, in turn, was responsible to the School Committee who undertook to uphold his authority 'as long as it is exercised with temper and discretion'. The Committee required of him that he exercise 'strict discipline, prompt obedience and perfect regularity' and that, whilst doing so, he was 'to bear in mind that gentleness and kind treatment must be the rule, punishment and severity the exception'. Boys were normally admitted between the ages of ten and fourteen, although some were younger, and usually stayed up to six months, during which time parents and friends were only allowed to visit them on the first Saturday of every month at noon, 'and then only by order of the Chairman ... The Chairman, however, is authorised under very special circumstances to use his discretion in giving orders on the other days.' The careful restriction of visits, together with the rule that a boy might not leave the Asylum without an express order in writing from the Committee and with the consent of his parents, if any, was intended to allow the system of reform to operate on the boys to maximum effect. 'Our system is mildness, constant inspection, constant labour or amusement, constant innocent occupation', Brenton told the Select Committee. 'I may say we never punish, except with solitary confinement for a few hours; or privation of animal food.' If this last comment arouses the uneasy feeling that perhaps, after all, there was a good deal more in common between the regime of the *Euryalus* and the Asylum than one had been led to believe, it is a feeling soon dispelled by reading the rules set out in a pamphlet issued in 1833 by Brenton's society under its original name, the Society for the Suppression of Juvenile Vagrancy:[1]

[1] *Report of the Hackney Wick School Sub-Committee*, 1833, pp. 6–7.

Rule 9. During the Summer half year, the boys to rise at 6 a.m., and in the winter at 7 a.m., time allowed for dressing and washing to be half an hour; reading the Scriptures, prayers and general education, from half-past six or half-past seven to eight a.m.

Rule 10. At 8, breakfast; from 9 until 12, employment in the field or garden [in the ten acres of ground attached to the Asylum] weather permitting.

From 12 until 2 o'clock, dinner and recreation.

From 2 until 5 in the Summer and from 1 until 4 in the Winter, employment in the field or garden.

From 5 to 6, wash and supper.

From 6 to 8, reading, to close with admonitions and prayers.

At 8, the names of the boys to be called over and retire to bed.

Rule 13. When the weather is unfavourable for field labour, the boys to be employed in learning some useful trade, such as the Committee may from time to time approve. They should be taught also to grind their own corn in hand mills, make their own bread and cook their own meat.

Compared with the *Euryalus*, the Asylum was indeed Elysium for those fortunate enough to be admitted. Even the use of punishment, inevitable with so mixed and often 'refractory' a group of boys, was differently conceived. True, the Master of the Asylum might resort to solitary confinement as a means of discipline, but only in the precise circumstances laid down by the Committee:

Any boy found guilty of falsehood to be placed in solitary confinement for three hours, and for any repetition of the offence, one hour additional . . . The punishment for every oath or bad language to be the same as above. For stealing, from six to seven hours solitary confinement, on bread and water diet, with lecture; and for every repetition of the offence, two hours additional confinement.

All minor offences were to be immediately punished at the discretion of the Master, 'but flogging or blows are strictly forbidden, and no task to be given from Scripture, as a punishment'. Offences in which the boys persisted were to be reported by the Master to the Committee, who dealt with them at their own discretion. Bullying of the kind so vividly described by Dexter, was specifically ruled against by the Committee. They gave the Master clear instructions that he was to watch the Monitors, each of whom was responsible to him for the behaviour of the boys in the 'divisions' into which the classes of the Asylum were divided, to make sure that they did not abuse their authority. Any Monitor who did abuse the trust placed in him by either bullying or lying, was immediately deprived of his position and not appointed again until after a very long probation.[1]

The ultimate aim of such training that the Asylum could give in a limited time to the children it accepted was to apprentice them in the colonies, mostly as farm or house servants, where specially appointed Committees were to receive them on arrival, arrange for their indentures and ensure that they were properly treated by their masters and mistresses. By 1835 a Committee was already established at Cape Town to look after boys sent out by the Society and steps were being taken to appoint a Ladies Committee to receive any girls sent out from the recently opened Royal Victoria Asylum. Efforts were also being made to recruit similar Committees in Canada.

If the numbers actually sent out appear small – between 1830 and 1834, some 278 boys and 37 girls emigrated under the auspices of the Society – the individual results were said to be very encouraging. 'Almost all do well according to the reports of the Committees and the children's own letters',[2] Brenton told the Select Committee. The real obstacle to his work was finance. 'I am perfectly at a loss to know why I am not supported by the government', he wrote to a friend. In practice, the Society depended on voluntary subscriptions of from 5s. upwards to supplement the charge it made of 4s. a week or a lump sum of £12 10s. for receiving a child from a parish or one placed by an institution such as the Refuge itself, Coldbath Fields Prison and the Foundling Hospital. Brenton himself was inclined to argue that one reason why the government should give his Society financial support was that it was cheaper to maintain a child in the Asylum than in the *Euryalus* and 'much cheaper to give them a decent training for life than to have to keep them idle in prison afterwards'.[3] Whether or not he was best advised to canvass support for his Society on the grounds of the economy of the service it could give to the public is rather doubtful.

---

[1] ibid., p. 8.

[2] ibid., p. 397.

[3] *Memoir of Captain Edward Pelham Brenton by his brother, Vice Admiral Sir Jahled Brenton, Bart.*, p. 88.

Certainly one of the reasons why it was dissolved in 1841, soon after his death, was lack of funds. Be this as it may, there is no doubt that members of the Select Committee were much impressed by the evidence they received from Brenton and others who were associated with reformatory schools which contrasted very favourably with the evidence they had heard relating to the confinement of young offenders in prisons and, above all, in the *Euryalus*. In their final report they spoke of 'the very beneficial effects' resulting from reformatory schools for juvenile offenders which had been established by voluntary societies, such as the Children's Friend Society which they particularly mentioned, and suggested that the system adopted in these schools might well be extended to 'public Establishments' which, unlike the voluntary reformatories, had powers of compulsory detention.[1]

The issue as to the most appropriate place to which the convicted delinquent should be committed was still confused with the manner in which juveniles were to be tried. In November 1835 Lord John Russell, then Secretary of State, directed the Commissioners on Criminal Law, 'to consider whether it would be advisable to make any distinction in the Mode of Trial between Adult and Juvenile Offenders'. In a Report published in 1837 it is clear that the Commissioners themselves, however hesitantly, were prepared to recommend summary powers for local justices with regard to the trial of juvenile offenders. Although, they argued, 'it would not be advisable to make any distinction in the mode of trial between adult and juvenile offenders, except by increasing the summary jurisdiction of magistrates . . . the extension of such summary jurisdiction, within certain limits, would be a safe and beneficial alteration of the law, and would tend materially to diminish juvenile crime'.[2] Their recommendations were quite precise. First, that on charges of larceny if the accused was under sixteen and the value of the property stolen under 10s. a single justice of the peace might be empowered to dismiss the alleged offence if, in his opinion, the circumstances were so trivial as to warrant it. Second, if the culprit were to confess his guilt, a magistrate might be allowed the discretionary power to imprison the

[1] op. cit., p. v.
[2] Third Report from the Commissioners on Criminal Law, *PP*, 1837, XXXI, p.5.

culprit for a period of six months, if the property stolen was less than 10s. in value, and up to twelve months if the value were between 10s. and £5. Third, they recommended that on summary charges where the value of the property stolen did not exceed 10s. two justices, sitting together, might be empowered to hear evidence for both the prosecution and the defence, adjudicate upon it if they should think proper, and, in case of conviction, sentence the offender to imprisonment for not longer than twelve months.

Despite a caution with regard to the trial of petty thieves which would today appear remarkable, the recommendations of the Law Commissioners were noted but not adopted. Instead, one of the ideas of the earlier House of Lords Select Committee on Gaols and Houses of Correction, that a separate prison for juvenile offenders be established, was presented to Parliament in the Parkhurst Bill, 1838, and it was this proposal which eventually gained parliamentary approval.[1] For over twenty years the merits of the rival systems of separate juvenile prisons and the reformatory school system had been argued by the protagonists of the two schools of thought, the one more concerned that anti-social groups should be deterred, the other that the malleable young offender should be reformed. Despite the considerable success of the reformatory schools it was, however, the deterrent principle which now temporarily secured ascendancy in the Parkhurst Act which established for the first time in England a separate prison for juvenile offenders.

From the outset Parkhurst was the subject of criticism. Among its more formidable detractors was Mary Carpenter, the famous advocate of the reformatory system. One of Miss Carpenter's many criticisms of the Parkhurst Prison was that it represented an essentially negative approach to the problem of juvenile delinquency. At first glance, the actual wording of the Act might make such a criticism seem far from just. The explanatory preamble to the Act begins: 'Whereas it may be of great public advantage that a Prison be provided in which young Offenders may be detailed and corrected, and may receive such Instruction and be subject to such Discipline as shall appear most conducive to their Reformation and to the Repression of Crime . . .'. As is often the case, however, the real flaw in the

[1] 1 & 2 Vict., c. 82.

Act was not so much to be found in its individual clauses but in what was not explicitly laid down in any one of them. Although the idea of a separate prison for juveniles had been canvassed and debated in England for some considerable time, the legislation on which the first such prison was based was curiously vague about the system on which the prison was to be run. The type of prisoner to be held in Parkhurst and the terms of imprisonment were laid down quite clearly:

> Any young Offender, Male or Female, as well as those under sentence or Order of Transportation as those under Sentence of Imprisonment, who, having been examined by an experienced Surgeon or Apothecary, shall appear to be free from any putrid or infectious distemper, and fit to be removed from the Gaol, Prison or Place in which the such Offender shall be confined ... Every Offender who shall be so removed to Parkhurst Prison shall continue there until he or she shall be transported according to Law, or shall become entitled to his or her Liberty, or until the Secretary of State shall direct the removal of such Offender.

Offenders who proved too difficult or 'incorrigible', were to be removed from Parkhurst and returned to an ordinary prison, there to serve the full period of their original sentence. Clauses VI, VII and VIII, however, which purported to lay down the way in which the prison was actually to be run, are a good deal less precise. The Governor was to have 'the same powers ... as are incident to the Office of a Sheriff or Gaoler'; the Secretary of State was empowered 'from time to time to make rules for the Government and Regulation of Parkhurst Prison, and for the Discipline of the Offenders imprisoned therein, and to subscribe a Certificate that they are fit to be enforced'. Moreover: 'It shall be lawful for the Secretary of State from time to time to specify ... such offences which, if committed in Parkhurst Prison by Male Convicts, shall appear to him deserving of corporal Punishment ... and the Governor ... shall have Power to inflict such Punishment.'

It was to the obscurity of these particular clauses that Lord Lyndhurst addressed himself during the course of the debates on the draft Bill in the House of Lords.[1]

Looking at the preamble he found that part of the object of the Bill

[1] Hansard, 3rd series, vol. XLIV 1838, col. 760.

was to reform and instruct juvenile offenders. The object was therefore highly laudable, and in proportion to the importance of the
object was the importance of considering the manner in which that
object was to be effected; but he did not find on the face of the Bill,
nor in the statement of the noble Marquess [the Marquess of
Lansdowne, who had introduced the Bill in the Lords] either today
or on a former occasion anything which could give them any insight
into the system which was intended . . . if they intended to adopt
anything like the separate system [under which each offender was
rigorously kept from any association with any other prisoner] he
protested vehemently against it.

In his reply, Lord Lansdowne rebutted any suggestion that
Parkhurst was to adopt this particular system – but he carefully
avoided detailing the nature of the system which it was intended
to adopt.[1] In effect, therefore, Parkhurst was left to approach
the problem of how the objects of the Act might be achieved in
practice in a largely empirical manner, the success or failure of
which necessarily depended on the sympathy and flexibility of
mind of those who held office in the prison.

The earliest reports do not encourage much optimism on this
score. In December 1838 102 boys arrived in Parkhurst drawn
from hulks and Metropolitan prisons and serving sentences
varying from two years' imprisonment to fifteen years' transportation. 'The Penal Discipline', reported the Governor,
Robert Woolcombe, 'consists of deprivation of liberty, wearing
an iron on the leg, a strongly marked prison dress, a diet
reduced to its minimum, the enforcement of silence on all
occasions of instruction and duty and an uninterrupted surveill-
ance by officers.'[2] The first four 'fit and discreet' men appointed
under the Act to visit the prison at least once a month and
enquire into the behaviour and conditions of the prisoners did
not seem disposed to adopt a less negative approach, although
one of them was William Crawford of the Philanthropic Society.
Despite an expression of the belief that 'the utmost care must
be taken to avoid any species of discipline which is inconsistent
with the habits and character of youth or calculated in any degree
to harden and corrupt', they were quite clear about their major
objectives. The prison, they suggested, should provide 'a

[1] ibid., cols 766–7.
[2] Quoted J. Carlebach, *Caring for Children in Trouble*, p. 27.

judicious course of moral, religious and industrial training; but the means adopted for this purpose should not be of such a nature as to counteract the wholesale effects of corrective discipline'. Further they argued 'that every comfort and indulgence' which was not essential to preserve health of mind and body should be excluded, and that there should be nothing in the arrangements of the prison which might tend to 'weaken the terror of the law or to lessen in the minds of the juvenile population at large, or of their parents, the dread of being committed to prison'.[1]

Almost immediately, however, attempts were made to modify and improve the régime. In February 1839 the Home Office instructed the Governor that leg-irons could be removed for good conduct and in September 1840 leg-irons were abolished altogether. It took rather longer to improve the prison diet, concerning which successive Annual Reports are curiously reticent, but in the Report for 1844 it is noted that 'the previous diet had not been considered sufficiently nourishing to sustain the vigour of growing boys kept in continual and active employment', and that a new diet had been introduced in November 1843 and an improvement in the boys' 'health and energy' was recorded.[2] Meantime, while the chaplain endeavoured to discover what type of boy found his way into prison, the Governor set out to discover some principles which might be applied in the management of his institution. He divided his charges into three classes:

1. Probationary class. Boys were not permitted 'that intercourse with each other which is inseparable from youthful exercise'. Whilst in this class a boy's capabilities and habits were noted and he was treated accordingly.

2. Ordinary class. Boys in this class were not subject to corporal punishment.

3. Refractory class. Received very rough treatment.

By 1842 numbers in the prison were growing so rapidly that new constructions were begun and additional staff drafted to the prison. The first groups of boys were sent on conditional pardon to Western Australia where they were apprenticed to

---

[1] ibid., p. 26, n. 3.
[2] ibid., p. 28.

settlers. But the boys were restless, the treatment uncertain, and the results doubtful. A few boys attempted to escape from the prison each year and the numbers in the Refractory Ward increased. In spite of solitary confinement, bread and water, extra drill and whipping, some boys proved too tough to handle and were either transported as convicts or returned to ordinary prisons.

A good deal of the difficulty experienced in handling the boys arose from the very crude nature of the classification which the first governor had adopted. In 1843, the new Governor, Captain George Hall, embarked on a more sophisticated scheme. The prison was now divided into:[1]

1. The General Ward for boys of 14 and over.
2. The Junior Ward for boys below 14.
3. The Probationary Ward for boys for the first four months after admission.
4. The Refractory Ward for punishment.
5. The Infirmary Ward for boys needing in-patient treatment.

The boys worked an average of seven hours a day, mainly indoors, and almost half their time was spent in classrooms, a fact which Captain Hall believed contributed in no small measure to the restlessness of many of the boys in his care who had never been accustomed to so sedentary and confined an existence. He advised the visitors that the 'physical and moral advantages of giving to the prisoners healthful and interesting employment in the open air and training them to handicrafts whereby they may readily earn for themselves a comfortable subsistence in the Colonies, are too obvious'. In their Report for 1849 the visitors expressed dissatisfaction with the general progress of the prison and introduced a number of changes, including several suggested by the Governor himself, which greatly changed the approach to the management of the boys. Boys were to be graded into first, second, and third class prisoners; schooling was to be cut and emphasis was to be placed on outdoor, agricultural, training. This last, entirely desirable, development was to have disastrous consequences. When the new scheme was put into practice, and the boys sent to work outside the prison walls for the first time, the largest number ever (thirty-

[1] ibid. , pp. 28–9.

four) attempted to escape. In order to allay public anxiety, a small military guard was provided to check escapes from the farm. Although it remained for no more than four years, this guard, together with the leg-irons used in the first two years, became the symbols of Parkhurst not merely for its critics in the nineteenth century but for a large number of twentieth-century writers on the treatment of juvenile delinquency.[1]

The responsibility for this must rest largely with Mary Carpenter herself and is mainly due to the influence her books wielded and still wield today. Her main thesis was quite simple and today would be readily acceptable: prisons were no fit place for the detention of children. To establish this, however, she did not scruple to generalise from particular instances; the technique of extracting items of information which supported her arguments, and ignoring the context in which they were provided, typified her writings, both in attacking ideas and people she disliked and in supporting ideas and people she approved of. It was a technique which was to alienate many who basically shared her views, just as it was to prove effective in persuading opinion in favour of extending the sphere of the voluntary reformatory schools rather than in increasing the number of institutions based on the Parkhurst model.

Mary Carpenter, the eldest child of a Unitarian Minister, already had a wide range of experience of work among children long before she developed a particular interest in juvenile delinquency. While still a girl she assisted her father in teaching the pupils in his private school. In 1831 when she was twenty-four, she became superintendent of a Sunday School in Bristol, and it was there that she first became aware of the problems of the poor. Four years later she became secretary of the Working and Visiting Society which her father had established in Bristol for visiting the homes of the poor of the Sunday school. The plight of those children continued to engage her interest after her father's death and, in 1846, having studied the results of John Ponds' Ragged School Movement and the success of Sheriff Watson's Industrial Feeding School in Scotland, she decided to

---

[1] Cf. H. T. Holmes, *Reform of the Reformatories*, p. 2. C. E. B. Russell and L. M. Rigby, *The Making of the Criminal*, pp. 207–8. M. C. Barnett, *Young Delinquents, A Study of Reformatory and Industrial Schools*, p. 18. M. A. Speilman, *The Romance of Child Reformation, London Reformatory and Refuge Union*, pp. 61–2.

open a Ragged School at Lewin's Mead, Bristol. Experience at Lewin's Mead convinced Miss Carpenter that this type of school needed supplementing by an altogether different type; a school where young criminals could be kept under some form of detention and trained by a mixture of discipline and kindness. Lewin's Mead itself had proved an immediate success and plans had to be made to enlarge it the same year that it was opened. The difficulty which faced Mary Carpenter, however, was that among her pupils there were many whose attendance was punctuated by short sojourns in the local gaols. When they reappeared in class, she found that they entered without shame and were greeted 'with respect' by their fellows. In the following year, therefore, she acquired the land around her school and turned it into a residental settlement for selected families. The study of 'the vagrant and lawless class' around her began to absorb more and more of her interest, and she started to correspond with some of the better known prison chaplains, the Rev. T. Carter of Liverpool and the Rev. John Clay of Preston among them. She also wrote to Sheriff Watson himself and, perhaps most important of all, began a long correspondence with Matthew Davenport Hill, then Recorder of Birmingham.

Like Mary Carpenter, Matthew Davenport Hill came from a Unitarian background, and he too had taught in his father's school for a time. His real talent, however, was for the law, and it was whilst practising his profession at the Warwickshire Quarter Sessions that his interest in the treatment of the juvenile offender was first aroused. Since 1817, it had been the policy of the Warwickshire County magistrates, whenever possible, to return a first offender to the care of his parents and of his employer, thus giving him a second chance by putting him on 'probation'. Where the offender had no friend, family or employer to look after him, rather than commit him to prison, they would sent him to their Asylum at Stretton-on-Dunsmore, which they had financed from their own pockets and from public subscriptions. The Asylum was a sort of industrial school run on lines very similar to those adopted in the later Approved Schools. If the boys ran away, they could be punished by the justices on the grounds that they were hired by the Master of the Asylum as 'Servants in Husbandry and Handicraft', a device which solved one of the major problems of detention in voluntary institutions. If the boys behaved badly during their stay, they were promptly sent to the local House of Correction for a period of solitary confinement.

Limited in its work by available finance, the size of the Asylum was necessarily small. When it first opened, it could only accept six boys, and even fourteen years later, there was only accommodation for thirty. Nevertheless, its success as a reformatory was said to be considerable.

So impressed was Davenport Hill by the activities of the County magistrates, particularly their 'probation' policy, that as far as possible he adopted the same policy himself on becoming Recorder of Birmingham in 1839, securing a good deal of publicity for his views on the appropriate treatment of the young offender through the help of some leading journals. Several times he invited employers who had taken back juvenile delinquents to meet with prominent citizens of Birmingham and representatives of the local churches. The *Spectator* for 20 January 1844 carried an article which gives some indication of how successful Davenport Hill and his friends had already been in stimulating public interest in the 'Warwickshire plan'. This was described as 'so far an adoption of what we conceive to be the sound principle of correctional discipline; and, so far it is a departure from the principle of retributive punishment, the source of so much embarrassment in the existing system.' The plan was soon adopted in several other parts of the country, but when the Middlesex magistrates tried to apply it to London they failed because 'hardly any delinquents in the Metropolis had either employer, parents or friends to look after them'. The alternative to the Warwickshire plan, that children should be remitted to a voluntary reformatory institution, proved scarcely more easy to adopt, since the number of places in the existing institutions was far below the number required, a situation which was far from unique to London.[1]

From 1846, to call attention to this urgent problem and to recruit the public support necessary to make a demand for state action effective, meetings were held up and down the country addressed by eminent supporters of the reformatory movement. In London itself Mr Charles Pearson, a distinguished City

[1] Cf. R. and F. Davenport Hill, *The Recorder of Birmingham: A Memoir of Matthew Davenport Hill*, p. 156.

solicitor, proposed at a meeting held in the Mansion House that special asylums for criminal and destitute children, in place of ordinary prisons, should be maintained and directed by the state. In the same year, 1846, Davenport Hill drafted his *Report upon the Principles of Punishment*, which formed the basis of a *Memorial* to the House of Commons on behalf of the Law Amendment Society, in which similar state action was urged.

Meanwhile Sydney Turner, Chaplain to the Philanthropic Society, and Thomas Paynter, a London magistrate and a member of the Society's Committee, had visited the French reformatory at Mettrai. On their return, they published a detailed report. The report pointed out that Mettrai was so carefully adapted to the requirements of the French national character that there could be no question of transplanting such an institution in this country, but they did find in Mettrai five principles which could well be adapted to an English setting. These were first, the employment of trained staff; second, the division of the inmates into family groups living in a homely setting (one of the original ideas of the Philanthropic Society itself); third, the use of persuasion rather than force; fourth, active outdoor employment such as gardening and agriculture to 'prevent the constant communication and intercourse which could scarcely be avoided when the boys are collected together in sedentary trades'; and fifth, the combination of the charity of individuals with the support and sanction of the government.[1]

Addressed to the public, the report was largely read by those already converted to the reformatory cause: magistrates and legal officers, prison chaplains and voluntary social workers. In the 1840s, far more prominent social questions were occupying the minds of the majority of people in England: the Corn Laws and the Free Trade issue, Factory Reform, Public Health and Local Government Reform. Besides these, the subject of delinquency and criminal law reform seemed of far less urgent importance. The concerned minority, however, continued to press their case. In 1847 Lord Brougham presented to the House of Lords a *Memorial* from the magistrates of Liverpool, praying for the amendment of the criminal law, on the reception of which Brougham successfully moved for a Select Committee of the House which was appointed 'to enquire into the Execution

[1] Carlebach, op. cit. p. 21.

of the Criminal Law especially respecting Juvenile Offenders and Transportation'.

The Report of this particular Select Committee is important for a number of reasons, not the least being that it was the first Select Committee of either House specifically appointed to enquire into the problem of juvenile delinquency. It recommended the abolition of transportation as a punishment for young offenders and heard evidence from the most prominent of those working among juvenile delinquents as to their own views on how such children might best be treated under the law. 'The evidence throws some light upon the treatment of young offenders. That the Contamination of a Gaol as Gaols are usually managed may often prove fatal, and must always be hurtful to Boys committed for a first Offence, and that thus for a very trifling Act, they may become trained to the worst of Crimes is clear enough', stated the Committee's final Report. 'But the Evidence gives a frightful picture of the Effects which are thus produced. In Liverpool, of Fourteen Cases selected at random by the Magistrates, there were several of the Boys under Twelve who in the space of three or four years had been above Fifteen Times committed, and the average of the whole Fourteen was no less than Nine Times.'[1] The Report then inevitably proceeded to ways and means of curtailing the practice of committing first offenders to prison, and commended the scheme already operating in Birmingham, of 'a judiciously exercised discretion in discharging Boys, especially when apprehended for the first time . . . upon taking the Recognisances of Parents or Masters for the good behaviour of the Party.'[2] As to the limits of the power of summary jurisdiction which might be extended to local magistrates, the Committee were a little cautious.[3]

The opinions of competent Judges, especially on the Bench, vary as to the Expediency of giving to Magistrates a Power of Summary Conviction in such Cases; but the inclination of Opinion is in favour of confining this to professional Persons exercising Judicial or

[1] Second Report from the Select Committee of the House of Lords appointed to inquire into the Execution of the Criminal Law, especially respecting Juvenile Offenders and Transportation, *PP*, 1847, VII, p. 5.

[2] ibid., pp. 5–6.

[3] ibid.

Police functions; or, if Two ordinary Justices should be entrusted with it, to interposing the check of a Jury, composed, however, not of Twelve but of Three or Four Persons . . . The principal Difficulty of giving a summary Jurisdiction arises from the Difficulty of fixing a limit in the point of Age, and of ascertaining in each case that the Party comes within the Line. But the Committee are strongly inclined to think that much of this might be got over, even without appointing special Justices, by enabling the Magistrates in Petty Sessions to exercise the summary Power, with the previous consent of the Parties themselves to submit to such Tribunal, confining the Jurisdiction to certain Offences, and the Punishment to Six Months Imprisonment, with or without Labour, or to the infliction of Whipping in the Presence of certain appointed Officers, with or without such Imprisonment.

So far the Select Committee had gone a long way in support of some of the more radical ideas canvassed before them concerning the mode of trial of young offenders. They were more hesitant, however, in supporting the view that reformatory schools should be the principal place of committal, not just a possible alternative. It was on this score that their Report aroused the impassioned criticism of Mary Carpenter.

That some magistrates did use local asylums as an alternative to the local gaol or House of Correction we have already seen but it was not a practice which received much official encouragement. On the contrary, Mr Serjeant Adams pointed out to the Committee, the specific provision of the Parkhurst Act, which allowed young offenders sentenced to transportation, or a term of imprisonment, to be granted a Royal Pardon on condition that they entered one of the charitable reformatories, had very soon become a dead letter because of the intervention of the Prison Inspectorate. The view of the Inspectors was that criminal children were 'children of the State and unfit objects for Private Benevolence'.[1] This view the Select Committee were not disposed to set aside. Instead, they chose to recommend the establishment of more institutions on Parkhurst lines. It was this proposal for what Mary Carpenter described as a 'plague of Parkhursts' that fired her to write her famous book *Reformatory Schools for the Children of the Perishing and Dangerous Classes and for Juvenile Offenders* which she published in the winter of 1851.

[1] Cf. Serjeant Adam's evidence, ibid., pp. 12–17.

So immoderate was her attack on Parkhurst and all it stood for, and so embedded have her criticisms of it become in later thinking and writing about that establishment, that it is worth noting the principal reasons why the Select Committee saw fit to commend it as a model. First and foremost they were convinced that it was unwise to commit young offenders to ordinary prisons where they could only be contaminated by the older, more hardened, criminals. Hence they supported the movement for the more effective classification of prisoners, and the complete segregation of the young offenders from the old. Further they believed that Parkhurst represented a serious attempt to work out some system of training which would both reform the boys and equip them for a useful life after they were released:[1]

> The Question of Punishment of juvenile Offenders is a further and distinct one beside that of the Jurisdiction and Power of Conviction in their Case. Very important Evidence has been given in favour of dealing with such Offenders, at least on first Convictions, by means of reformatory Asylums on the Principle of Parkhurst Prison, rather than by ordinary Imprisonment; the Punishment in such Asylums being hardly more than what is implied in Confinement and Restraint, and Reformation and industrial training being the main Features of the Process. Without going beyond the Principle which should be followed on this Question, the Committee are disposed to recommend the Adoption, by way of trial, of the Reformatory Asylums as above described, combined with a moderate use of Corporal Punishment. The Committee also recommend the trial of a Suggestion made by Witnesses who have given much attention to this Subject, that, wherever it is possible, part of the Cost attending the Conviction and Punishment of Juvenile Offenders should be legally chargeable on their Parents . . .

With this last suggestion, since it was a policy she herself had very much at heart, Mary Carpenter did not quarrel. Her real quarrel was with the idea that Parkhurst could in fact operate as an agency of reform. To demonstrate her argument she asserted that, although well organised, it was 'a prison in name and in fact'; that in one year alone 34 boys had tried to escape; that 165 were whipped; and that 79 had been returned to Millbank Prison as incorrigible. She insisted that, 'it is utterly vain to look for any real reformation where the heart is

[1] ibid., pp. 5–6.

not touched', and that this 'cannot possibly be done for children under the mechanical and military discipline of Parkhurst'.[1] Since Miss Carpenter did not herself visit Parkhurst until 1856, she was obliged to rely for her statistics on official reports on its work which were published annually, any unbiassed scrutiny of which would reveal that the figures she chose to publish were highly selective. As we have already seen, there were particular reasons for the number of attempted escapes in 1849, reasons which were far from discreditable to the prison and its then Governor.[2]

> Neither that, nor the figure quoted of the number of whippings at Parkhurst, the number for 1844, were typical illustrations. In the two previous years, and in each succeedings year up to and including the publication of her book, there were in fact no whippings at all. As to the number of boys returned to Millbank, it should be remembered that it was in this prison that boys were assembled from local gaols all over the country before being passed on to Parkhurst. The boys lived in one room in Millbank, which served as a dormitory and workshop, under appalling conditions, usually for a period of fourteen months. By the time they reached Parkhurst, the task of reforming them had been made infinitely more difficult.

More impressive than Miss Carpenter's third-hand accounts of life at Parkhurst, was the analysis she made of the extent of juvenile crime and the plight of lower-class children. She made a clear distinction between destitute, neglected and criminal children, and suggested free day schools, compulsory industrial feeding schools and reformatory schools as the best method of dealing with the three groups. These proposals attracted the attention of a large number of people who had been conscious of the need for action and who had been waiting for just such a comprehensive and able review of the situation. The response to her book encouraged Mary Carpenter, with the support of Matthew Davenport Hill, now a resident of Bristol and a personal friend, to call a conference of like-minded people in December 1851, in Birmingham, for the purpose of considering 'the condition and treatment of the Perishing and Dangerous Classes of Children and Juvenile Offenders', and the remedies which their condition demanded. The Conference did not attract

---

[1] *Reformatory Schools . . .*, pp. 312, 319–22.
[2] Carlebach, op. cit., p. 40.

as much attention as she had hoped and the attendance was small, but it did lead to a *Resolution* advocating the threefold system of schools being laid before the Secretary of State for Home Affairs (Sir George Grey) who told a deputation from the conference that there was not sufficient interest to warrant legislation. To prove him wrong, the principal figures of the conference formed a permanent committee to carry on the work and to form a lobby to press their cause 'throughout the length and breadth of the land'.

In May 1852 Mr Adderley (later Lord Norton) moved in the House of Commons for a Committee of the House to enquire into the treatment of criminal and destitute juveniles. The day before doing so, he wrote to Davenport Hill, 'I move tomorrow for the Committee . . . Do pray come up. And give me at once, an outline of the men to be examined, the best sources of written information, and the line and drift to start upon. We want you terribly now.'[1] A Committee was indeed appointed and presented its Report in the year following. Mary Carpenter herself gave evidence. 'I do not believe', she stated, 'that reformation is compatible with the general system adopted at Parkhurst', explaining that she had never visited the prison personally. She agreed that particularly difficult boys should be sent there, but denied all knowledge of the major changes which had been introduced in 1849.[2]

While the Committee continued its laborious task of sifting the mass of evidence presented to it, Mary Carpenter was anxious herself to demonstrate the advantages of the reformatory schools she so vigorously advocated. The opportunity came to her to set up such a school on her own lines when some vacant buildings, situated near the village of Kingswood, four miles from Bristol, came on the market. The house had been built by Wesley himself and twelve hundred children could be accommodated in the buildings which were surrounded by many acres of land. The place seemed to Mary Carpenter to be an ideal background for her work with delinquent city children. The property was purchased for her by Mr Russell Scott of Bath, who had been much impressed by a visit to the 'Rauhe Haus', the cottage-village for juvenile delinquents founded in 1833 by

[1] Quoted Davenport Hill, op. cit., p. 163.
[2] *PP*, 1852, VII, p. 102.

Emmanuel Wichern at Hamburg and the model for the juvenile prison at Mettrai. Other friends helped with gifts of money, furniture and fittings. In September 1852 Kingswood School was opened as a mixed reformatory.

Mary Carpenter was to outline the principles on which she worked at Kingswood in her new book *Juvenile Delinquents, – their Conditions and Treatment*, which appeared early in 1853:[1]

> The child . . . must be placed where the prevailing principle will be, as far as practicable, carried out, – where he will be gradually restored to the true position of childhood. He must be brought to a sense of dependence by re-awakening in him new and healthy desires which he cannot by himself gratify, and by finding that there is a power far greater than his own to which he is indebted for the gratification of those desires. He must perceive by manifestations which he cannot mistake, that this power, whilst controlling him, is guided by wisdom and love; he must have his affections called forth by the obvious personal interest felt in his own individual well-being by those around him; he must, in short, be placed in a *family*. Faith in those around him being once thoroughly established, he will soon yield his own will in ready submission to those who are working for his good; it will thus gradually be subdued and trained, and he will work with them in his reformation and training, trusting, where he cannot perceive the reason of the measures they adopt to correct or eradicate the evil in him. This, it is apprehended, is the fundamental principle of all true reformatory action with the young, and in every case where striking results have followed such efforts, it will be traceable to the greater development of the principle, to a more true and powerful action on the soul of the child, by those who have assumed the holy duties of a parent.

The purpose of *Juvenile Delinquents* was not, however, merely to outline more clearly the principles on which she herself worked, but once more to attack the Parkhurst system. Other workers in the field of juvenile delinquency had been advocating to the House of Commons Committee a term of imprisonment prior to admission to reformatories; in fact, draft legislation was being prepared to this effect. This plan 'filled her with alarm' and in her book she not only supported the results of her own experience with accounts of the successful reformatories in America, on the Continent and at Redhill, in England. She

[1] Carpenter, op. cit., p. 298.

also wrote of the 'failure' of Parkhurst, referring to 'those unhappy young persons who have become, to their unspeakable misfortune, the children of the State'. She made particular play on the account sent to her by a gentleman who had recently spent all of five hours at Parkhurst in which he vividly referred to the armed guard which had been introduced to allay local anxiety at the employment of the boys outside the prison, and who walked along the hedges of the fields in which the boys were at work 'muskets loaded, and bayonets fixed'. She concluded that Parkhurst was 'most costly, most inefficacious for any end but to prepare the child for a life of crime'.[1]

Her remarks stung Joshua Jebb, now Director of Convict Prisons and a visitor at Parkhurst since its inception, to write her a bitterly reproachful letter.[2]

This, the only establishment which has been formed for receiving young criminals from prison and making any endeavour to combine the punishment due to crime with a reformatory and industrial training, is held up as a warning against the formation of any such for the future. It has been stated in proof of this failure that boys run away and rob, that they set fire to the prison, attempt to murder the warders, and crouching with fear all the day long, are only kept in subjection by brute force, that sentries with loaded muskets and fixed bayonets are ready to shoot them and that the entire expense so far as the assumed object is concerned is thrown away.

Now all this may be true of several individuals among the hundreds of desperate characters who have passed through Parkhurst within the last twelve or fourteen years, but if anyone argues on the isolated and exceptional cases, the very best and most cultivated society in his countryside may be placed in a light that would be a disgrace to the savage tribes who wander over the wilds of Australia.

It is altogether unfair, and what is worse, being based upon single facts, wholly inapplicable as arguments, it conveys an absolutely false impression.

Such impression being made, however, is productive of the same results as if it were true, Hence the widespread mischief that will be the consequence of the diligence with which Parkhurst has been vilified.

It will take years of prudent and energetic exertion on the part of those who have been thus engaged to regain what they them-

[1] ibid., p. 202.
[2] Quoted Carlebach, op. cit., p. 51.

selves have lost by such misdirected efforts. They have shaken the confidence of Parkhurst and the public in such an institution and it will not be easy to win it back.

As we now know, confidence in Parkhurst was in fact never regained. Children were sent there in decreasing numbers, expecially after the passing of the Youthful Offenders Act. The boys' section of Parkhurst was closed finally in April 1864 when the last seventy-eight inmates were escorted to Dartmoor by Captain Hall, who was then retired but who, as Governor of Parkhurst, had worked so devotedly for the good of those committed to his charge. The impression of the Parkhurst experiment which successive generations have inherited is heavily coloured by the lurid hues in which Mary Carpenter painted her pictures of it.

Some little while after the publication of *Juvenile Delinquents,* the House of Commons Committee presented their Report in which the case for the voluntary reformatories as suitable institutions to which juvenile offenders might be committed by the courts was generally admitted. The legislation which embodied this and related proposals reached Parliament too late in the session for it to be successful, but the encouragement given to the reformatory movement, both by the Committee's Report and the draft legislation, gave a fresh impetus to its activities. A second Conference was called in November 1853. 'We are going to renew our Conference at Birmingham', Davenport Hill wrote to Lord Brougham. 'We find from the sort of men who give it their adhesion what a vast progress the principle of reformatory discipline has made in the public mind in the last two years.'[1] Since the aim of the Conference was to gain publicity and public support, the number of people invited was very much larger than before and included both the expert and the amateur as well as those who were more generally interested in the problem of juvenile delinquency. 'We are here to correct public opinion', Davenport Hill told them. 'It requires even more reformation than the children of whom we have been speaking. It is to this ignorant and cruel public opinion that the existence of the vice of thousands of our fellow creatures in prison is owing.'[2] Fired by his enthusiasm, the Conference proceeded to

[1] Davenport Hill, op. cit., p. 164.
[2] ibid., p. 166.

discuss and adopt various suggestions which were incorporated into a Bill which Mr Adderley introduced into the next session of Parliament under the title of the Youthful Offenders Act[1] which, in an amended form, became law in 1854.

Under the Act, voluntary societies were authorised to establish reformatory schools which were to be allowed the necessary powers of compulsory detention. Each school was to be governed by the 'Managers', the body of subscribers who were to frame their school's rules. The Home Secretary was to certify the schools as satisfactory, and was given the right to veto any rules he thought undesirable and the power to withdraw certification if the Managers, after due notice, failed to meet any request with regard to the modification of their rules. Wherever possible, parents were to be required to make some financial contribution to the upkeep of their children whilst in the school.

During its passage through Parliament the draft Bill had been subject to the very amendment which Mary Carpenter had most feared. Although the general tenor of the Act was to substitute reformatory treatment for retributive punishment, a concession was made to the older principle by including in its final provisions a clause under which children were to serve a fourteen days' period of imprisonment, an expiation for their crime before they were remitted to the custody of a reformatory. Nevertheless, Matthew Davenport Hill hailed the Act as the Magna Carta of juvenile delinquents. He wrote enthusiastically on 2 August 1854 to William Miles, M.P.:[2]

You have established three great principles. First, the value of voluntary action in the institution and conduct of Reformatory Schools. Secondly, the substitution of reformatory treatment for retributive punishment as the rule, subject, however, to exceptions which may or may not, if I had been a dictator, venture to go as a first step. Thirdly, you have recognised the duty of the parent to maintain his offspring, and not to cast the burden on the public. These, my dear sir, are great principles. Although little thought of now by the world at large, I firmly believe that their solemn recognition and confirmation by the Legislature will be considered in future times to form a great epoch in the jurisprudence of this country.

[1] 17 & 18 Vict., c. 86.
[2] Davenport Hill, op. cit., pp. 168–9.

2. *From Punishment to Prevention*

Within four years of the Act authorising their establishment there were over fifty reformatory schools, almost the highest number at any time in the nineteenth century. Since offenders were now legally detained, the schools no longer exerted themselves to attract children to stay by the facilities and provisions they offered. 'There is [now] little of the petting and bribery which at the outset obtained here and there', wrote the Inspector of Reformatory Schools in 1859. 'The principle of duty is more clearly insisted on; persuasions less trusted to.'[1] There was a good deal of theoretical material and practical experience to guide those who were setting up new institutions all over the country. Both English and Continental institutions had been described and frequently reported on, and a whole series of Blue Books and private publications between 1835 and 1853 provided an extensive literature on which new institutions could be established. But in practice other pressures and stresses determined the shape and form of the schools.[2]

Once the voluntary principle had been accepted it was open to any respectable person in the country to establish a reformatory school. Most of the early managers disregarded the problem of suitability of staff and appear to have assumed that any calibre of staff under proper supervision would be sufficient to the task. The very first report of the Inspector of Reformatory Schools made particular reference to this, remarking on the lack of efficient staff and noting that 'some have still to be retained who are but ill-suited to the work'.[3] Some institutions experienced a continuous series of staff changes and the difficulties associated with it, while others were more fortunate in appointing, more or less by chance, officers with a natural inclination for residential work, who then assumed real control of the institution. The inspectorate saw clearly the importance of defining the respective roles of voluntary managers and paid staff, but it was a long time before they felt sufficiently strong and influential to intervene with bad management on behalf of good staff.[4]

[1] Second Report of the Inspector of Reformatory Schools, *PP*, 1859, XIII pt II, pp. 15–16.
[2] Carlebach, op. cit., p. 66.
[3] Quoted ibid., p. 66 n. 2.
[4] ibid., p. 67.

Even when the staff employed was of the right quality, they came without training, very often without experience and sometimes with very rigid ideas. As a result, the discipline in the reformatories became very quickly more and more penal and restrictive, some schools introducing the barred windows, locked doors and cropped hair which continued to be a feature of some schools until the 1920s, thus making a mockery of the bitter battle which had been fought by some pioneers against the use of an exclusively restrictive policy in training children.[1]

It had been the intention of the pioneers that the voluntary reformatories should independently and individually develop their systems of reformation, but at the same time they were well aware of the advantage of the exchange of information and experience between those engaged in the day to day operation of the schools. To achieve this, the Preventative and Reformatory Schools Committee, which had met for the first time during the 1851 Birmingham Conference, promoted five years later the Reformatory and Refuge Union with the threefold object:[2]

1. To collect and diffuse information as to the operations and results of all such Institutions: to afford a means of communication between their promoters, and of concerted action with reference to the Government, the Legislature, and public bodies in general.
2. To facilitate the establishment of new Institutions, the selecting and training of efficient masters, matrons and assistants, the procurement of books and school material for educational or industrial work, and the ultimate provision for inmates by emigration or situations of permanent employment.
3. To promote the religious, intellectual, and industrial education of such Institutions and, without interfering in their management, to encourage those who conduct them in every effort to elevate and reclaim the neglected and criminal class, by educating them in the fear of God and the knowledge of the Holy Scriptures.

The energy with which the Union set to work, no less than the piety of its objects, did a great deal to influence public opinion in favour of the reformatories and to encourage magistrates to use them. In November 1857 after correspondence with

[1] ibid., p. 68.
[2] *Fifty Years Record of Child Saving and Reformatory Work* (*1856–1906*), being the *Jubilee Report of the Reformatory and Refuge Union*, p. 7.

the managers of the reformatory schools, the Management Committee of the Union found themselves in a position to be able to advise the magistrates as to which reformatories were ready to receive and were most suitable for the various classes of 'criminal children', and a communication was addressed to the Metropolitan magistrates to that effect, offering to help them in the matter. The offer was accepted, and over the years the Reformatory and Refuge Union (after 1933 known as the Children's Aid Society) co-operated with magistrates all over the country in placing juvenile delinquents in the voluntary reformatory schools.

Meanwhile the Union organised national conferences of managers, superintendents and matrons, held triennially after 1869, at which ideas and policies relating to reformatories could be discussed by those most closely associated with them. It was at the 1869 Conference that special reference was made by the chairman to the recognition and approval now accorded to the reformatories:[1]

> It used to be said that the only duty which those who are engaged in making and administering the law had to perform, was the protection of society by the punishment of criminals. That the reformation of a criminal was something quite out of their province, in which kind and charitable, though somewhat quixotic, individuals were in the habit of busying themselves, and might continue to do so, provided they did not interfere with justice or discipline. I remember it was said about fifteen years ago that no judge above the age of sixty believed in Reformatory treatment. That opinion, whether accurate or not in the particular application of it, described pretty well the scepticism of the public at the time. Most of us can remember that the first suggestions in reference to Reformatory treatment, as a system to be carried out generally under authority, fell upon the ears of an incredulous and unsympathetic community. I believe, indeed, that it was to one whose labours are over that the sarcastic prediction was addressed: 'some morning you will get up and find yourself the only spoon in the house.'

Yet with the growth of public recognition and an established place in the community for the reformatory schools had come an increasing conservatism among those responsible for manag-

[1] *Report of the Conference of Managers of Reformatory and Industrial Institutions,* 1869, pp. 17–18.

ing them, a development which some saw as inevitable, even desirable. The same speaker continued:[1]

> with the general recognition of the system has come a corresponding necessity for caution among those who work it. So long as they were unrecognised and unsupported, it mattered little what means were used by the benevolent pioneers of this movement. They might have failed or they might have succeeded in the few isolated experiments they made, without exercising any apparent effect on society generally. The reformation of criminals, whether under Government Inspection or not, is now, as it were, a recognised branch of the public service; drawing large sums from the public purse, either directly through Government allowance, or by means of voluntary contributions, which have reached a very considerable amount.

The 'caution' referred to here with such complacency was even then beginning to diminish the work of people such as Jebb, Turner and Mary Carpenter herself, none of whom had assigned undue importance to financial and administrative problems.[2]

> There was, first of all, a gradual trend from work carried out for training purposes to work which would increase profit. A number of institutions eventually confined themselves to employments which were not only useless in the training sense, but which were very harmful to the children in order to achieve maximum profit from their labour. Amongst such employments were brick-making, wood-chopping and paper salvage for boys, and laundry work for girls. Most institutions soon realised that the most valuable worker in terms of profitability was the older inmate, who had the training and the experience to maintain a high level of production. Not surprisingly, therefore, there was an almost universal tendency to retain the services of these inmates for as long as possible. Reformation criteria for readiness of release on licence were largely ignored and many youngsters were detained for almost the full five years provided for under the Act, so that their period under licence was sometimes not longer than a few weeks. Nor was there much incentive to develop a licensing system in a satisfactory way, and the frequent description of discharged children as 'doubtful' or 'not known', demonstrated the reluctance of managers to maintain contact with discharged inmates if this involved them in any great expenditure. The corollary of excessive labour in institutions to

[1] ibid., p. 18.
[2] Carlebach, op. cit., pp. 68–9.

minimise *per capita* expenditure was to provide a minimum of provisions and services. In many institutions, buildings were hopelessly inadequate, food insufficient both in quantity and quality, and clothing quite inadequate to protect the children, particularly those who had to work all the year round in exposed areas in every kind of weather. Finally, the Government system of paying a *per capita* allowance for every child admitted, led many institutions to admit more children than they could properly cater for, and children too young, too ill or too handicapped to benefit from such training as they could offer.

There were also two other factors which led to ambivalent attitudes to the schools. The first was concerned with the fear of offering the offender advantages which were denied to his honest counterpart, and the second was concerned with the question of preliminary imprisonment.

The movement for the establishment of voluntary reformatory schools was at its strongest some twenty years before the establishment of compulsory education in England, and at a time when the children of very large sections of the population lived in states of extreme poverty and social deprivation. It was not surprising that a constantly recurring criticism of the provisions for young delinquents was based on the argument that it was only by committing a crime that a child could gain access to education and industrial training. Lord Chief Justice Denman expressed a widely felt attitude when he said: 'I am myself extremely jealous of the gratuitous instruction of the young felon in a trade, merely because he is a felon.'[1] The managers of the reformatories were always acutely aware of this difficulty and endeavoured to find a practical solution by providing what they did in a manner unlikely to attract and be pleasant to the offender. Thus, the education provided was often poor in quality, the work hard, the bulk of the money earned by the children retained by the institution, and the buildings, food and clothing left much to be desired. Some managers took this attitude even further by denying the right of any former inmate of a reformatory to achieve a 'specially good appointment in the world'.

Once compulsory education was established, however, and all children of the lower classes had been afforded access to elemen-

[1] Quoted ibid., p. 71.

tary education, there was a pronounced and continuous process of change for the better in the material, educational and industrial facilities offered by the reformatories.[1]

The pioneers of the reformatory schools were pioneers in the sense that they were responsible for the formulation and introduction of social change, but once compulsory education had been introduced, their ideas which had once been revolutionary tended to become reactionary, and from the mid-seventies onwards the founders of the reformatories and the many who had followed in their wake were overtaken by social forces which some of them could not accept. The central issue in which the managers became involved was the question of whether or not a convicted juvenile delinquent should undergo a short period of imprisonment before entering a reformatory. Three reasons were usually offered to justify preliminary imprisonment. One was simply administrative. It took some time after a committal to find a school and ascertain if the managers were prepared to accept the particular child. During this time the child had to be detained somewhere, and prison seemed the obvious choice; indeed, in the absence of remand homes, often the only choice. A second reason was that a reformatory was concerned only with reforming offenders. Since a crime had been committed, there should also be a punishment. If it was not the business of the reformatory to punish, then punishment must be carried out prior to admission – in prison. Thirdly, it was argued that a young offender, following his committal, would be in a state of 'high excitement', which was not conducive to the start of reformation. Hence, it was argued, a calming period in prison would create in him a proper state of mind receptive to what the reformatory itself had to offer.[2]

These considerations had lain behind the insertion of the previous imprisonment clause in the Youthful Offenders Act of 1854. Increasingly, however, their wisdom came into question. Those who were opposed to the principle of previous imprisonment put forward counter-arguments. They said that the practice deprived prison of its terrors; that it corrupted children by bringing them into contact with older, more experienced criminals; that it cast a taint on their characters and added to

[1] ibid., p. 71.
[2] ibid., p. 73.

the offender's difficulties when he resumed life in the community. By the 1880s the judiciary, the inspectorate, the managers of Scottish schools and public opinion had hardened considerably against the continuation of the practice of previous imprisonment for youthful offenders. The managers of the English reformatories, however, held out with surprising obstinacy. Speaking at the Conference of Managers of Reformatory and Industrial Institutions in 1881, the Rev. S. C. Baker declared himself as in no doubt as to the advisability and necessity of retaining the practice:

'My experience of thirty years (eight years as a Chaplain of a County Prison and twenty-two as a Reformatory manager) gives me an ever strengthening conviction that there is no punishment for a juvenile offender whom you want to reform like imprisonment in a separate cell in a well-ordered prison.' It was good, he argued, because it was prolonged, unlike flogging, which could be braved out. Referring to magistrates whom he had heard object to imprisonment as 'enough to break the poor boy's heart', which, 'practically means to break down his rebellious spirit', he declared, 'such breaking down is most disagreeable in the boy's view of it, but most desirable in *ours*. We want that wicked spirit of his broken; and if any contrition is added to its brokenness, then he becomes, so far, that "broken and contrite heart" which God does not "despise" . . .'[1]

Year after year, when the imprisonment clause of the Youthful Offenders Act came up for discussion at the Conferences of the Reformatory and Refuge Union, similar opinions were voiced and even in the 1890s the majority of those attending such conferences were prepared to accept them as valid. Outside the Union, however, their validity was seen more and more as dubious.

Concern at the complacency of the Union, hints that conditions in the schools were sometimes far from satisfactory, and attempts by such men as Sir William Harcourt to amend the Youthful Offenders Act so as to abolish the imprisonment clause – all these contributed to the appointment of the Reformatory and Industrial Schools Commission in 1883.

The object of the Commission was 'to enquire and report

[1] *Report of the Conference of Managers of Reformatory and Industrial Institutions,* 1881, p. 14.

upon the operation management, control, inspection, financial arrangements and conditions generally of certified Reformatories . . . in order to run such institutions more efficiently for the object with which they were established.' The Report of the Commission, published in 1884, was surprisingly weak and indecisive, and stands in marked contrast to that of the Commission which sat and reported twelve years later. After considering a substantial amount of evidence, it was reported that the[1]

> effect . . . has on the whole been very satisfactory. They are credited. we believe justly, with having broken up the gangs of young criminals in the large towns; with putting to an end the training of boys as professional thieves; and with rescuing children fallen into crime from becoming habitual or hardened offenders, while they have undoubtedly had the effect of preventing large numbers of children from entering a life of crime. These conclusions are confirmed by the statistics of the juvenile commitment to prison in England and Wales since 1856 . . . in 1856, the number of these commitments was 13,981; in 1866, 9,356; in 1876, 7,138. Since that time, the number has decreased regularly and had fallen in 1881 to 5,483.

Moreover, the Commissioners believed that the diminution in the numbers of hardened adult offenders was also largely the result of the successful reformative treatment of juvenile offenders.

On the whole, however, they were not much interested in the method of treatment of children in the schools except in so far as they were concerned to make sure that there was no scandalous abuse in State-approved institutions, and that the education provided in these particular schools did not compare unfavourably with that then given in the elementary schools for non-offenders. Some witnesses had argued that only a greater degree of governmental control could ensure protection, but the Commission was not persuaded:[2]

> We are convinced that the children who are committed to these institutions need a degree of personal care and interest which no mere official system could provide, and that, scattered as these

[1] Report of the Reformatory and Industrial Schools Commission, *PP*, 1884, XLV, p. x.
[2] ibid., p. xiii.

schools are . . . and small as they often are in size and numbers of inmates, they are particularly unsuitable for central management. And while we desire to retain the great advantages arising from the personal care, supervision and interest of their present managers, we also attach some importance to the pecuniary aid which they derive from the voluntary contributions of philanthropic persons in every part of the three kingdoms. Moreover, the religious zeal which often prompts the efforts of the present managers, and their missionary work in the schools, are of the highest value. Only under unofficial management can such efforts have such free scope.

In spite of this the Commission clearly saw the need to ensure that such limited responsibility as the government accepted should be efficiently discharged.[1]

The Executive should satisfy itself, by frequent and thorough inspection, that the local management is a reality, and that the committee meets regularly, and exercises due supervision and control over the superintendent. Otherwise some gross irregularity or mutinous outbreak may startle the public and the Executive by the appearance of evils which would never have arisen under proper management, such as the inspector should require, as a condition of the Treasury grant.

In the Commission's view, the proper and adequate sanction against persistent mismanagement was the negative one of withdrawal of the Home Secretary's certificate, the *sine qua non* of government finance.

As regards the standard of elementary education given to the inmates of the schools, the Commission declined to make any more positive proposals for its improvement, even though they were agreed that, in many schools, its quality left a great deal to be desired.[2]

The teachers employed are frequently insufficient in number, and of inferior quality although a strong and highly qualified teaching staff is needed in consequence of the inferiority of the material. The attendance at school is sometimes unnecessarily subordinated to the industrial training, or the farm, or to casual interruptions; the energies of the teacher are frequently wearied . . . before and after school hours, by other duties; those hours are sometimes unsuitably early or so late in the evening that the children are unfitted for

[1] ibid., pp. xiii–xiv.
[2] ibid., p. xvi.

mental study by bodily fatigue; the timetable may be excellent, but there is no security for its enforcement; no check exists upon the withdrawal of children during schools hours for industrial labour, except in rare cases where the teacher voluntarily keeps a school-register, such as should be universally required; and the methods and appliances of the school are often antiquated and second-rate and do not come up to the requirements of the Education Department in public elementary schools.

To meet these several difficulties, the Commission suggested that not only were more inspectors needed, but that the duty of educational inspection should be transferred to the Education Department. That the Education Department should in fact take over completely the care and supervision of children in this group of schools (as is in fact done today), the Commission could not agree.[1]

> We do not think that the function of seeing to the reformatory treatment of such children could, with any advantage, be removed from the Home Office, which is closely connected with the judicial and police systems of the country, and the administration of prisons, and be transferred to a department exclusively charged with educational duties.

It was scarcely to be expected that a Commission so wedded to the *status quo*, so cautious not to depart too far from it, would recommend any radical modification of the existing law regarding the committal of young offenders to reformatory and industrial schools, nor did they in fact do so. Inevitably confronted with the much debated issue of the previous imprisonment clause, the Commissioners drew attention – not, one suspects, without some relief – to the sharp division of opinion amongst those who had presented evidence on the desirability of its retention. In the absence of a consensus of opinion favourable to change, the Commission were able to commend a policy of the least possible interference. Children should, they believed, be subjected to some short but sufficiently sharp punishment before the reformatory treatment began. In most cases this would continue to take the form of a term of imprisonment, but for boys under the age of fourteen they recommended that magistrates should have the alternative of ordering them to be whipped at the police station. As

[1] ibid., p. xvii.

for girls, they might have a period of solitary confinement – seven days for those under twelve, fourteen for those aged twelve and upwards – which could be passed in properly fitted cells in or near to the reformatory to which they had been committed. In addition they expressed the belief that when a child under fourteen, or on a first conviction, was sent to a reformatory, a special report should be submitted by the convicting magistrates to the Home Secretary, stating their reasons for such a step, and such children should only be committed up to the age of sixteen or for a period of from three to five years.

Finally, the Commissioners made six recommendations designed to restrict the use of punishment in reformatories and advocated the establishment of special reformatories for 'refractory cases' with a proviso that children sent to such schools must be paid for by the reformatory sending them there, so as not to swamp the new institutions with all the children who might be expected to present any form of difficult behaviour. They also wanted to see more half-way hostels for children discharged on licence, and they wanted more care and accuracy in the returns submitted by the managers in the disposal and success of the inmates.

The Royal Commission of 1884 did not question the need for the kind of schools they were dealing with. The 1896 Departmental Committee, on the other hand, tackled their job very much more thoroughly and at considerably greater depth. Furthermore, they had the courage to examine the rightness or wrongness of these principles and to comment on them, even though this led to serious conflict within the Committee itself.

The other outstanding feature of the 1896 Report was the importance which it attached to the child. The previous Commission took the view that the reformatory and industrial schools were essential to the protection of the community. While they recognised that the offender had a right to be fairly and properly treated in the institution, they nevertheless regarded the institution as being more important in relation to society than the child itself. The 1896 Committee on the other hand, anticipating twentieth-century practice, regarded the child and his welfare as the most important single factor in the operation of these schools, and viewed the schools primarily as instruments for offering children a happy and constructive environment.[1]

Precisely because they differed from the managers in their understanding of the function of reformatories, the Committee decided that reformatory and industrial schools should be treated as one because 'there is no substantial difference in the discipline and regime beyond what can be accounted for by difference of age'.[2] While the Committee's observations were undoubtedly correct, they were nevertheless based on a confusion of principle. The reformatories had been established in 1854 to deal with young offenders: industrial schools were added three years later to absorb 'those who have not yet fallen into actual crime but who are almost certain from their ignorance, destitution, and the circumstances in which they are growing up, to do so if a helping hand be not extended to them'. Industrial schools, that is to say, were intended for what Mary Carpenter called children of the 'perishing classes'; vagrant and destitute children, not convicted of any criminal offence.

By the end of the nineteenth century, therefore, the trend of development in the institutional care of the young delinquent was the opposite of what the original schools had found to be effective. Whereas they had introduced a division of intake and management for their populations, the system now moved towards unification. With the abolition of imprisonment before admission to the reformatories in 1899, the external differentiation between the two types of school disappeared.[3]

The vigour with which the abolition of the previous imprisonment clause was resisted by the schools themselves had meanwhile only added to the doubts entertained by magistrates, judges, philanthropists and politicians regarding the desirability of such institutions, and prompted them to seek alternative ways of dealing with young offenders.

The Summary Jurisdiction Act of 1879[4] had allowed one possible alternative to either imprisonment or institutional treatment in that it had provided that a juvenile could, for petty offences of which he was undoubtedly guilty, be let off with an

---

[1] Carlebach, op. cit., p. 80 n.
[2] ibid., p. 80.
[3] ibid.
[4] 42 & 43 Vict., c. 49.

'admonition' instead of a formal conviction. Subsequently the growing conviction of the futility of short sentences of imprisonment and of the undesirability of committing children to prison at all brought the 'admonitary method' into prominence in discussions of the treatment of juvenile delinquents.

Four years later a different though related alternative was provided by the Probation of First Offenders Act, 1887.[1] Colonel Vincent, who introduced the Bill, explained his motives for doing so to the Fifth Conference of the National Association of Certified and Industrial Schools (scarcely the most sympathetic of audiences, judging by the Council's Report which inveighs against 'the growth of that morbid sentimentality which so often manifests itself in sympathy with the individual wrongdoer at the expense of public morality').[2] 'I have always felt', declared the Colonel, undeterred, 'that imprisonment with all its lifelong taint, its never-ending self-reproach, its unnecessary torture of possible denunciation to a trusting employer, an unsuspecting wife or family, is to be avoided, so far as is practicable, in the young.'[3] His Bill, therefore, gave magistrates discretionary powers to release, on his own recognisance, any delinquent convicted of an offence punishable by not more than two years' imprisonment.

Important in principle, since it provided a middle course between admonition and imprisonment, the Probation of First Offenders Act nevertheless had two substantial drawbacks, compared with the system of probation operating today. First, its application necessarily involved the formal conviction of the offender. Second, unlike the system of probation which had been operating in the United States for some years in Massachusetts and Michigan, where the offender was returned to his family under the supervision of a specially designated probation officer, no provision was made in England for the supervision of those on probation. Because of this, magistrates were, in practice, reluctant to invoke the Act and preferred to send offenders to industrial schools.

It was to this particular deficiency of the Act that the Howard

---

[1] An Act to Permit the conditional Release of First Offenders in Certain Cases, 50 & 51 Vict., c. 25.

[2] *Report of the Fifth Conference of the National Association of Certified and Industrial Schools*, 1891, p. 13.

[3] ibid., pp. 89–90.

Association made repeated reference in its campaign to keep juvenile offenders not merely free from the taint of imprisonment but out of the reformatory schools of which they were no admirers. The Association's Annual Report for 1896 drew attention to the latest criminal statistics, which showed that whilst 'crime on the whole had diminished . . . unfortunately, the proportion of juvenile offenders, and especially of offenders between the ages of 16 and 21, had increased appreciably'. This, the Report commented, called for careful examination of the causes.[1]

> Considering the large extent to which, of recent years, juvenile offenders have been committed to Reformatories instead of to Prisons, the system of Reformatory management may possibly have some bearing upon this increase of juvenile crime. But it is a delicate thing even to make such a suggestion. For many good people assume that Reformatories are almost an unlimited success. And whenever any question on this point is raised, figures are promptly quoted which show that by far the greatest number of the former inmates of Reformatories turn out well. Both in Great Britain and the United States, a sort of INSTITUTION CRAZE has taken hold of the public fancy. Reformatories do reform. But a certain residuum of their boys are very bad. These institutions need more attention. They are often carried on too much for mere pecuniary profit. The boy's moral interest being made secondary.

The following year, 1897, the Association's Annual Report carried an attack on the continued committal of the children to prison, noting that 'The imprisonment of children is a subject to which fresh public attention was recently aroused by a long and interesting letter in the *London Daily Chronicle* by Mr Oscar Wilde, and also by a subsequent letter in the *Nineteenth Century* by Major White.' Referring to the Association's own communication to the Home Office, urging the abolition of imprisonment of children under the age of fourteen except for serious crimes, the Report quotes a letter of support which it received from Ruggles-Brise, the Chairman of the Prison Commission, in which he described the imprisonment of children as 'as foolish as it is inappropriate . . . Every alternative should be exhausted before this is done . . .'[2]

[1] *Annual Report of the Howard Association*, 1896, p. 6.
[2] ibid., 1897, pp. 10–11.

On grounds of economy as well as efficacy, the best alternative, both to imprisonment and to committal to a reformatory was, in the view of the Howard Association, a properly organised and supervised system of probation. In this they had the strong support of Mr Stewart, stipendiary magistrate for Liverpool, who had himself used the services of local school-board officials to gain information concerning the social background of the offenders who appeared before him, thus avoiding sentences inappropriate to the individual child. The result, he claimed, was beneficial both to the child and to the community.

Increasing advocacy of the merits of the probation system for the young offender; strong opinion against the desirability of imprisonment of children; growing criticisms of the reformatory schools in which, according to a letter in *The Times*, 'Most of us are losing faith . . . by herds and battalions,'[1] paved the way for further reforms which had the influential support of Sir William Harcourt (the 'most humane Home Secretary that John Bright had ever known'). Not only was the previous imprisonment clause withdrawn in 1899,[2] but the Youthful Offenders Act of 1901[3] and the Probation Act of 1907[4] effectively established the form of probation urged by the Howard Association, and which is familiar to us today. The following year, the monumental Children Act,[5] in establishing separate juvenile courts, confirmed the ascendancy of the view that juvenile delinquents were not most appropriately or most effectively dealt with by the same processes of law and the same punishments as adult criminals, and, by so doing, reflected a revolutionary change of attitude from the days when the young offender was regarded as a small adult, fully responsible for his crime.

Although, like probation, the juvenile court system was immediately copied from the United States, a proposal for such a system had originally been made many years before by Benjamin Waugh in *The Gaol Cradle – Who Rocks It?*, first published in 1875. The book, 'written in popular style', was an all-out attack on the existing English penal system for children. According to Waugh some 28,000 children annually appeared

---

[1] *Annual Report of the Howard Association*, 1899, p. 4.
[2] Reformatory Schools Act, 62 & 63 Vict., c. 12.
[3] 64 Vict., c. 20.
[4] 7 Edw. VII, c. 17.
[5] 8 Edw. VII, c. 67.

in the courts as 'prisoners at the bar', and many of them were committed to prison to become habitual criminals:[1]

> The gaol inures them to crime; it rears them for its own family. In short, the work of the gaol is to rock its own cradle . . . The time will come when Englishmen will be ashamed that they ever dealt with the naughtiness of a child by police courts and prisons, as they are ashamed that they ever traded in slaves, and that a Christian could ever be party to such proceedings will amaze them.

Illustrating his argument by reference to numerous case-histories he had investigated, Waugh made an impassioned plea for the abolition of imprisonment for children and for the establishment of separate district tribunals for young offenders.

Although the book made an immediate impact on public discussion of juvenile delinquency and went through four editions in five years, no action on the proposals it contained was taken here for another thirty years; hence the credit for establishing the first juvenile court must go to Illinois where, by the Act to Regulate the Treatment and Control of Dependent, Neglected and Delinquent Children, 1899, special courts of equity jurisdiction were established. A more enlightened approach to adjudication of cases involving juveniles in this country waited upon the Children Act of 1908, the outcome of informed and sympathetic debate in Parliament, in the course of which it was claimed that 'the Courts should be agencies for the rescue as well as the punishment of children.'[2] Under the Act children were to be kept separate from adult criminals at their trial and afterwards were to receive treatment suited to their special needs and not punishment fitted to the crime. For the first time juvenile courts were set up in which young offenders and non-offenders were charged and heard in a separate room or at a separate time from the adult court, and the public not actually concerned with the hearing were excluded. The imprisonment of children under the age of sixteen was abolished, and special places of detention, remand homes, aided by Treasury grants and under the supervision of the police, were set up to avoid any child being kept in prison, while awaiting his trial.

The whole trend of the 'Children's Charter' of 1908 was

---

[1] op. cit., p. 4.
[2] Jean Heywood, *Children in Care*, p. 109.

aimed at a more comprehensive and child-oriented legal system and at more generous and liberal provisions for children in all walks of life. The Act differentiated between reformatory and industrial schools by providing for local education payments for children in industrial schools, at the same time widening the scope of their intake to cover all classes of deprived children, whilst reformatory schools were to receive payments from municipal and county councils. But the Act also brought the schools together by making transfers between them possible, thus following the trend set by the Committee of 1896. The distinction between the two types of school was now becoming largely artificial except that reformatories were used for children who had committed offences against the law and, generally, were above school leaving age. Almost twenty years later the Departmental Committee on the Treatment of Young Offenders was to recommend the final abolition of any distinction between the two types of school, the catchment area of all of them being now defined as 'all classes of neglected and delinquent children'.

The Departmental Committee appointed in 1925 did not include anyone connected with the schools and its report, issued two years later, had relatively little new to say. Apart from the decision that the names Reformatory and Industrial should be dropped in favour of the appellation 'Approved' for both categories, the only significant recommendation was that the managers be deprived of the right to refuse admission to a child sent by the court. The proposal was unanimously, but unsuccessfully, rejected by the managers themselves, an ironic outcome of the work of a Committee for which the schools had pressed so hard and hoped so much.

The main provisions of the Children and Young Persons Act of 1933,[1] a consolidating Act of great importance, were largely based on the administrative recommendations of this Committee. It forged a much closer link between the work for neglected and delinquent children and the work of the local education authorities, dealt with the procedure and constitution of juvenile courts, the duties and responsibilities of education authorities in this field and the treatment of boys and girls brought before the courts. The object of the juvenile court was now to be not punishment alone – 'the Court shall have regard to the welfare

[1] 23 & 24 Geo. V, c. 12.

of the child' – but rehabilitation and even social service, and justices were to be specially selected for it on the grounds of experience and interest. Local education authorities had a duty now to provide the magistrates with information about the family and school background of the children who appeared before their courts. Emphasis on the constructive and educational purpose of the remand home was seen now in the transfer from the police to the local education authorities of the duty to provide them. The distinction between the reformatory and industrial schools was finally abolished, and they both became 'approved' by the Home Office to give short term training to enable children to take their place as useful, happy citizens in society. They thus became known as Approved Schools, and a maximum period was determined and laid down for the detention of children in them.

Far more important than any of the Act's individual provisions, however, was the standard of welfare and rehabilitation it set for the delinquent child. Ideas and philosophies which had required treatment to be based on hard work and stigmatization were now finally discarded and a constructive concept of social training in the interests of the child took its place. The welfare of the child, not the judgment of society, was now paramount even for those who had 'offended' against society's rules.

XVII

◇◇

The Release of Children
from Pauperism

◇◇

INEXTRICABLE from the problem of delinquency was the problem of destitution. As in the eighteenth century, so in the early nineteenth, children figured large among those who sought relief from the overseers of a Poor Law which measured its successfulness by its cheapness. Attempts to make poor children contribute to their own upkeep had conspicuously failed. The eighteenth-century workhouse movement, of which so much had been hoped, had proved hopelessly unprofitable. The original schemes for training and educating children in separate institutions had broken down, with the result that children mingled with thieves, prostitutes, the physically handicapped and the mentally afflicted, the idle and the shiftless, in the overcrowded workhouses on which Eden had commented so trenchantly in 1797. Outside the workhouses, poor law apprenticeship, devised at the end of the sixteenth century for the education and training of the poor child in private houses, had deteriorated into a form of cheap boarding out. Apprenticeship, as such, was decreasingly useful in the growing towns where developing conditions of modern industry rendered it largely irrelevant. Some, like Robert Blincoe, were apprenticed in textile mills, others in the mines and collieries, others again to unskilled trades. Most were only taken for the sake of the premium each brought with him, in return for which there was no longer any guarantee of instruction in a craft by the practice of which he could later hope to maintain himself. In the rural areas, where attempts continued to billet poor apprentices on farmers compulsorily, the system was bitterly resented[1] and, instead of being trained in the skills of husbandry and the crafts of housewifery, the children were used as field-labourers and domestic drudges, and released from their indentures ignorant and unskilled. In those areas of the country where the Speenhamland system of outdoor relief operated, children and young people swelled the ranks of the unemployed applying for the miserable weekly allowance fixed by the local justices. Elsewhere they joined the ranks of those forced to beg for their bread.

In London the number of beggars swarming on the streets and in the alleys became as much a matter for concern in the early nineteenth century as it had been four hundred years earlier, and was the subject of two successive Reports in 1815 and 1816, of a specially appointed Select Committee of the House of Commons.[2] The first of these Reports drew attention to an enquiry into the numbers of beggars in London made by a Mr Martin in 1803. According to Martin's estimates, these totalled some 15,288, of whom 9,288 were children. A considerable proportion of the children came from outside London – Martin believed virtually one-third to be Irish – and more than one witness was to deplore the social and moral effects of this addition to London's already considerable number of beggars. The Rector of St Clement Dane's, for example, told the Committee that he had seen hundreds of children among the groups of poor on the road from Birmingham, 'all begging their way to London. They get a dreadful habit by coming to the metropolis, a habit of idleness and drinking; and these children

---

[1] One particularly articulate critic was William Cobbett, who, in his *Weekly Political Register*, drew attention to the considerable burden the system imposed on men such as himself:

'Just after Easter Tuesday, the officers of the several Parishes held a meeting, at which, by the way of lottery, they distributed amongst the most able parishioners, *young paupers* to be kept by the said parishioners and brought up in their own homes, or at any rate maintained by them, clothed, fed, lodged, and doctored at their own particular expense, until they grow up men and women.

Luckily I have last had drawn for me in this lottery: a girl about 10 or 12 years of age . . . if I had had all my share of paupers quartered upon me as this girl was, I should have had about twenty eight of all ages . . .' 18 May 1816.

[2] The Select Committee on the State of Mendicity in the Metropolis, First Report, *PP*, 1814–15, III; Second Report, *PP*, 1816, V.

are annually instructed in idleness and drinking, and of course lying; idleness is sure to bring on lying and theft. I dare say that there are few of these Mendicant children who are not trained up to pilfer as well as to beg; . . . '[1] Martin himself had a sympathy with the plight of the poor that the majority of witnesses did not share. He wrote to the Committee that he believed that, 'in many cases, beggary was the effect of misfortune rather than of choice; of the want of means, rather than the want of will to maintain themselves', adding that 'even industry on the individual's part cannot in all cases oppose an effectual barrier against beggary'.[2] The weight of other opinion was in a contrary direction. One of the witnesses, Mr J. Daughty, 'a benevolent tradesman', asked for his own opinion, replied; 'They are idle and worthless; the visitors of the Spitalfields Benevolent Society with which I am connected, having been led to adopt as a maxim "That street beggars are, with very few exceptions, so utterly worthless and incorrigible as to be undeserving of the attention of such a society." '[3] A member of the Select Committee itself, Mr J. Butterworth, declared that 'In the course of my observations I have noticed many beggars . . . and I am persuaded that they are the most profligate and idle description of character: I am convinced that very few, if any, honest, industrious and sober people have recourse to begging.'[4] Special emphasis was placed on the exploitation of children by unscrupulous parents and others. The ex-overseer of St Giles was asked: 'Do you think children beg at the instigation of their parents?' 'Most assuredly' came the reply. 'They are sent out as soon as it is possible for them to extort relief, and distributed about; one perhaps takes a broom, and if they do not bring home, more or less according to their size, they are beaten for it; a family is the greatest recourse of such persons.'[5] The Chaplain of Bridewell went further, alleging that in Whitechapel there was a central beggars' depot where children were taken to be hired out to women for work either as beggars or prostitutes,[6] whilst yet another witness gave evidence of a 'night

[1] *Minutes of Evidence, PP*, 1814–15, III p. 29.
[2] ibid., p. 91.
[3] ibid., p. 73.
[4] ibid., p. 48.
[5] ibid., p. 53.
[6] ibid., p. 22.

school' in St Giles, where children, young girls in particular, were taught all the tricks of begging and petty theft.[1]

Commenting on this evidence, the Committee's second Report urged the need for some kind of Parliamentary intervention: 'Your Committee cannot quit this part of the subject respecting Children, without expressing an anxious hope that it will be considered as worthy the immediate and serious attention of Parliament; . . . to prevent their growing up in habits of vice and idleness destructive to themselves and most highly dangerous to society.'[2] In the event it was not Parliament but men such as Peter Bedford – whose own work with the Spitalfields Benevolent Society had not forced him to so pessimistic a view of human nature as Mr Daughty – who were to engage in this work of rescue and moral welfare among children. The statutory Poor Law continued in its policy of not seeking out the children for whom such care was needed; its purpose being only to relieve a need when actually required to do so, and to give as little relief as statute prescribed and the local rates were obliged to support.

The effects of this minimal relief in the workhouses were well illustrated in the Report of the 1832–4 Poor Law Commission, where children were described as having been 'trained in idleness, ignorance and vice . . . not one third found any respectable employment. The majority dropped almost automatically into the ranks of pauperism and crime.'[3] – a description to which the detailed evidence added substance and colour. The Master of the St Pancras Workhouse, for example, stated that:[4]

> if we get them places they throw them up, or misconduct themselves so as to lose them, and return to the workhouse as a matter of course, because they prefer the security and certainty of that mode of life to the slightest exercise of forebearance or diligence. As little or no classification can take place, the younger soon acquire all the bad habits of the older, and become for the most part as virtuous. This is particularly the case with respect to young girls. We are obliged to have many prostitutes among our inmates: they decoy the young girls, with whom they have met in the house, to leave it, and addict themselves to the same abandoned course.

[1] ibid., p. 87.
[2] op. cit., p. 4.
[3] Cf. Report of the Royal Commission on the Poor Laws and the Relief of Distress, *PP*, 1909, XXXVIII, pt I, p. 618.
[4] *PP*, 1834, XXXVI, p. 242.

F

Apart from poor law apprenticeship, which they proposed to retain, the Commissioners' Report, however, only dealt with children incidentally, their assumption being that children should be relieved in the same manner as their parents. Hence they recommended the children of the aged, sick and impotent should be given outdoor relief, whilst the children of the able-bodied poor, to whom outdoor relief was to be denied, should go with their parents into the workhouse, where they be accommodated in a separate building, under separate superintendence, so as to be educated by 'a person properly qualified to act as a schoolmaster'. The principle that 'children should follow their parents' was adopted in the 1834 Poor Law Amendment Act, with the result that, in practice, there was wide variation of treatment largely depending on whether or not they lived in unions governed by the Outdoor Labour Test Order – which allowed the domiciliary relief of the able-bodied poor. The number of children who were relieved in the workhouses was nevertheless considerable. By 1838, it had reached 42,767, nearly half the total workhouse population: two years later, it had risen to 64,570.[1] The sheer size of their number and fears that they might become permanently pauperised by inadequate attention in the workhouses to their special needs, prompted the administrators of the new Poor Law to look once again at the consequences of relieving children in the workhouses of the old regime, and to propose modifications for their treatment in those of the new.

The Fourth Annual Report of the Poor Law Commissioners contained an unequivocal condemnation of the workhouse practices before the formation of the unions:[2]

The children, who were for the most part orphans, bastards and deserted children, continued to remain inmates of the workhouse long after the period at which they might have earned their subsistence by their own exertions; and those who obtained situations, or were apprenticed by means of the parish funds, turned out as might be expected of children whose education was utterly neglected or at best confined to the supervision of a pauper. They rarely remained long with an employer, but returned to the Workhouse – which so far from being to them an object of dislike, they regarded

[1] Cf. Sidney and Beatrice Webb, *English Poor Law Policy*, p. 45.
[2] *PP*, 1838, XXVIII, p. 60.

as their home, and which they looked forward to as the ultimate asylum of their old age. In this manner, the workhouse, instead of diminishing, increased pauperism by keeping up a constant supply of that class of persons who most frequently, and for the longest period, become its inmates. Pauperism, however, was only one of the evils which resulted from the neglect to provide the proper means of instruction for the children. Those who have ascertained the early history of persons who in a greater or lesser degree have offended against the laws, have found that a large proportion of these have passed their infancy and youth in the workhouse, and can trace the formation of the habits which have led them to the commission of crime to the entire want of training in these institutions.

Very early in their work, therefore, the Poor Law Commissioners became aware that containing and reducing pauperism was fundamentally connected with a more positive approach to the relief of children than the principle of less eligibility, introduced by the new Act, readily allowed. The problem which confronted them was how to achieve the one without weakening the deterrent effects of the other.

Their first step was to attempt to ensure that two policies recommended in the original Poor Law Report and incorporated in the 1834 legislation were fully and efficiently implemented. The first provided that children should be separated from adults in the workhouses by the introduction of a proper system of classification; the second, that they should be provided with a basic education. In the first Orders and Regulations issued in 1835 for the management of a workhouse, the Commissioners stressed the necessity of paying particular attention to the accommodation of children under the age of seven years. They 'shall be placed either in a ward by themselves, or in such of the wards appropriated to the female paupers as the board of guardians shall direct. The mothers of such children to be permitted to have access to them at all reasonable times.'[1] Further, the local guardians were required to see to it that: 'The boys and girls who are inmates of the workhouse shall, for three working hours at least, every day, be respectively instructed in reading and writing and in the principles of the Christian religion; and such other instructions shall be imparted to them

[1] First Annual Report of the Poor Law Commission, *PP*, 1835, XXXV, Appendix A, p. 60.

as are calculated to train them to habits of usefulness, industry and virtue.'[1] To achieve this, the Orders provided for the appointment of a schoolmaster and a schoolmistress in each union workhouse. The duty of seeing that the Orders were implemented was laid on the visiting committees of the local guardians who were to obtain answers to a number of specific questions: 'Are the schools regularly attended to by the master and mistress? Are the youths, boys and girls properly instructed and set to work, and due care taken to fit them for becoming useful and respectable members of the community? Are the children kept clean in their persons and does their general conduct and behaviour appear to be properly attended to and regulated?'[2]

Educational developments in the workhouses were considerably hampered, however, by the difficulty of obtaining the services of competent teachers. An example of the standard of teacher employed is seen at Salisbury, where the schoolmistress could not write and the schoolmaster was a pauper who had found his way into the workhouse through excessive drink; whilst at Southampton the schoolmaster was a deaf old man completely unable to control his pupils. At a time when skilled teachers were difficult to obtain even for the well-to-do, the salaries offered by the new unions were in the vast majority of cases too small to attract people of the calibre required to teach children often of limited ability and even more restricted interest. To some extent, the low salaries offered were one of the inevitable consequences of the basic units of administration remaining too small, even under the revised Poor Law. Even had the unions been more financially viable, however, it is extremely doubtful whether there would have been any marked tendency to advertise and pay for teachers of better quality. In too many instances, both guardians and overseers were reluctant to provide, even at a minimal level, a service which they believed to be a subsidy to the idle and an infringement of the principle of less eligibility. Thus, at the request of his board of guardians, the Clerk of Bedford Union wrote to the Poor Law Commissioners in 1836, asking for their sanction to[3]

[1] ibid.
[2] ibid., p. 61.
[3] Second Annual Report of the Poor Law Commission, *PP*, 1836, XXIX, p. 529.

have writing omitted as part of the schoolmaster's instruction in the workhouse, and that he teach *reading only*. The Board do not recommend this on the score of economy, but on that of principle, as they are desirous of avoiding a greater advantage to the inmates of the workhouse than to the poor child out of it, withdrawing thereby as much as possible any premium or inducement to the frequenting of the workhouse.

Rejecting this request, the Commissioners replied:[1]

The Commissioners think it of the greatest importance that the workhouse child should be so taught as to give them the greatest attainable chance of earning an honest and adequate maintenance for the remainder of their lives, and they cannot conceal from themselves that the acquisition of the power of writing greatly increases this chance.

More significantly, they went on to advocate a more generous attitude to the relief of the poor child than the enquiry from the Bedford guardians displayed.

They [the Commissioners] think also that the workhouse children should not be so treated as to fix upon them any permanent stigma which should be likely to attach to them in after life. All other children who learn to read also learn to write; to have acquired a knowledge of reading, being at the same time altogether ignorant of the art of writing would become the distinguishing mark of those who had received a workhouse education . . .

It would be a mistake to assume that the Commissioners necessarily saw this advice as constituting a breach in the application of the principle of less eligibility. Indeed, in their Third Report, issued in 1837, they specifically expressed their conviction that such was not the case since[2]

it is found that it is *maintenance* alone, and not the advantage of obtaining an ordinary education, which operates as an inducement on the parents to throw the burden of maintaining them [i.e. their children] upon the rate payers . . . In respect of the *maintenance* of children, the same principle is applicable to them that is applicable to young adult paupers.

The following year, however, they were to receive a report

[1] ibid.
[2] *PP*, 1837, XXXI, Appendix A, p. 54.

from an Assistant Commissioner, Dr Kay – later Sir James Kay-Shuttleworth – in which he advocated both the principle of equal, not less, eligibility as regards the maintenance of children in the workhouses and also, as regards their education, the principle of greater eligibility in localities where the standard of education outside the workhouses was low. In marked contrast to many of his contemporaries, who believed that the only effective way to discourage pauperism was to operate a punitive system of relief for young and old alike, Kay firmly believed that children should receive a far more sympathetic treatment.

> A child cannot be a pauper in the sense in which that term is commonly understood, that is, he cannot be indigent as the consequence of his own want of industry, skill, frugality or forethought . . . The pauper children, maintained in union workhouses are dependent not as a consequence of their errors, but of their misfortunes. They have not necessarily contracted any of the taint of pauperism. They are orphans or deserted children, or bastards, or children of idiots, or of cripples, or felons, or they are resident in the workhouse with their parents who seek a brief refuge there.

To many of these children, Kay asserted that the Poor Law Commissioners really stood *in loco parentis*:

> The dependence of certain of these classes of children cannot be transient. The care of their natural guardians is at an end, or is suspended for so considerable a period, that the children have claims on the Board of Guardians not for food and clothing merely, but for that moral sustenance which may enable them, at the earliest period, to attain independence.

Thus, he argued, that not only should the workhouse child be given clothes, food and lodging equal to that of the child of the self-supporting labourer:[1]

> But whenever the community encounters the responsibility of providing for the education of children who have no natural guardians, it is impossible to adopt as a standard for the training of such children the average amount of care and skill now bestowed on the moral and religious culture of the labouring classes generally, or to decide that their secular instruction should be confined within the limits confessedly so meagre and inadequate . . . The duty of pro-

[1] Fourth Annual Report of the Poor Law Commission, *PP*, 1838, XXVIII, Appendix B, No. 3, pp. 145–6.

viding a suitable training for pauper children is simple and positive and is not to be evaded on the plea of the deficiency of such instruction among the self-supported classes. Education is to be regarded as one of the most important means of eradicating the genus of pauperism from the rising generation, and of securing in the minds and the morals of the people the best protection for the institutions of society.

It was clear to Kay and some of the other Assistant Commissioners, such as Hickson who also signed the report, and to Carleton Tufnell who was making his own investigations, that the education which pauper children so much needed was not to be expected in the individual workhouse schools which were too small to be efficient. What seemed to be required, and what they urged, was that groups of neighbouring unions should combine to establish district schools, capable of taking some five hundred children, for whom a better quality of education, given by better paid teachers, could be provided in an establishment separated from the workhouse and free of its stigmatising influences.

In the Metropolitan area there was already an example to hand of several workhouses sending children to one large school, Mr Aubin's private establishment at Norwood, of which Kay knew. This and other types of private establishment had grown up as a consequence of Hanway's Act of 1767 which had required that pauper children under the age of six years were to be maintained at the cost of their respective parishes at a distance of three to five miles from the Metropolis, in the interest of their health. Although originally intended for the very young, the system of 'farming out' pauper children to private individuals who contracted to house and educate them in return for payment from the overseers had been used for much older children. Hence at the time of Kay's report Mr Aubin's school contained about 1,000 children of up to fifteen years. First acquaintance with Norwood had revealed almost its only virtue to be its size.[1]

> The means adopted for the religious instruction of the children were inadequate, and were not in conformity with the provisions of the law; the moral training of the children was in every respect extremely defective . . . The industrial instruction of the boys was confined

[1] Fifth Annual Report of the Poor Law Commission, *PP*, 1839, XX, Appendix C, no. 1, p. 91.

to the sorting of bristles and senna, and the making of hooks and eyes; occupations of the most cheerless description, incapable of exercising the ingenuity of the children, useless in preparing them for any future duties, and pernicious because they disgusted them with labour. The girls were taught to sort bristles, to thread hooks and eyes upon cards, and were instructed in needlework; they were also partially employed in making the beds and cleaning the rooms.

Basically, Kay disliked the whole idea of contracting out pauper children for profit. Nevertheless, since the farming out of children was allowed under the law, and because the contractors themselves had invested considerable sums in their establishments in the hope of making a profit from the children's labour, he advised the Commissioners in 1839 that they 'should be afforded a period of probation . . . that they might be enabled to render their establishments more satisfactory in all that related to the training and management of the children'.[1]

Within a matter of months a chaplain was appointed to Norwood by the Commissioners themselves, the services of more skilled teachers obtained – although a good deal of the teaching was on the monitorial method, with the older children teaching the younger – and the curriculum for both boys and girls extended and improved. Soon Mr Aubin's school had become a model for guardians wishing to provide large children's institutions in their own locality. In 1841 a deputation from the Manchester board of guardians made a special visit to Norwood which now took between 1,200 and 1,300 children and were delighted with the teaching they found there. The infants' school where the children were from three to five years of age particularly impressed them: 'We listened with delight to the long exhibition of their knowledge of many subjects contained in the scriptures.'[2] The older children, instead of sorting bristles and making hooks and eyes, were now being trained by competent instructors in skills which were not only useful for the institution but likely to be profitable when they eventually left it. Boys were trained in tin-plate working, joinering, iron and brass work and shoe making; whilst the girls were trained as domestic servants, making and repairing clothes, working

[1] ibid.
[2] Sixth Annual Report of the Poor Law Commission, *PP*, 1841, XI, Appendix B, p. 138.

in the laundry and learning to cook in the school's kitchen.[1]

Kay himself was not slow to recognise the considerable improvements that had been achieved in the school, noting the greater willingness of local employers to take children from the institution now that they had had some better training, and commented particularly on the fact that 'the Children now at least display in their features evidence of happiness . . .'. Yet he still believed that contractors' schools, in which educational efficiency had constantly to be weighed against private profit, were not in fact the best way of providing the education and training which he regarded as so necessary for the pauper child. 'My experience leads me to say that the defects apparently inseparable from contractor's establishments, are such as to render their extension in the highest degree impolitic; and to induce me to add, that a right regulation of such houses can generally only be secured by incessant and painful vigilance.'[2] On the other hand, the Commissioners clearly lacked the necessary powers to authorise the large, district schools which Kay and his colleagues advocated so strongly. Successive representations on this matter in their annual reports resulted in legislation being passed in 1844[3] which permitted parishes and unions to combine to set up residential district schools, with boards of managers representing the several parishes. No part of the district was to be more than fifteen miles from any other part, and the sums raised for providing the necessary building were not to exceed one-fifth of the previous three years' annual poor rate of any of the participating unions. The Act also repealed Hanway's Act, so that the London unions were no longer obliged to send even their youngest children into the country unless they so wished.

The Commissioners had hoped that the concept of the district school would have wide appeal throughout the country, but in this they were to be disappointed. In fact, no order establishing a school district was issued under this Act until three years after its passing and no district school established until 1849. To some extent, the drafting of the Act itself had made the Commissioners'

---

[1] ibid.

[2] Fifth Annual Report of the Poor Law Commission, *PP*, 1839, XX, Appendix C, no. 1, p. 97.

[3] 78 & 79 Vict., c. 101.

disappointment inevitable. The limitation of the size of each district made the organisation of district schools virtually impossible in sparsely populated areas, and the careful limitation on the sums which might be used to provide the necessary accommodation severely hampered those who might otherwise have applied for authority to build. But to an even greater extent, failure to adopt the Act was rooted in local opposition to its provisions. Local boards of guardians, especially those in rural areas, objected to the idea on several grounds. First, they disliked the idea of still another authority operating in the sphere of poor law relief. Second, they did not want to bear their share of the very great expense that these vast State boarding schools entailed. Third, they objected to the principle of greater eligibility for the pauper child which the district schools seemed to imply. In London, where the contractors' establishments had made the guardians accustomed to the idea of large schools, there was less opposition to the concept of district schools, but no very marked enthusiasm for abandoning the use of the older establishments in their favour. The final impetus for this came early in 1849, when a hundred and eighty children lost their lives in an outbreak of Asiatic cholera at Mr Drouet's Pauper Establishment at Tooting, which housed 1,394 children from parishes all over London. In the scandal caused by the arraignment of the proprietor for manslaughter, it was revealed that some guardians, warned of the outbreak by the newly created Board of Health, had refused absolutely to remove their children to less overcrowded conditions, although for several days between fourteen and twenty children died each day.[1] No case could have more adequately justified Dr Kay's reservations concerning contractors' schools, nor could any tragedy more amply have justified the decision to abolish these establishments as such. Drouet's establishment was closed down, as were several smaller establishments. Aubin's school at Norwood was handed over to the management committee of London's first school district, the Central London School District, and Aubin himself was retained as the salaried superintendent.

So ended the last vestiges of the eighteenth-century method of 'farming the poor' and so appeared the very first of the district

---

[1]General Board of Health, Report on Quarantine, *PP*, 1849, XXIV, p. 27 et seq.

schools. A year before, legislation had been passed to encourage guardians in agricultural districts by allowing the formation of larger school districts than permitted under the original Act, and in their first report the new Poor Law Board mentioned that there were two plans to set up district schools, one in Hampshire and one in Surrey. But district schools never became popular. In all there were never more than ten or eleven and of these six belonged to the Metropolitan area. For the rest of the century the district schools were to have their passionate advocates and their violent critics, but at this early stage the critics were not the reformers but the reactionary elements in the local authorities concerned. Meanwhile the majority of pauper children received such education as they were given in the workhouse schools. To improve their standards Parliament voted £15,000 towards the payment of the teachers' salaries, the continuation of the grant being dependent upon their maintaining a required standard of efficiency. For the purpose of checking this separate inspectors of workhouse schools were appointed, under the control of the Committee of Council of Education.

Since parish apprenticeship had not been abandoned by the reformed Poor Law, however, an alternative system of instructing pauper children in some useful skill still remained for the older among them. Up to 1834 the local overseers had been accustomed to give a premium to employers for any poor law apprentice they accepted, and the child itself was given a complete outfit of clothes. Even before the introduction of the principle of less eligibility into the administration of poor relief, there had been some anxiety lest the pauper child, by superior training, should occupy a position which might otherwise have fallen to his superiors. After the 1834 Poor Law Reform Act, objections to the payment of a premium were voiced very strongly indeed on the grounds that the custom was unfair to the independent labourer, whose application to an employer on behalf of his own children would be turned down in favour of the pauper child for whose acceptance the employer received a premium, paid from the local poor rates. Tufnell made specific reference to this, to him, undesirable aspect of poor law apprenticeship, in his report to the Commissioners in 1837, claiming that, since employers actually needed child labour, there was no cause to offer them a bribe to accept it.[1] Both he and the Commissioners themselves were in fact very critical of the whole operation of poor law apprenticeship, and not always on narrow grounds of finance. The growing emphasis on the quality of the education and training necessary to prevent children becoming permanently pauperised, together with a growing awareness of the dangers of exploitation inherent in the apprenticeship system, led to revisions of the regulations governing the binding of pauper apprentices which, amplified and consolidated in 1847, remained operative until the end of the century. Under the new code[2] a child under the age of nine (other than the deaf and dumb) who could not read and write his own name was not to be apprenticed by the guardians. In future apprentices were not to be bound for more than eight years, and there were close restrictions on the qualifications of people to whom a child might be bound. No premium, other than clothing, was to be given for any apprentice bound above the age of sixteen unless 'such a person be maimed, deformed, or suffering from some permanent bodily infirmity, such as may render him unfit for certain trades or sorts of work'. Where premiums were given part had to be given to the apprentice himself, in the form of clothing, and only a portion of the money was to be paid to the master at the time of his accepting the apprentice, the remainder being held back until the end of the first year of the binding – a device to protect apprentices from being turned out-of-doors with no training whatsoever by unscrupulous masters. Further the forced acceptance of apprentices was abolished altogether, thus removing a longstanding grievance in country districts.

Unfortunately concern for the quality of education and training under the Poor Law, which was gradually but inevitably modifying the application of the principle of less eligibility in this particular area of relief, had not also led the Commissioners to encourage the more progressive guardians to give the children they trained any assistance in actually establishing themselves as independent, self-respecting work-people. In 1846 the Board of Guardians of Norwich Union opened a Working Boys' Home

[1] Third Annual Report of the Poor Law Commission, *PP*, 1837, XXXI, Appendix B, p. 89.
[2] Contained in the *General Consolidated Order* of 24 July 1847, issued by the Poor Law Commissioners.

where those who had been in the workhouse, but were now employed outside it, might be given subsidised accommodation whilst their earnings were too low to enable them to live decently elsewhere. This early attempt at 'after care' the Commissioners did all in their power to discourage, questioning the legality of subsidising such a scheme out of the poor rates.[1]

The formation of the Poor Law Board in 1848 brought no marked change from this highly cautious approach to the liberalising of the Poor Law as it affected children. Since in most cases the inspectors were the same, this is scarcely surprising. Yet the inspectors' own experience, now as in the past, sometimes moved them to different views of the interpretation of the duty of the State to the poor child, and these views they conveyed to the Board itself in their reports. Hence the process of the self-education of the administration continued. 'What happened was a slow and almost unselfconscious development of a supplementary policy in respect of certain favoured classes, notably children and the sick classes which had been practically ignored in the 1834 Report.'[2] This supplementary policy was openly based not on minimum relief and deterrence but on the need of supplying whatever was necessary for adequate training and treatment. Where such a policy was pursued – and it was far from being accepted by all poor law administrators – the persons thus dealt with 'were in a position of positive advantage as compared with the lowest class of independent labourers'. In all this Parliament took little interest. According to the Webbs, 'Parliament had in fact ceased to be interested in the Poor Law, and furnished for many years neither independent criticism nor initiative'. They add that the Poor Law Board 'got from Parliament just what additional powers it chose to ask for'.[3]

The work of improving workhouse schools and encouraging the building of new district schools, the merits of which the inspectors still enthusiastically canvassed, continued. However, the difficulty of getting good teachers in either was never overcome. Rates of pay – £20, £30 and £40 a year – remained hopelessly inadequate to attract men and women to instruct the children in reading and writing, and occasionally arithmetic,

[1] Webb, op. cit., pp. 109–10.
[2] ibid.
[3] ibid.

give various forms of 'industrial training' and constantly supervise them during all their waking hours. The 'training' most constantly recommended by the Board's inspectors was 'of an agricultural nature', which in practice turned out to consist of digging a few acres of ground surrounding the workhouse. After a very short period of this the boys were almost invariably reported to show great improvement in health and happiness. The girls were easier to deal with. They could be given the ordinary work of the house, and thus be said to receive 'domestic training'. The teacher was supposed to be able to teach them to sew and to knit. Occasionally, where the guardians could be induced to buy a cow and the girls taught to milk it, girls were also reported to be trained in dairy work. But the real problem with regard to the training of girls, as the inspectors themselves freely admitted, was that it was very often impossible to separate them from the adult women inmates who instructed them in different avocations.

Such was the reality of the 'education' and 'training' given to workhouse children. Outside the workhouses thousands of pauper children were left with no education at all. Indeed, a circular issued by the Commissioners in 1844 specifically emphasised that pauper children were not to be educated at the expense of the rates. The Manchester guardians had for years been trying to get outdoor pauper children to school, and even maintained a primitive school for their own for this purpose. The Commissioners refused to sanction this, forbade its extension and questioned its legality. From 1850 to 1855 they constantly complained to the Manchester guardians regarding the continuation of a policy which they believed *ultra vires*. In 1855, however, the Education of Poor Children Act (Denison's Act)[1] was given the Royal Assent. This allowed local boards of guardians to pay for the schooling of their outdoor pauper children of between four and sixteen years of age, but it was expressly forbidden to make the granting of relief to parents conditional on their sending their children to school. The Poor Law Board, drawing the attention of local guardians to this new legislation, stressed its permissive nature but, interestingly enough in the light of their recent correspondence with the Manchester guardians, expressed the hope that it would soon

[1] 18 & 19 Vict., c. 34.

be brought into extensive operation. That there was an undoubted need for a rapid growth of this sort of local provision was illustrated in the poor law statistics for the following year, which showed that of the 200,000 children on outdoor relief only 3,936 were at school.[1] That such growth was unlikely to be achieved by Denison's Act was made clear in the Report of the Royal Commission on the Education of Neglected Children (the Newcastle Commission) published in 1861, where it was recommended that, far from prohibiting guardians from bringing pressure to bear on the poor to have their children educated, the Act should be amended to allow relief to the parents to be conditional on their children's attendance at school.[2]

The Newcastle Commission also proposed that pressure should be put on the boards of guardians themselves to combine to form the district schools for which, as seventeen years' experience had now proved, they had little enthusiasm. The Commission pointed to the considerable evidence they had collected which showed that 'children bred and born as paupers furnish the great mass of the pauper and criminal population'. They argued that this was the inevitable consequence of allowing each union to assert its right to provide for the education and training of the poor in their own workhouse schools, rather than forcing them to collaborate with their neighbours in establishing larger schools with better facilities, independent of the workhouses in which, despite the creation of separate children's wards, the minds and morals of the young were continually corrupted. Sir James Kay-Shuttleworth and Carleton Tufnell, both members of the Commission and both architects of the original plan for district schools, contributed their own evidence of the continuing necessity to remove children to such establishments. Kay-Shuttleworth claimed to have discovered from the Master of Greenwich Workhouse that, of girls brought up there, 'by far the majority had turned to prostitution'. He estimated himself that 'at least one third of all London prostitutes were brought up in workhouses'.[3] The boys were said to take to crime. Tufnell alleged that in one workhouse, of a group of thirty-nine boys, two had subsequently been transported for ten years; four for

[1] *PP*, 1856, XLIX, p. 345.
[2] *PP*, 1861, XXI, pt I, p. 383.
[3] *PP*, 1861, XXI, pt I, p. 353.

fourteen years; one for twenty years; two had been imprisoned for an unspecified length of time, and of the thirty-nine only seven were said to be doing well.[1] Elsewhere, Tufnell was to claim that only two per cent of children entirely educated and trained in schools separated from the workhouses were not 'de-pauperised'.[2]

Incensed by what they correctly interpreted as a thorough-going criticism of the inadequacy of their arrangements for the education and training of the vast majority of pauper children, the inspectors of the Poor Law Board penned lengthy criticisms of all the findings of the Newcastle Commission, particularly those which related to the institutions for which they were ultimately responsible. They were against the compulsory school attendance of the children of those on outdoor relief. They protested against the proposed extension of district schools, holding that vast improvements had taken place in all the workhouse schools since the early criticism of Kay and Tufnell, pointing to the disadvantages of the district schools which already existed. There was evidence to show, it was argued, that children brought up in such large establishments showed lack of initiative and, in contradiction to Tufnell's estimate, they claimed that large numbers of children brought up in district schools were still returning to the workhouses as adult paupers, the one basic trend which they were supposed to abolish. One thing the inspectors did not do was to recommend any alternative either to the workhouse schools, which even they did not claim to be a panacea for the treatment of juvenile pauperism, or to the district schools of which they were so critical. The merits of the so-called 'separate schools', residential establishments which had been set up under the provisions of the 1844 Act by some individual unions, apart from their workhouses, they failed to discuss at all.

Underlying the inspectors' angry reaction against the Report and recommendations of the Commission was not only a belief that large district schools had inherent disadvantages, but also a disapproval of any provision for the poor child better than was available to the children of the self-supporting. They quoted in full the evidence submitted to the Commission itself by one,

[1] *PP*, 1861, XXI, pt. I, p. 353.
[2] 'The Education of Pauper Children', *TNAPSS*, 1862.

George Coode, declaring themselves to agree entirely with the sentiments he expressed. Among other things, Coode had grumbled at the great expense of the district school, estimating that the cost to the rate payers was £20 a year for each child. This, he claimed, amounted to more than four times the value of the normal education of the free labourer's child. Again, he protested, why should the pauper child be provided for in the schools up to the age of sixteen, when the child of the independent labourer often worked from the age of ten years? Indignantly, he remarked that such schools were raising the pauper child 'as it were, above Eton and Harrow, and the rest of our schools, for the education of our nobility and gentry . . .'.[1] The Commissioners had feared for the corrupting effects of the public workhouses: the inspectors feared no less for the demoralising influences of the private Homes, such as Louisa Twining and her Workhouse Visiting Society were anxious to establish for the benefit of pauper girls. The purpose of such Homes was to give the girls the training in domestic skills which they all too evidently were not given in the workhouse. W. Hawley, one of the inspectors, strongly objected to the idea. 'I beg to express my entire dissent to it', he wrote. Above all else, he apparently objected to these charitable institutions being called 'homes',[2]

> because, misled by a name, the children may be induced to consider them as really their homes, and contrasting the kindness and indulgence they receive there with the sterner realities of actual life, they will feel indisposed to retain service under smart mistresses when they know that they have these refuges to fall back upon . . . The 'home', as I take it, of these young persons just entering upon life, is the wide world . . . and helps of all descriptions only neutralise the incentives to prudence and independence.

Happily for many hundreds of neglected children, women such as Miss Twining and her friends neither shared, nor were influenced by, this bleak view of the lot of the deprived and underprivileged child. Mary Carpenter had already engaged herself on their behalf, and had been running Homes for destitute children for some years. The Ragged Schools and the Shaftesbury Homes were growing in number, and within a few years,

[1] *PP*, 1862, XLIX, p. 520.
[2] ibid., p. 535.

Barnardo was to start his own great work for the under-privileged child. The second half of the nineteenth century was in fact to be the period in which most of the great voluntary societies for the care of destitute children came into being as a positive response to the social and moral consequences of the continuing negativism of the Hawleys and Coodes of their generation, and the abject failure of the Poor Law to achieve the very task which the 1834 Commissioners had set it, the elimination of child pauperism.

Nevertheless the criticisms the inspectors had levelled against the large 'barrack' schools – and some of them were very large, the schools at Hanwell and Sutton having been originally built to accommodate 1,200 children and more – were soon to be substantiated. The new constructive educational policy of the Poor Law as it was expressed in the district schools was found to be ineffective both in developing intelligence and in forming character, while in 1872, serious outbreaks of ophthalmia occurred among the children in several of the London schools. In fact, ophthalmia and skin eruptions began to distinguish the institutionalised child. Moreover, it was found that the district schools, which their original promotors had claimed could be justified 'on grounds of economy', actually cost more than any other form of provision for children, and it was only on the outskirts of the large towns such as Manchester, London, Liverpool and Leeds, that they were in practice used as an expedient method of care.

The trend towards the adoption of district schools was halted incidentally by the Education Act of 1870. By making education of the poor a national duty, this Act made it possible for guardians to provide alternative forms of care under which the children could be sent out to schools in the general community. Even so, education by itself was increasingly recognised as no answer to pauperism and the delinquency which so often accompanied it. 'We all know from unhappy experience', said W. E. Forster, the prime mover in the 1870 Act, 'that knowledge is not virtue, much less is elementary education, and that education alone does not give the power of resisting temptation.'[1]

More positive reasons for abandoning the development of district schools were revealed in two reports, both published in

---

[1] Quoted Heywood, *Children in Care*, pp. 71–2.

1874 and both relating to the schools in the Metropolitan area. One was a report on the health of the children in the schools. As a result of recurrent outbreaks of contagious ophthalmia, Mr Nettleship, an ophthalmic surgeon, was commissioned by the Local Government Board, which had now replaced the Poor Law Board, to examine the children of the Metropolitan Pauper Schools, in all of which contagious ophthalmia was more or less rife between 1872 and 1874. Reporting in December 1874,[1] Nettleship pointed out that the generally low physical condition of the children, a consequence of the destitute conditions in which they had been born and bred, inevitably made them easy victims for such a disease. But he went further, commenting on specific causes 'which not only accounted for its current prevalence, but would ensure its continuance'. These were general overcrowding, bad ventilation, defective provision for exercise and open air and, above all, the bringing together of 'masses' of children in large institutions where they slept in huge dormitories, and worked together in large, ill-ventilated work-rooms. Such conditions, he claimed, were a menace to child health. The schools were like a piled up bonfire, to which any imported cases of ophthalmia acted as so many firebrands.

The second report,[2] also made at the request of the Local Government Board, was from Mrs Nassau Senior, daughter-in-law of William Nassau Senior, one of the authors of the 1834 Report on the reform of the Poor Laws and one of the original Poor Law Commissioners. The Board had become so concerned about the difficulty of successfully training, educating and caring for pauper children so that they grew up into self-supporting and useful citizens that, in 1873, it asked Mrs Nassau Senior, who later became the first of its women inspectors, to make a report to them with particular reference to the education and training of pauper girls. Large numbers of these girls, it had been alleged, were being sent back to the workhouse from the situations which had been found for them as being sullen, dirty and utterly untrained in domestic work. Her conclusions sounded the death knell of the large, institutional tradition and began a

[1] Printed in the Fourth Annual Report of the Local Government Board, *PP*, 1875, XXXI, p. 114.
[2] Printed in the Third Annual Report of the Local Government Board, *PP*, 1874, XXV.

gradual move away from the administratively convenient device of the 'barrack' home to the family system we have today. She reported that:[1]

> With regard to the physical state of the girls who left school in 1868, I cannot consider it satisfactory. The girls whom I have been able to trace are, without exception, stunted in size, and a large proportion are delicate in health . . . I am told that stunted growth, and weakly health are natural and inevitable in children of a low class . . . But the fact remains, that children in these schools are subject to constant ophthalmic and skin diseases and that their small size is much against their success in the world . . . the boys are often rejected for the Army and Navy, and the girls in service repeatedly tell me that they would have no chance in getting into a 'good family' because they are so little.

Of the basic education given in the schools, Mrs Nassau Senior did not complain, indeed she believed it to be better than the children would have received outside, but she very strongly condemned the failure of the schools to encourage the children to develop an interest in their work and initiative in performing it. She concluded:[2]

> That the massing of girls in large numbers was bad, and must issue in failure: that their physical condition when in the schools and their moral condition on leaving them was disappointing and unsatisfactory; and that, while the scholastic training of both boys and girls in the Metropolitan pauper schools was first rate on all other points, the system of education did not answer in the case of girls, even at the very best separate and district schools, and that many of them were, in general intelligence, below children of the same class educated at home.

Attached to her report to the Board were recommendations which attempted to classify the different needs of the children and to meet them. These were: an extension of boarding out, but for orphan children only; the separate education of deserted children and casual children in schools of a more homelike character, such as those at Mettrai, where each 'family' cottage contained no more than twenty to thirty children of all ages; separate training for permanent and casual inmates; and a system of after care for girls when they were placed out in the

[1] ibid., pp. 343–4.
[2] ibid., p. 347.

world. It was in this climate of opinion that the guardians, while not abandoning the district schools for another twenty years, turned their attention to boarding out and cottage homes.

To the extension of the system of boarding out, Mrs Nassau Senior had attached an especial significance:[1]

> The whole Poor Law system is a necessary evil, and I believe the time will come when its provisions will be no longer necessary, when education and improved social arrangements will have triumphed over pauperism. The enormous buildings that are erected for the reception of pauper children, seem to point to a belief that we are to have an ever-increasing race of paupers throughout the centuries to come. Against such a belief boarding out is a protest.

Of course, she exaggerated, but it is difficult to believe that many still shared the optimistic hope of the original advocates of the large schools, that they would be a sure and swift means of eradicating pauperism; or that so investment-conscious a generation would have become increasingly interested in a form of property investment which they were confident would soon have little use or capital value.

On the other hand, there were already signs that some authorities were themselves beginning to investigate alternative methods of providing for their pauper children. Indeed, in 1870, as one of its last acts before being succeeded by the Local Government Board, the Poor Law Board had itself sanctioned boarding out, the very scheme to which Mrs Nassau Senior attached so much importance.

As a system, boarding out had a long history in England dating back to Tudor times. Babies from the Foundling Hospital were boarded out in the eighteenth century; and in the nineteenth, the practice of boarding out within the boundaries of their unions was used by some few boards of guardians under the reformed Poor Law, which had not actually prohibited it as a form of out-relief. Such a system was certainly operating, for example, in Warminster Union about 1849; in Sandbach about 1852; and in Ringwood in 1857; and was apparently introduced as an alternative to existing methods of institutional care which were proving unsatisfactory for girls. In the same year, 1857, the guardians of Leominster adopted the boarding-out system for its poor orphans, as a means of rescuing them from the mixed

[1] ibid., p. 343.

519

workhouses. Very large numbers were never involved. Ten years later this particular union had only dealt with a hundred and fifty children this way. The children were boarded out in 'superior' cottages only, given a good domestic training and their attendance at school was stipulated as a condition of receiving such a child. Foster parents were paid 2s. 6d. per week, without a clothes allowance, or 2s. a week, with clothes provided. Eton Union began a similar scheme. Their workhouse school had proved very unsatisfactory, a large proportion of the children brought up in it returning as adult paupers. They closed their school and sent all the children to the large Metropolitan district school at Hanwell, which proved almost equally unsatisfactory; thus, like the Leominster Union, they resorted to boarding out their orphan children with respectable cottagers, paying 3s. 6d. a week, and providing clothes and school fees.

Although the Eton Union appears to have boarded out both boys and girls, generally speaking, the revival of the boarding-out system was prompted by a concern to protect young girls. Thirteen years before Mrs Nassau Senior reported to the Local Government Board, Mrs Archer, the wife of an *ex officio* guardian who was chairman for many years of the Highworth and Swindon Board, published her own pamphlet drawing particular attention to the need for withdrawing young girls from the workhouses:[1]

> It is not that the little girls in the workhouse are not fed and clothed properly [an observation with which Mrs. Senior would scarcely have agreed], or that they have not a proper amount of school teaching, about which I am now raising a question; but I would wish it to be understood that under the workhouse system of bringing them up, their minds are contracted and their affections stifled to such a degree that they are unfitted for being placed out in those situations of life where they would be most likely to make a favourable impression, and gain the goodwill of respectable employers. To remedy this evil I would propose that we should use our influence with Guardians to get all such children placed with trustworthy cottagers under whose care they may have the same advantages as other children, and the opportunity of gaining a proper knowledge of life before being thrown on their own resources.

Attendance at a good elementary school was made part of the

[1] Hannah Archer, *A Scheme for Befriending Orphan Pauper Girls*, 1861.

scheme which, the same year, Mrs Archer persuaded her own union to try out. The guardians granted 2s. a week for board and lodging, and 10s. 6d. a quarter for clothing. These sums did not cover all the expenses involved, but Mrs Archer hoped some of the cost would be met by gifts. The combination of state aid and voluntary help was an important feature of her plan.

The schemes outlined so far were all concerned with the boarding out of children within the unions. Boarding children in an area outside the union was not at issue, yet in Scotland, such a system was almost universal. Children from the densely populated cities were boarded out in rural districts with the small occupiers and crofters where there was more chance of employment and also, even in the country districts, a well-established system of education. Knowledge of the effectiveness of the Scottish system spread to England and in 1868, for the first time, guardians applied to the Poor Law Board for leave to board certain classes of pauper children outside their own areas. In the following year the Board, which had been rather doubtful of the expediency of boarding out, gave permission for this development to be tried out, and directed poor law inspectors to report on how far boarding out in any form was adopted in their respective areas. At the same time they instructed one of their inspectors to investigate and report on the operation of boarding out in Scotland. Meanwhile, they displayed a sensitivity to the inherent problems of boarding out which stemmed from long experience of binding poor apprentices. In a letter to the Evesham board of guardians, for example, they pointed to the difficulty of exercising supervision and control over children removed from the workhouse; underlined the responsibility imposed on the guardians; and the danger of placing children in charge of those 'whose main object in taking the children would be to make a profit out of the sums allowed for their maintenance'. They also queried whether it would be practically possible to ensure the regular education of such children as were boarded out.[1]

In fact in the late sixties only a very few children were being boarded out by local guardians in England. The Board's enquiry showed that only twenty-one unions practised boarding out within their areas and that a mere 347 children were dealt with

[1] Cf. Heywood, op. cit., p. 81 passim.

in this way. Hundreds more, however, were boarded out at the expense of private individuals or of charitable societies, many of whom, like Mrs Archer, and like the members of the Workhouse Visiting Society, had come to the conclusion that for children, and for girls in particular, institutional provision was positively harmful. Numerous lectures, pamphlets and books were devoted to this theme. Amongst its most notable advocates was Florence Davenport Hill whose widely read and much quoted *Children of the State*[1] showed to a hitherto ignorant public that boarding out was no novelty in England; that it was a highly efficient system when carefully organised; that it was cheaper than any other method – a very telling point to many; that it already flourished successfully in Scotland and Ireland; and that 'it made for the greater happiness of the children than any other method of dealing with children on the rates'. Boarding-Out Associations were formed to press the government to agree to the principle of boarding out children in homes beyond the strict limits of union boundaries, and a crisis was reached when Miss Annette Preusser made arrangements to take a group of children from Bethnal Green Union to Westmorland. Immediately, the arrangements were vetoed by the Poor Law Board, and the dispute between them was only solved by the lady in question taking the children off the guardians' hands for nothing. The Board had won a battle, but not the war. In the end, bowing to pressure from many quarters, not least from guardians, they issued an Order, sanctioning the boarding out of pauper children beyond the boundaries of their own unions, under the care of a certified committee of voluntary workers.

The Order was precise, carefully thought out with every contingency thought of, and intended to ensure that boarding out beyond the union should not be immediately discredited by any failure of the Board to provide for the welfare of the children involved. So meticulously was it drawn that twenty-six years later, when the system was being closely reviewed, no substantial changes were advocated other than those that were purely administrative. In brief, the Board laid down that only children between two and ten years of age could be boarded out. Their prospective foster parents were to be carefully chosen, and no child was to be placed with foster parents of a different

[1] Published 1868.

religious creed. Inspection of foster homes, both before the child was placed and at regular intervals afterwards, was insisted upon, and boarding-out committees were set up in the receiving areas, on whom the duty of inspection was laid. Foster homes had to be within a mile and a half of a school, and within five miles of the residence of some member of the boarding-out committee. The weekly sum payable for the child's maintenance was limited to 4s.; payments for clothing, which on no account were to distinguish the wearer from other children, school money and medical attention were left to the discretion of the individual boards of guardians. Instructions about overcrowding and accommodation in the foster home were also contained in the explanatory letter accompanying the Order which was issued only to unions and parishes in large, populous towns to enable them to carry out a system of boarding out in country areas where foster parents were more plentiful and conditions better for the children. Within a year thirty certified committees had been formed to obtain homes, and place and visit children sent to them by guardians into whose care they had been received.

The Local Government Board, who inherited the Order, were themselves something less than enthusiastic. Along with the first boarding-out Order, they wrote that they watched the boarding out of children in populous places 'with grave anxiety'. Tufnell, although not one of the Board's officers at the time, was so opposed to it that he advised the Board to suppress the whole practice. There were fierce protests from other quarters. In his *Pauperism: Its Causes and Remedies* (1871), Professor Henry Fawcett objected on the grounds of 'political economy', by which he meant that the conditions under which pauper children might now be boarded out virtually guaranteed them a level of treatment better than that which an ordinary labourer, whose total week's wage often did not amount to more than 10s., could afford to give his own child. The scheme thus inevitably made pauperism a desirable profession, he claimed, since 'a reward will be given to improvidence and a stimulus given to immorality'.

For many other critics than Professor Fawcett, the fear that the Order would encourage immorality and increase the already large proportion of illegitimate pauper children, was a very real one. In contrast to the practice previously adopted by guardians boarding out children within their unions, which had been limited to orphans, the new Order specifically included the illegitimate and the deserted. When the boarding out of such children had been touched on ten years before, official objections to the idea had been raised, on the grounds that it would exert an injurious effect on the morals of the lower classes if the children of sin were to be observably treated in the same way as the orphans of the 'respectable' poor. Now, however, there was to be no bar to illegitimate children being boarded out under an Order, which laid down standards of maintenance well above those which a literal application of the principle of less eligibility would have required. Far from being a cheaper system, Fawcett argued, boarding out under these circumstances must inevitably prove at least as, if not more, expensive, since it would encourage illegitimacy and desertion so extensively that the great increase in the numbers of such children would effectively cancel out any difference of cost between it and other systems of maintenance, notably that provided by district schools. Such schools, he claimed, were good and efficient, and if they could not offer to their inmates the care and comforts of a normal home, by the same token they did not encourage illegitimacy, vice and desertion. With typical shrewdness, Fawcett went on to point out that in Scotland, the very country whose practice English guardians were urged to copy, one in six of all births were illegitimate, as compared with one in ten in England.

The twofold allegation that boarding out would not prove less expensive, and would necessarily increase immorality among the poor, was to prove far more detrimental to the official adoption of the scheme than the fear expressed by others, who believed that boarding out did not really make for the happiness of the children. It was simpler to answer objections of practical detail – that not enough 'superior cottages' were available, or that the children were not properly supervised, and were therefore victimised in their new homes – than it was to counter the objections to the basic principles of the scheme which, by appealing to prejudice, Fawcett's book had raised in so many minds. A quarter of a century later, *Pauperism: Its Causes and Remedies* was still recognised as influential, and witnesses before the Mundella Committee on Poor Law Schools, 1896, were constantly pressed to say whether or not they shared its *laissez-faire* attitude to the treatment of the pauper child.

Meanwhile, one of the other alternatives to the large school to which Mrs Nassau Senior had drawn attention in 1874, the 'cottage home' was being experimented with by some boards of guardians. The idea of cottage homes, based on the continental experiments at Hamburg and Mettrai, had been advocated in a paper submitted by Mr Joseph Fletcher in 1851 to the Statistical Society of London, *Statistics of the Farm School System of the Continent, and of its applicability to the Preventive and Reformatory Education of Paupers and Criminal Children in England*. He thought that England could well learn from the Continental experiments the value of moral and industrial training based on family and farm training, which could be provided at a fraction of the cost required to keep children in workhouses with such unsatisfactory results.[1]

> Labour must be the staple of the poor man's training. To live is the first necessity . . . And in all the best continental institutions for these classes, therefore, labour on the land and industry in the workshop is the first desideratum, religious and moral training on example realised in daily life the next, and intellectual culture . . . used rather as a relief from other occupations than as the greatest feature of a pauper school.

About the same time, and inspired by the same Continental examples, Mary Carpenter had also pleaded for the establishment of cottage homes in England – although her own immediate interest was in the delinquent or potentially delinquent child, rather than pauper children.

The effective introduction of the principle of cottage homes, both in the public and the private provision for the deprived child, waited for more than twenty years. For children receiving indoor relief from the Poor Law authorities, the idea appears to have been revived in a report to the Local Government Board by the Rev. Dr Clutterbuck, inspector of the Western District, which was published in the fourth annual report of the Board, 1875. Like Joseph Fletcher and Mary Carpenter, Clutterbuck was impressed by the record of Mettrai, and advocated that a version of this cottage home system should be adopted by the English Poor Law authorities. Two years later, another

---

[1] Quoted Heywood, op. cit., p. 73.

inspector, Mr Andrew Doyle, wrote a letter to the Swansea board of guardians, suggesting that the Swansea Union should join with the two neighbouring unions of Neath and Bridgend to provide for their children by a district school established on the cottage home principle. In the end, each union built a separate establishment, but in the report of the Local Government Board for 1877–8, there is approval for plans for three more unions (West Derby, West Ham and Bolton) to build district schools on cottage home lines. In practice the schools were to be large establishments, broken down into groups of children in cottages. Bolton, for example, was to establish a school for three hundred children, housed in groups of thirty. The Swansea school was to have eighty children, living in groups of twenty: Neath, forty-four, in groups of twenty and twelve: and Bridgend and Cowbridge, which joined together, sixty children in groups of ten.

As the system seemed likely to develop, due to the growing disillusion of the guardians in the merits of both the workhouse and the district schools, the Local Government Board turned its attention in 1878 to the experiments being made by voluntary organisations in the cottage home system, and organised an investigation into the work of six voluntary homes all based more or less strictly on the family system and 'aiming to bring up destitute or criminal children in habits of religion and virtue'. One of these was the Village Home for Girls which Dr Barnardo, who was responsible for carrying the idea of cottage homes into the sphere of voluntary organisation, had opened two years before in 1876.

Barnardo's own account of how he came to open this Home is an interesting illustration of how increasing familiarity with institutional provision on traditional lines could lead to a growing appreciation of its inherent drawbacks. Barnardo had opened his first home for destitute boys in Stepney in 1870. After his marriage in 1873, he opened a similar institution for girls attached to his own home, Mossford Lodge at Barkingside. He soon learnt his mistake.

> My first attempt really took shape as a small institute on what would now be called the barrack-system. Forty little girls were housed simply in a remodelled coach-house, with a simple upper floor added to it at the back of our own dwelling, Mossford Lodge.

The forty soon grew to sixty; and then the seriousness of the situation was borne in upon me with such overwhelming force, that one night I came to the conclusion that I must stop it all. I felt that the system was a bad one, though I still knew of no better.

Disturbed at the degraded and exceptional behaviour of the girls, he thought hard about the problem until at last:[1]

I saw at a glance what I ought to do. Instead of a big house with sixty girls clad in a dull uniform, I would arrange for a number of little ivy-clad cottages to arise, each presided over by a kindly Christian woman who would be the 'Mother'. The children would be of all ages, from the baby-in-arms to the girl well on in her teens, training for service. They should be dressed as simply and with as much variety as possible, and there should be nothing in the way of uniform. Anything approaching institutionalism would be scrupulously excluded. In such a home, and in such at atmosphere, the affectionate ties of family life and family love would have a chance of being created and fostered in the experience of the children, while the daily performance of commonplace duties would tend to fit them for their future career. Surely the family is God's way, for 'He setteth the solitary in families.'

The cottage homes at Ilford each housed twenty-five to thirty girls, under the charge of a 'mother'. In the other villages of cottage homes visited by the inspectors in 1878 the numbers in each 'family' were roughly the same, with the exception of Princess Mary's Village Home, Addleston, where the girls lived in groups of ten. Those which accepted only girls operated under a system of housemothers on whose selection and character everything depended. Where boys were accepted, as at the Farmingham Home, each 'family' was headed by a man and his wife who were 'father' and 'mother' to the children in their house.

In making their report on these examples of villages of cottage homes, Dr Mouat and Captain Bowley recalled the earlier findings of the late Sir James Kay-Shuttleworth who had believed that the degraded condition of pauper children made it imperative that they should receive special care in education and training to correct defects which were considered inseparable from their birth and upbringing. They thus believed that a corrective environment had to be provided through vocational education which concentrated on physical improvement, moral

[1] ibid., pp. 52-3.

instruction and industrial training to fit them to become independent by their own labour. The cottage home or farm school system appeared to fulfil all these requirements, and the inspectors recommended that, where it was adopted, each family should number between twelve and twenty children, boys and girls being brought up together until the boys reached the age of ten.

To those suspicious of the boarding-out system, unattracted to the large barrack schools and dissatisfied with the results of the workhouse schools, the cottage home had enormous appeal, and the new system spread. But for all the individual attention to character and health, the industrial training and the greater freedom and variety of life which the villages could provide, life within them was still artificial. The children were still kept separate from normal, everyday life. They still met no other children except those of their own community. The cottage with twenty children living in it could never be a home in the full sense of the word. In time, the villages became too self-contained; too out of touch with the world; their inhabitants unable to learn by the experience of joining in the experiences of other people.

The 'scattered home' system, developed by the Sheffield guardians from 1892 onwards, was an attempt to blend the best features of the cottage home with the advantages of boarding out. Convinced as far back as 1883 that children should be removed from their workhouse, the guardians had been unable to find any alternative which was exactly what they wanted.[1]

> We came to the conclusion . . . that no system that was in existence was exactly what we wanted, that boarding out [which they actually tried] was not universally applicable . . . then we saw the disadvantages, or some of the disadvantages, of the cottage-homes village, and we said to ourselves, 'Can we not obtain a system which would be a combination of the two, which will have a good many of the best features of boarding out in family life, mixing with the outside population, and yet where we shall be able to select our own mothers and our own localities, and where we shall be able to deal with children of all sorts?' And this idea of isolated homes as a means of meeting the two difficulties appeared to us the best.

By 1896 the Sheffield guardians had set up nine scattered

[1] ibid., pp. 77–8.

homes by purchasing ordinary working-class houses, indistinguishable from other such houses in the districts in which they were situated. In each home they placed about twelve children under the care of a foster mother, whom they themselves appointed and paid. The children attended the local elementary schools along with the other children of the neighbourhood. Small boys were allowed to live in the girls' houses, so that there would be a more normal family atmosphere, and the older girls were taught domestic skills such as any child might learn in an ordinary home.

The guardians also set up a reception centre into which, instead of the workhouse, all children coming into their care for indoor relief were admitted, and from which they were drafted into the scattered homes. Special care was taken to provide for the religious needs of these children, and there were both Roman Catholic and Protestant homes, situated within easy distance from their denominational schools – a wise precaution in view of the unhappy litigation in which Barnardo had been involved a short while before.[1]

Religious instruction had always been a sensitive issue in England, and the 1834 Poor Law Act had ruled that no workhouse child was to be educated in the workhouse in any other creed than that of its parents or, if an orphan, of its godparents. It had thus required the boards of guardians to accord facilities and free entry for the ministers of the children's own persuasion, whether Catholic or Protestant. In evidence to the 1861 Select Committee on Poor Relief, however, Roman Catholics strongly objected to the disadvantages attaching to Roman Catholic children in the workhouses and in poor law schools of all descriptions. They complained that the Anglican chaplains compelled children, regardless of creed, to attend Church of England services and to join in Anglican prayers. Teachers, alleged almost without exception to be Protestants, were said to poke fun at the Roman Catholic faith. Proper facilities for a priest to say Mass and instruct Roman Catholic children in their religious duties were said either to be denied or simply not provided. Special reference was made to the Metropolitan Unions, and in particular to Holborn and St Pancras where facilities were apparently worse than elsewhere. In these unions, Roman

[1] ibid., pp. 63–5.

Catholic children were said not to be allowed their own devotional books, although Protestant tracts were constantly distributed.[1]

To protect the consciences of Roman Catholic children, the Committee were asked not only to consider the introduction of more stringent regulations concerning religious observation in the workhouses, but also legislation to make it possible for pauper children to be removed from the workhouses and maintained at the expense of the guardians in voluntary homes established by the respective religious organisations. The model for such a provision which was constantly referred to was the Certified Industrial Schools Act, 1857, under which voluntary institutions caring for potentially delinquent children had been made eligible for grants from public funds.

Since the 1849 disaster, when 138 children had died of cholera in Mr Drouet's private school at Tooting, guardians had in fact been legally forbidden to send children to privately organised establishments. They were, however, allowed to send difficult and vagrant children to schools registered under the Industrial Schools Act, 1859, and it was for an extension of this principle of certification that witnesses now pleaded. Since the close association between deprivation and delinquency was repeatedly emphasised in all discussion of the treatment of the juvenile poor, the model was an obvious one. Indeed, it soon appeared from evidence presented by three ladies who took the opportunity afforded by the Committee's enquiry, that astute manipulation of the terms of the Industrial Schools Act had already enabled the more enterprising to receive other classes of children into their voluntary Homes at the ratepayers' expense. Mrs Emmeline Way, for example, described the organisation of the Home she had opened two years before, at Brockham, for the reception of orphaned or deserted girls whom she trained for domestic service. Some of the necessary funds were contributed by private individuals but, since Mrs Way had had the Home certified as an industrial school under the terms of the 1857 Act, she also received money from the Privy Council. In addition, however, she had also obtained money from some unions for the workhouse girls – forty in all so far

[1] *PP*, 1861, IX.

– whom she had taken from them to train as servants.[1] Miss Twining, who also gave evidence, revealed that she too received payment from a number of guardians for the upkeep of pauper girls in the Home she had opened for girls between fifteen and twenty-five years of age, with the object of giving them a thorough training as domestic servants. Questioned by members of the Committee, curious to know whether the Poor Law Board had expressed any opinion on this rather unusual type of out-door relief, Miss Twining, with typical candour, told them that indeed, the Board had decided as far back as December 1859 that it was quite illegal.[2] Although the Board's view clearly deterred neither Mrs Way nor Miss Twining, it nevertheless made the continuation and expansion of such work, by them-selves or by others, extremely dubious. Hence Miss Carpenter, who as much as anyone appreciated the merits of associating voluntary work with statutory finance, pressed the view that legislation should speedily be introduced to extend the principle of certification, already applying to voluntary Homes for the semi-delinquent, to voluntary Homes for the merely poor.[3]

The point was taken, and the following year, on 17 July 1862 an Act for the Education and Maintenance of Pauper Children in Certain Schools and Institutions[4] was given the Royal Assent. Under its provisions guardians were empowered to send children to voluntary institutions certified for the purpose by the Poor Law Board on application from their managers. As was the case with certified industrial schools, certification implied the accept-ance of inspection by the Poor Law Board. Payment up to the amount that would have been spent had the children been maintained in the workhouse was to be made by the guardians, who were themselves given rights of inspection. The Act applied to orphans and deserted children and to children whose own parents gave their assent. In no case was a child to be sent to a school belonging to a denomination other than its own.

During the years that followed certified schools were to be developed not only for the teaching of Roman Catholics and the training of servant girls, but also to meet the special needs of

[1] ibid., p. 648.
[2] ibid., p. 616.
[3] ibid., p. 628.
[4] 25 & 26 Vict., c. 43.

G

handicapped children: the blind, the deaf and dumb, the mentally defective, and boys and girls needing treatment because of particular disabilities. By 1878 seventy-seven certified schools were in existence, of which thirty-seven were training institutions. By 1896, their number had increased to 215, and they accommodated almost one in five of all children receiving indoor relief.

The certified schools were regarded by some as complementary to the boarding-out system, the particular merits of which continued to be vigorously debated. No less than four speakers at various meetings of the British Association held between 1876 and 1886 gave papers on its advantages. Numerous papers were presented and discussed at the Annual Conferences of the National Association for the Promotion of Social Science. An Association for the Advancement of Boarding Out was started in 1885, with Miss Brodie Hall as Honorary Secretary, the object being 'generally to arouse interest in the subject' by printing pamphlets, reprinting public lectures and advising guardians on the subject.

The Local Government Board continued to act with characteristic caution. Perhaps because boarding out within the unions had never been so popular as boarding out elsewhere, no Order regulating it was issued until 1877, when both the relieving officer and a medical officer were directed to visit each child regularly and report on its condition. Eight years later, in 1885, the Board appointed a special inspector, Miss Mason, whose duties were to visit all children boarded out in unions other than their own; to inspect the work of the local boarding-out committees; and help them with advice concerning the placing and supervision of the children. Less impressed by the arrangements made for the children than some of her male colleagues, Miss Mason's critical comments lay behind the two revised boarding-out Orders issued by the Board in 1889. The new Order, which applied to all unions and separate parishes in England and Wales, provided that boarding-out committees could be set up for the boarding out of children within the union, and insisted that every committee should consist of not less than three persons, of whom one at least was to be a woman. (On the need for the inclusion of women, Miss Mason's observations had been most emphatic.) Miss Mason's other observations were reflected in the circular letter from the Board which accompanied the Order.[1]

> The Board desire that the members of the boarding-out committee should bear in mind that they are jointly responsible for all children entrusted to the care of the committee, and that the visitation of each child should not be entirely left in the hands of an individual member of the committee. The Board have reason to believe that in some instances, persons have consented to become members of committees under a misapprehension as to the responsibility they would thereby incur.

How much easier it was to call for adequate supervision of boarded-out children than to ensure it through the work of voluntary committees, experience was to show, and since for boarding out within the union even this protection for the child was not compulsory, the welfare of boarded-out children still rested on precarious foundations. Even so their numbers increased. In 1885 1,774 children were boarded out within their own union and 1,026 boarded beyond it. Ten years later the respective numbers had increased to 3,778 and 1,794 – an increase of from 2,799 to 5,572 in the total number of children involved in the system. To these numbers must be added those of the voluntary societies who operated their own boarding-out arrangements. The Waifs and Strays Society, for example, founded in 1881, had boarded out many of its children from the start and as a general rule all children under seven years of age were thus dealt with. Barnardo, still not satisfied that even his cottage homes were the proper means of caring for girls, had started boarding them out in 1886, and found it to be the best of all his systems. Ten years later he was boarding out more children than all the Poor Law authorities of the country, although the total number of children in the charge of these authorities was more than ten times as many as the children in the care of his organisation.

In the light of the several alternative methods of indoor relief for the juvenile poor in existence, in 1894 the Local Government Board appointed a Departmental Committee to enquire into their operation in the Metropolitan area and to advise the Board on any changes in them that they thought necessary. This

---

[1] Eighteenth Annual Report of the Local Government Board, *PP*, 1889, XXXV, Appendix A, p. 35.

Committee, usually referred to as the Mundella Committee on Poor Law Schools, reported two years later, and although its investigations were restricted by its terms of reference to one area only, its published findings were taken by the general public to have reference to the situation over the whole country.

The Committee's work was thorough, their approach sensitive and their advice to the Board balanced. Once again, they emphasised the need to emancipate children from their pauper associations and assimilate their lives more closely to those of the self-respecting working classes. They saw that variety was needed in the treatment of children, some responding to boarding out, some to care in scattered homes or voluntary homes, or finding their best hope of success in emigration. The large district schools they condemned. To the system of boarding out they paid particular attention. It had now been running officially for some twenty-five years, and they felt bound to weigh the arguments both for and against it, to look at its relative cost and to decide whether to adapt, abolish or maintain it. They interviewed representatives of nearly every institution that had a boarding-out system in operation, and solicited the views of those who did not operate it. They invited evidence not only from Scotland but from Australia where boarding out was widely operated in New South Wales, in Victoria and in Southern Australia. Among the witnesses who appeared before the Committee were Miss Mason, Miss Brodie Hall and Barnardo himself.

Of the difficulties of adequately supervising boarded-out children, they were in no doubt. Nor did they overlook the fact that such children, very often brought up by those who themselves had no specialised skills, did not receive the industrial training which, in theory at least, was available to them in the district schools and cottage homes. For boys, they saw this as a particular disadvantage, since it meant that large numbers of them went to swell the already over-large ranks of the unskilled. The girls were often no better equipped when they looked for work. They got the ordinary domestic training of the working-class home which did not fit them for the higher grades of domestic service where wages were relatively good and positions more secure. Although they usually appeared to fare better than the girls from the institutions, largely because their initiative had not been undermined by being brought up in cohorts, girls tended to become domestic drudges unless, by accident of their fostering, they found jobs in local factories and shops.

Despite these disadvantages the Committee were convinced that boarding out was in principle sound and should be pursued, but still limited to the orphaned, deserted, and the illegitimate. There is no doubt that in reaching their decision the Committee were impressed by the fact that boarding out had proved to be a great deal less expensive to the ratepayers than the district schools or the cottage homes. On the other hand, the welfare of the child, just as much as a care for economy, obviously weighed heavily on the Committee when drawing up their Report. Hence their emphasis on the fact that children were brought up in a normal home atmosphere, in which their affections as well as their talents might be encouraged to develop; on the evidence which showed that ophthalmia, still the curse of the institutional child, was practically unknown; and, above all, their stress on boarding out as a system which not only separated the poor child from adult paupers but freed him from the taint of pauperism.

Despite this strong, official commendation of boarding out and the renewed confidence it gave to the supporters of the system, the proportion of children receiving indoor relief who were boarded out by the guardians remained small, certainly far smaller than was the case in Barnardo's organisation, which boarded out two in every five children who came into its care. According to the local guardians, suitable homes were said to be difficult to find, a fact which Miss Mason believed to be associated with a resentment of inspection and a fear of interference amongst those who might have been suitable foster parents. More important was the difficulty of forming local committees to provide the necessary supervision of children boarded out in foster homes, which itself was associated in no small degree with a fear that the standard of maintenance for boarded-out children required by the Local Government Board gave to such children advantages not so readily available to children not in receipt of public relief.

By the end of the nineteenth century, very considerable improvements in the standard of provision for the pauper child had been introduced by the more enlightened guardians. The Local Government Board itself advocated the removal of children from the workhouses, so that its stigma might not set them apart and permanently brand them pauper in fact as well as name. Nevertheless the doctrine of less eligibility and the belief in the virtues of some element of deterrence in the administration of the poor laws still lingered. The Hon. Mrs Cropper, a guardian of the Kendal Union, addressing the Annual Central Poor Law Conference in 1900 on the 'Removal of Children from the Workhouse', urged that alternative types of accommodation, such as cottage homes, should not be made so attractive as to inhibit the poor from maintaining their own. 'If their lot is to be an enviable one in Cottage Homes, with many a privilege, with specially good food and industrial training, we can scarcely expect that relations . . . will come forward as generously as they have done . . . I am not sure that there is not something to be said for a distinctive dress in Cottage Homes in order that every deterrent may not be recklessly swept away.' Such sentiments may not have been anything like so widespread in 1900 as they had certainly been seventy years before, but their continued existence made it possible for some local guardians to continue to ignore both the pressures of the Local Government Board and the example of the philanthropic organisations to provide suitable and adequate indoor relief for the children in their care. To this, the authors of the Majority Report of the 1905–9 Poor Law Commission referred at length:[1]

> Notwithstanding all the efforts which have been made in the last seventy years, a very large number of children are still maintained in the workhouses . . . On January 1st, 1903, out of 62,426 indoor pauper children, 16,221 were maintained in workhouses, a considerable number of whom were under medical treatment . . . we have ourselves seen that the condition of such children is sometimes far from satisfactory. In many Unions indeed, the children are treated with the utmost kindness and care. Elsewhere we have ourselves found children in surroundings so dreary that it seems strange that Guardians who have families of their own could acquiesce to them. The following are instances of some of the places visited by us:
>
> (1) The nursery was bad, very messy, and the children looked miserable; some of the infants were being nursed by old women,

[1] *PP*, 1909, XXXVIII, pt I, p. 186.

some lay in cradles with wet bedding, and were provided with 'comforters' . . . The infirm and children over three are in the same building, apart from the main body of the house. The children are under the care of a woman who has been there twenty-seven years and has two helpers. She is a fairly capable, roughish sort of woman, hardly fit for such a responsible position. She was reluctant to show anything, and I had to push my way in everywhere. The three-year-old children were in a bare and desolate room, sitting about on the floor and on wooden benches, and in dismal workhouse dress. The older ones had all gone out to school . . . except a cripple, and a dreary little girl who sat in a cold room with bare legs and her feet in a pail of water as a 'cure' for broken chilblains. The washing arrangements are unsatisfactory; the children have no tooth-brushes, and very few hairbrushes. They do not wear workhouse dress to go to school, but I saw some coming in from school in the rain who were not properly dressed for a wet day. Altogether there is great need for reform in the treatment of the children.

(2) The children (thirty-nine girls and twenty-three boys) are housed in the workhouse under the care of a male and a female industrial trainer, but they are not kept separate from the adult inmates. Indeed the children's wards left on our minds a marked impression of confusion and defective administration . . . In appearance the children were dirty, untidy, ill-kept, and almost neglected. Their clothes might be described with very little exaggeration as ragged, and when the inspector told a group of children to take off their right boots large holes were displayed in six stockings out of thirteen. The eyes of some of the children seemed suspiciously 'weak', and in two or three cases to be suffering from some serious inflammation.

(3) In the nursery we found the babies of one to two years of age preparing for their afternoon sleep. They were seated in rows on wooden benches in front of a wooden table. On the table was a long narrow cushion, and when the babies were sufficiently exhausted they fell forward upon this to sleep. The position seemed most uncomfortable and likely to be injurious. We were told that the system was an invention of the Matron's and had been in use for a long time.

The Minority Report of the Commission, a burning piece of invective against the failure of the Poor Law to provide for the poor, had its own comments to make and its own illustrations to offer on the continued presence of children in workhouses.[1]

[1] ibid., pt II, p. 802.

With regard to the children who are still living in the General Mixed Workhouses of England and Wales, we need do no more than emphasise the universal condemnation of such a method of providing for the rearing of the young. 'The retention of children in Workhouses [reports our own Children's Investigator] is always unsatisfactory. Even where they have special attendants they are never completely separated from the ordinary inmates. In York certainly the children were dull and inert; they stood about like moulting crows, and did not seem able to employ themselves with any enthusiasm or vigour. The arrangements for their tendance and training are never as good as in an establishment wholly given up to them; the separation from the ordinary inmates of the Workhouse was very incomplete in each case I saw.' Despairing of being able to induce the Destitution Authorities to send the children away to proper residential schools, the Local Government Board for England and Wales has, during recent years, contented itself with pressing the smaller Unions to let the children in the Workhouses attend the public elementary day schools. This is doubtless an advance on the old school within the Workhouse walls; but we cannot too emphatically express our disagreement with those who accept this as any excuse for retaining children in the Workhouse at all. The day school accounts for only about one-third of the child's waking life. The Local Government Board Inspectors themselves point out that it leaves the children, in practice, exposed to the contamination of 'communication with the adult inmates whose influence is often hideously depraving.'

'It is a serious drawback [says the Inspector] that every Saturday and Sunday, to say nothing of summer and winter holidays, have, for the most part, to be spent in the Workhouse, where they either live under rigid discipline and get no freedom, or else if left to themselves are likely to come under the evil influence of adult inmates. The Workhouse is at best a dreary place for children to spend their lives in, and I should like to see them quite cut off from it.'

In view of the Majority Report, such reforms as were necessary in the interests of the pauper child could be brought about by building on the existing poor law structure, improving the character of its administration, and supplementing it by voluntary aid. The Minority Report recommended nothing less than a complete breaking up of the Poor Law and the transfer of its functions on a specialised basis to appropriate departments of the local authorities. Already failure to recognise the wisdom and the necessity for this was creating anomalies and confusion in the care of children, under the different authorities now responsible for child welfare.[1]

> What stands out is the extraordinary lack of co-ordination or even of mutual consciousness of each other's existence, between the operations of the Destitution Authority and the Authorities administering the Industrial and Reformatory School Acts ... 'The fact of children being sent to one kind (of school) or to the other, is [we are informed] largely accidental' depending, as we gather, when no offence against the criminal law has been committed, chiefly on which Authority gets hold of the case first. ... No fewer than 113 cases were brought to our notice in which, within a single year, in London alone, the same family had been relieved out of the same fund of rates and taxes, by one or more children being sent to Industrial Schools, whilst other children, together with their parents, were being maintained (often as Ins-and-Outs) in one or other Poor Law institution.

Meanwhile, as the Minority Report pointed out, the local education authorities were forging ahead with medical inspection and feeding for schoolchildren, and were effectively invading the sphere of the Poor Law authorities in areas which the physical condition of thousands of poor children showed those authorities scarcely to have operated. It was because the education authorities were so conspicuously succeeding where the Poor Law authorities had lamentably failed, that the authors of the Minority Report believed that the duties of the Poor Law towards destitute children should cease, and that they should be superseded by the local education authorities.[2]

> The failure [they said] of the Boards of Guardians in the great centres of population ... to relieve so much of the child destitution, is rooted in the very fact that they are Destitution Authorities, with a long established tradition of 'relieving' such persons as voluntarily come forward and prove themselves 'destitute'. What is required is some social machinery, of sufficient scope, to bring automatically to light, irrespective of the parent's application, or even that of the children, whatever child destitution exists ... An Authority dealing with the child, or with the family, merely at the crisis of destitution, having no excuse for intervening before or after this crisis, can never cope with the conditions here revealed.

[1] ibid., p. 828.
[2] ibid., p. 840.

The propaganda and publicity arranged for the Minority Report by one of its signatories, Mrs Webb, created active agitation for the reform of the Poor Laws for the next two or three years, but no direct legislation followed as a result. Instead, the president of the Local Government Board undertook what he called 'revolution by administration'. Already the Board had been taking its own measures to remedy the disadvantages of boarding out which stemmed from inadequate supervision. Two more women inspectors had been appointed, the first in 1899, the second in 1902, to assist Miss Mason in her pioneer work in establishing basic principles and standards for its operation by the local boards of guardians. Their every effort was devoted to checking that the guardians' allowances were actually spent on the children themselves, that ill-health was reported and treated, and that the children were properly educated. Although far from complacent about the effectiveness of these checks, the Board had decided in 1905 to extend the practice of boarding out to those children in relation to whom the guardians were *in loco parentis* having exercised their rights of adoption under the 1889 and 1899 Acts.[1]

Fresh regulations were issued by the Board in 1909, under which the appointment of boarding-out committees became compulsory whether the children were boarded out within or without their union. Two years later, by an Order which unified the regulations for boarding out, a universal requirement was imposed that one-third of all boarding-out committees were to consist of women, and relieving officers were excluded from the duties of making weekly payments to foster parents as part of a policy to exclude them altogether from dealing with boarded-out children. The same Order withdrew the principle of a 'minimum age' below which children were not to be boarded out.

In the last full annual report made by the Local Government Board before the outbreak of the First World War, it was clear that the encouragement the Board had intended to give to the practice of boarding out was having effect. Both absolutely and relatively, the numbers of poor law children provided for by this method had increased. So too had the numbers of children cared for in residential schools, cottage homes and scattered

[1] 52 & 53 Vict., c. 56.

homes, with the result that between 31 March 1906 and 1 January 1913 the number of children over three years of age being maintained in workhouses had dropped from 11,072 to 8,206, although the total number of children receiving indoor relief had risen from 56,991 to 70,676. Determined now to drive the established trend to its logical conclusion, in 1913 the Local Government Board issued the Poor Law Institution Order, which finally made it illegal to retain a healthy child over the age of three years in a workhouse for more than six weeks. After many generations children had been released from the punitive aspects of English poor law policy.

For another thirty years and more, much remained to be done. With the outbreak of war, and the inevitable suspension of building programmes, it was impracticable to enforce the Order, which had to be suspended. In the interwar years, economic depression and large-scale unemployment resulted in increased pauperism and almost intolerable pressures on social services ill-equipped both in skilled manpower and special resources. Although foster homes now became easier to find, because of the regular payments which fostering guaranteed, the quality did not necessarily improve; nor was the supply of staff trained to supervise and advise on placement anywhere adequate. Nevertheless, step by step the social provision for the poor and neglected child moved forward. Higher standards were gradually required in medical and dental care. In education a concept with which our Tudor forebears would have been familiar but which had been lost for so long as to appear something of a novelty in the twentieth century, began to re-emerge. A code issued in 1919 by the Board of Education, to whose elementary schools so many poor children were sent, defined the purpose of these schools as 'to form and strengthen the character, and to develop the intelligence of the children entrusted to it, and to make the best use of the school years available, in assisting both boys and girls, according to their different needs, to fit themselves practically as well as intellectually for the work of life'.[1] It was a purpose which Vives would well have understood.

The lack of integration of social provision for children, which the Minority Report of the Poor Law Commission had vigorously condemned, remained. Twenty years later (in 1927) the

[1] Quoted Heywood, op. cit., p. 122.

Departmental Committee on the Treatment of Young Offenders was itself concerned about the different ways in which neglected children were dealt with administratively. Some were brought before the courts and committed to industrial schools (where they might be boarded out), or to the care of fit persons; and others, by far the largest number, whose unsatisfactory parents were destitute, received into the care of the Poor Law, where they too were either boarded out, or placed in workhouses or infirmaries, in poor law schools, cottage homes, scattered homes or certified voluntary homes.[1]

> We have referred to children under the poor law in some detail [they state], because it appears to us an integral part of the whole question of neglected children. It is not within our functions to make any recommendations as regards the administration of the poor law. We would point out, however, that if under any proposals for the reform of the Poor Laws the powers and duties of Boards of Guardians are transferred to the ordinary local authorities, the separation of Poor Law children from other classes of neglected children would tend to disappear, and it would be possible to secure greater measure on unity and consistency in this treatment.

The reform of the Poor Law referred to in the Report, for which support had been growing since 1909, finally became embodied in the legislation of 1929[2] by which the boards of guardians were abolished and their duties taken over by the Councils of the Counties and the County Boroughs. The duties of the poor law to visit child-life protection cases, under the 1908 Children Act, now became the responsibility of the local authority health departments, and the care of the destitute child, who was either physically or mentally handicapped, but educable, became an educational provision. By the Poor Law Act of 1930,[3] every County Council and every County Borough was required to set up a Public Assistance Committee, which continued the administration of services for children in poor law care, but might delegate its functions to other appropriate committees of the Council.

Since both these statutes directly contributed to the development of specialised children's services, they also, in the long run,

[1] ibid., p. 125.
[2] 19 Geo. V, c. 60.
[3] 20 Geo. V, c. 17.

contributed to the development of highly sophisticated techniques in this area of case work. For some children, alas, this development came too late. The 1937–8 Report of the Ministry of Health complained bitterly of the still large number of instances of children living for considerable periods in bad conditions which were definitely prejudicial to their welfare 'without anything being done about it'.[1] Not for the first time, the plea was made for 'specially trained women children's officers' as a vital part of the administration of boarding out in each local authority.

The outbreak of the Second World War prevented the issue being pressed further. Instead, many children previously ineligible for boarding out were now evacuated from urban centres and billeted in what were intended as temporary foster homes. So beneficial was the enforced experiment found, however, that a government circular was issued in 1944 suggesting to the responsible authorities that, if parents were willing, the children might be allowed to stay where they were. The following January the situation was regularised by making boarding out applicable to all classes of children in the care of the public assistance authorities. After eighty years the protagonists of boarding out had finally triumphed. That same month Dennis O'Neill died of cruelty and neglect in his foster home, Bank Farm.

Dennis and his two younger brothers and sister had been removed from their own home in 1939 by an inspector of the National Society for the Prevention of Cruelty to Children. The three boys had been committed to the care of the local authority as being in need of care and protection, and the girl to the care of her maternal grandmother. The boys had been boarded out in the area of another local authority in successive foster homes, finally being placed at Bank Farm, Minsterly, in 1944. That a child, removed from his own home because of its bad conditions, and entrusted for his greater good to the public care, should yet experience even worse cruelty and neglect leading to his death caused widespread public concern and an official enquiry followed. Its report threw into startling relief both the lack of trained and skilled social workers to which the Ministry of Health had pointed almost ten years before, and also the confusion and

[1] *PP*, 1937–8, XI, p. 92.

defects of the administrative machinery provided for the care of children removed from their homes and committed to the care of the local authority (particularly where this involved placement outside that authority's own area) which had been the subject of adverse comment for forty years and more, and the theme of a considerable correspondence in *The Times* initiated by a letter from Lady Allen of Hurtwood in July, 1944.

Lady Allen followed up her letter with a pamphlet, *Whose Children?*, intended to inform public opinion about the conditions under which deprived children lived, and to stir the government and people into action. It was a pamphlet of immeasurable significance. It incorporated evidence from individuals who had been brought up or worked in children's homes, and contained complaints so similar, and so appalling, that they could not be disregarded. The publication, the following January, of the verdict of the coroner's jury in the O'Neill case, was an independent and dreadful confirmation of Lady Allen's urgent appeal for immediate reform.

The Government requested Sir Walter Monckton to conduct a public and independent legal inquiry into the circumstances of the O'Neill case, but long before the results of this particular investigation were available, they had already, in March 1945, invited Miss Myra Curtis to head an interdepartmental committee of enquiry 'into existing methods of providing for children who from loss of parents or from any cause whatever are deprived of a normal home life with their own parents or relatives; and to consider what further measures should be taken to ensure that these children are brought up under conditions best calculated to compensate them for the lack of parental care.'

The Committee's report is one of the most moving documents in the recent history of the public care and protection of the deprived child, indeed, the very adoption of the term 'deprived child' can almost be dated from its publication in 1946. On its recommendations is based the present-day administration of that care. They looked for a service both comprehensive and unified and they emphasised the need for trained workers to staff such a service. Although they envisaged the continuation of institutional care, provided from both public and private funds, they described adoption as the most completely satisfactory way of providing a substitute home, and boarding out as its best alternative. The Committee's proposals were embodied in the Children Act, 1948. It was a piece of legislation important not only for its administrative provision of a single, child care service under the Home Office, but also for the concept of children's rights on which such a service was to be based, rights not grudgingly conceded to the poor but openly acknowledged for children, rich and poor alike: the rights of support and security, of health and happiness, of development and fulfilment in the society whose children they are.

XVIII

<>-<>-<>-<>-<>-<>-<>-<>-<>-<>-<>-<>-<>-<>-<>-<>-<>-<>-<>-<>-<>-<>-<>-<>-<>-<>-<>

Transportation and Emigration

<>-<>-<>-<>-<>-<>-<>-<>-<>-<>-<>-<>-<>-<>-<>-<>-<>-<>-<>-<>-<>-<>-<>-<>-<>-<>-<>

Nor all voluntary or statutory schemes concerned with the
destitute and delinquent children were intended to keep them in
this country. The development of a colonial empire had created
a demand for men and women to populate and exploit the new
territories. A demand so great and so urgent that, for a time at
least, the colonies were willing to accept, sometimes even encourage, the emigration not merely of those anxious to seek their
fortunes in lands distant from the shores of England, but also
of those whom it was convenient for England to send abroad. In
other words, it was possible to view the planned emigration of
delinquents from this country as a service to both English and
colonial society – as well as a service to the delinquents themselves. Attempts first to export, then, after 1717, to transport
such children had been made in this country since the early
seventeenth century.[1] By the nineteenth century, it was at times
difficult in practice to distinguish between emigration and transportation. This was largely because voluntary societies who
promoted the assisted emigration of the destitute but law-
abiding frequently also dealt, and in a similar way, with delinquent and semi-delinquent children placed in their care and
supported by the State. It is hard to distinguish, for example,
between a delinquent boy sent to the Philanthropic Society's
Farm School at Redhill by the courts, the State paying for his

[1] Cf. vol. I, pp. 108–9.

upkeep, and later helped to emigrate by the Society under the strict rules of apprenticeship, and another boy who might have committed exactly the same crime, but sent to Parkhurst and subsequently sent to Australia as an official transport.

Moreover, whilst transportation from their native land was viewed by the law as a drastic punishment for the young offender, at least some of the 'objects' of the punishment saw it as a welcome release from a country in which they often had no family, few friends and little future. Thus removal to the colonies at an early date was advocated as an incentive for good behaviour whilst in the prison. In 1846 the Governor of Parkhurst wrote in his Report:[1]

> The desire to get their liberty by removal to the Colonies for good conduct has a very strong influence over the prisoners here. It appears to me that it would be of advantage to introduce some distinguishing mark or privilege which might be acquired by a prisoner at an earlier period of his confinement and which, being known as a recognition on the part of the Prison Authorities of good conduct so far, should operate as an encouragement and stimulus to the boy to persevere in the course of well-being, which will eventually procure for him a recommendation for liberty.

The fate of children transported to the colonies is not very easy to trace. Almost always they seem to have been apprenticed to a settler as a servant or as a labourer, and not set to work in one of the notorious convict gangs. The hope was that they would become reformed by the good influence of the settler and his family. Nevertheless there is evidence in the Report of the House of Lords Committee on Transportation, 1826, that in some places, where a settler complained and brought them before a magistrate, they got the identical punishment as the adult convicts: a flogging up to a maximum of fifty lashes. The convicts could be flogged for quite trivial offences. Frequent references are made in the magistrates' returns to 'laziness', 'insolence', and 'insubordination' as reasons for the floggings they ordered and supervised. The ages of the convicts concerned were not given but some entries certainly indicate that some of them must have been at least fairly young; 'A.B. sentenced to 30 lashes (a boy). Cried out much. Back turned black at 20th stroke.'[2]

---

[1] Carlebach, *Caring for Children in Trouble*, p. 29.
[2] *PP*, 1826, IV, p. 106.

This was not the kind of 'liberty' to which Parkhurst boys appear to have been urged. The liberty of which the Governor spoke was not all that different from the liberty of boys who were sent out under normal emigration schemes and apprenticed to settlers. The Parkhurst boys were sent to New South Wales, Van Dieman's Land, Western Australia and New Zealand. The most successful were those sent to Western Australia, where the Government appointed a Guardian of Juvenile Immigrants to look after them. He wrote annual reports which show, on the whole, that after a somewhat shaky start the scheme worked well and the boys were hard working and popular with the settlers, who were badly in need of help on their farms.[1] The boys were to be regarded as ordinary apprentices. This comes out very clearly in the reports. In one of them the Guardian asked that his hand be strengthened with the recalcitrant boys by giving him or someone else summary powers of punishment. It appears that the boys were only liable to ordinary prosecution and not the special justices' court to which adult convicts were sent. The visitors of Parkhurst were asked their opinion on this matter and, in reply, they signed a unanimous report in which they very much opposed the idea. Anything which made a distinction between these apprenticed boys and the other apprentices, sons of settlers and boys sent out under voluntary emigration schemes, was to be deplored, they argued. No good could come of it either to the boys or to their employers.[2] The Guardian himself reckoned that under 3 per cent relapsed into crime. High praise was also given to the boys by the Governor of Van Dieman's Land, but they were not popular in New South Wales or in New Zealand. In all 1,498 boys were sent to the colonies from Parkhurst between the years 1842 and 1853. After the first batch of boys to Western Australia proved successful, the Governor of the colony wrote asking for fifty more such boys, a request which not unnaturally gratified the Governor of Parkhurst who wrote that, with every draft of boys sent out to the colonies, 'a draught of fresh air' swept through the prison.[3]

Gradually, the whole idea of sending young criminals to the

[1] *PP*, 1847, XLVII, pp. 279, 291, 293.
[2] ibid., p. 67.
[3] Cf. Carlebach, op. cit., p. 29.

colonies dropped into disfavour and was ultimately abandoned.[1] The reformatory and industrial schools, however, still aimed at sending some of their young charges abroad, a policy which some of them had been pursuing long before Parkhurst was opened.

The Philanthropic Society, for example, had decided that emigration was a good way of helping some of the boys whom they trained, but they do not appear to have been particularly active in doing so in their earlier years as, by 1849, the Society had only sent out 55 boys. It was in 1849 that the Society opened its new farm school at Redhill. The training given to the boys there was ideal for emigrants and they consequently proceeded to develop this side of their work. Boys were apprenticed to carefully selected employers in the colonies for one or two years and were so successful there that it became possible to send out fifty every year.

The earliest society that appears to have made emigration one of its main objects, however, was the Society for the Suppression of Juvenile Vagrancy, later known as the Children's Friend Society. The aim was to train boys in some industrial or farm occupation and the girls in domestic service, and then send them to the colonies where they were to be apprenticed. The advantages of this method are as obvious as are its dangers. 'If the emigration agency succeeds in finding suitable foster parents, the child grows up familiar with colonial life, in healthy surroundings, and is absorbed into the ordinary population; on the other hand, if an unwise selection is made the child has little or no protection.'[2] The Society's experience was to show just how difficult it was to make a wise selection of foster parents and how great were the obstacles to providing adequate protection for the children. The first country chosen was the Cape, where the slaves had only recently been emancipated. By 1840, 440 children, 75 of them girls, had been sent there. Unfortunately for the work of the Society, rumours began to spread in England that the apprentices were being ill-treated, and a lurid

---

[1] In 1853, sentences of transportation for less than fourteen years were abolished, and penal servitude substituted. This practically put an end to juvenile transportation as juveniles were usually sentenced to less than fourteen years. Cf. S. G. Scholes, *Education for Empire Settlement*.

[2] Majority Report of the Royal Commission on the Poor Laws and the Relief of Distress, *PP*, 1909, XXXVIII, pt I, p. 194.

account of their lives appeared in the press. The Society, which kept in touch with the children, when it could, by letter, asked that an official enquiry should be made into the condition of every one of the children at the Cape. The request was granted and Sir George Napier, the Governor, deputed four magistrates to make a personal enquiry into the conditions of the children in the various districts in which they had been placed. The magistrates submitted their very extensive reports to the Governor who concluded that conditions on the whole were very satisfactory for the children and that they would have every chance at the end of their apprenticeship of earning good wages and setting up homes of their own. In fact, this was a rather sanguine interpretation of the facts presented by the magistrates. The children were mostly apprenticed to Boer farmers who understood little English and were thus only capable of giving limited instruction to their apprentices. The farms themselves were often very isolated, too far from a church or a school for the children to have any chance of improving their education, and quite a few of them remained totally illiterate. A substantial number of the children's own statements to the magistrates were thus signed with a rough cross. The major criticism that the magistrates themselves made referred to the type of occupation to which the boys were put, and this was also the main grumble of the boys themselves, who had apparently come out from England in the hope of being given the chance of learning a trade. The actual number of tradesmen and craftsmen in the towns who wanted boys was small, however, in relation to the number of boys seeking apprenticeship, and the majority had thus gone to the farmers who were in urgent need of labour. The farmers seem to have used the boys for 'dead end' jobs, mainly cattle herding. This had been a job relegated to aged slaves before the emancipation, but the farmers now found it almost impossible to obtain native labour. One magistrate wrote:[1]

Amongst the several employments to which some of the apprentices have been placed, I beg to point out the constant herding of oxen, which does not lead to any useful attainment . . . In this employment

[1] Report from the Governor of the Cape of Good Hope ... relative to the Condition and Treatment of Children sent out by the Children's Friend Society, *PP*, 1840, XXXIII, pp. 341–2.

his time is passed during the heat of the day, either in sleeping under a bush, or in strolling sluggard-like after the cattle: his only associate a stray Hottentot, and his only attainment indolent and slovenly habits.

Clothes were often insufficient and ragged, but food appeared to have been plentiful and the boys healthy. Bedding and sleeping accommodation, on the other hand, seem to have been far from satisfactory. Often they were given only a bundle of straw, or a mat, as a bed, on which they were expected to sleep in the kitchen or the hall. Sometimes they were put to sleep with the natives, men and women together, which one of the magistrates maintained led to 'loose and depraved' habits, especially on the isolated farms. Again, financial arrangements were not ideal and they did not always get what they earned. The arrangements with the Society were that they were to get 2d. a week given to them and a further 2d. a week put aside for them until they reached the age of sixteen. From sixteen to nineteen, they were to get 6d. a week, and thereafter 1s. a week. Many boys complained that they had not been paid for months.

Yet in spite of all these drawbacks the majority of the boys were happy and showed no desire to move. The arrangements for their arrival at the Cape and for their disposal were apparently good, although Mr Longmore, one of the magistrates, suggested that they might well be improved if four clergymen were appointed, whose sole duty it would be to travel around, supervising and instructing the boys. The wages of these four, he suggested, should be paid for by the farmers themselves, who were saving quite substantially by employing such cheap labour. This same magistrate concluded his own report with the comment:[1]

I consider however the best security for the apprentice is constant enquiry into his condition and as it appears that the attention of the public in England has been aroused and is very sensitive regarding the system of juvenile emigration, and that the Government on these occasions is called upon and is considered in some measure responsible that no oppressive treatment takes place, especially on the subject of apprentices and persons of colour, I take the liberty of suggesting that His Excellency the Governor, whenever he deems it advisable to appoint a commission, should institute an

[1] ibid., p. 349.

inquiry at unstated times, to report on this system, and the condition of the apprentices, as has been done in the present instance.

Mr Longmore's views were not shared by the majority of his fellow countrymen who were incensed that the enquiry should have been made at all, regarding any form of inspection as an unwarrantable interference with the individual employer who knew best what to do with his own apprentices, just as he had been supposed to know best how to deal with his slaves. Certainly the Governor himself had little patience with the notion that the condition of apprentices sent to the Cape by the Children's Friend Society needed special and regular scrutiny. In the covering letter he sent with the magistrates' reports to Lord Russell he wrote:[1]

> For myself, my Lord, although deeply regretting that an institution which promised well has been overthrown, as regards the Cape of Good Hope, by the effects of an evident disposition, if not a settled determination, on the part of many persons in England to pay implicit belief to every foolish report or misrepresentation to its discredit, I cannot but hope that the colony will be spared the pain of encountering any further inquiry through the continued operation of the Children's Friend Society.

Sir George had no need to concern himself. The scandal that had prompted the Society to ask for an official enquiry damaged its work irreparably. Subscriptions fell off, patrons withdrew their support, and the Society ceased to function on the death of its founder, Captain Brenton, the following year, 1841.

Although the parties of children sent out by the voluntary societies included some who had already embarked on a career of crime, since their aim was not merely the reform of the criminal but the prevention of crime itself, they also included destitute children, taken off the streets, trained by the societies, and sent overseas to earn an honest living in lands where, unlike England, labour was in short supply. The desirability of the State undertaking similar work on its own behalf, instead of indirectly assisting the charitable societies by placing children from the workhouses or the prisons in their care, had been urged some years previously, in 1826, in evidence to the Select Committee on Emigration from the United Kingdom by Robert

[1] ibid., p. 339.

Chambers, a London magistrate. 'I conceive that London has got too full of children',[1] he told them. His belief was that emigration would help rid London of 'this teeming mass' of children for whom there was no employment and who were thus forced to rob and steal. Further, Chambers pointed to the high cost of maintaining the large numbers of children committed for sleeping in the streets or sent to the workhouse as vagrant and destitute. Many of the London guardians, he claimed, precluded from apprenticing poor children in the factories of the north and clearly unable to find employment within the statutory forty-mile limit from London, would welcome the opportunity to send some of their charges to Canada. Not only this, but the poor themselves would welcome such a scheme. The guardians of St Luke's, Southwark, were quoted as saying that 'among the pauper poor, it is probable that a considerable number would gladly avail themselves [of a State assisted passage] . . . and relieve themselves from a burden which the increasing population of London and the decreasing call for labour render it difficult to sustain. It is very difficult at all times to obtain good masters for apprentices.'[2] Chambers, who was supported by the secretary of the Mendicity Society, an organisation which had paid special attention to the causes and consequences of child poverty, proposed that children should emigrate about the age of twelve, and be bound apprentice in Canada for a period of five or seven years.[3] The Committee itself, however, was by no means convinced that such a scheme would not encourage parents to abrogate their own responsibilities to their children, leaving them on the parish in the hope that they would be emigrated and thus no longer a burden on themselves. In their final Report, no mention of child emigration was included, but they did advocate the assisted emigration of adults, and when the Poor Law Amendment Act was passed in 1834, a clause to that effect was inserted.[4] The procedure to be followed by any parish wishing to raise money 'for Defraying the expenses of the Emigration of Poor Persons having Settlements in such Parish and willing to emigrate' was carefully laid

[1] *PP*, 1826, IV, p. 83.
[2] ibid., p. 85.
[3] ibid.
[4] 4 & 5 Vict., c. 76, s. 62.

down. The Act also stipulated that if an emigrant refused to go at the last moment, any money given to him was to be returned to the guardians at once, thus inhibiting any shrewd pauper from abusing the scheme. Children were not specifically mentioned as potential emigrants in the Act, although it was clearly assumed that they would accompany their parents. In the subsequent returns made from time to time regarding the numbers of 'statutory adults' emigrated by guardians of the poor, every two children under the age of fourteen were officially counted as one 'adult', a practice which makes it impossible to see either the number or the proportion of children emigrated in this way.

There had, in fact, been a clear recommendation on the part of two of the Assistant Commissioners of the 1834 Poor Law Commission that special attention be paid to the issue of emigrating workhouse children. Captain Pringle, for example, noted the slender chances of a workhouse child prospering in England, partly because of the excess of the supply of labour over demand for it and partly due to their original bad upbringing. Workhouse children, he stated, had few ties with their native land, and such as there were could be broken only to their profit. Moreover, according to Pringle, settlers in Australia and in Canada were so hard-pressed for labour that they would not only accept the workhouse children as apprentices but also pay a premium for children of nine or ten years, to cover the expenses of their passage out. The advantages of encouraging such emigration seemed to him both clear and substantial. It would save the parish any further expense in maintaining the children. It would ease the home labour market, which was much overcrowded. It would give the children themselves a better chance in life. All that was necessary for its success was that the scheme should be officially sponsored by the English Government, who would be responsible for supervising the children's passage out and for investigating and approving colonial applicants for the apprentices.[1]

For much the same reasons as the earlier Select Committee, the Poor Law Commissioners elected not to press these suggestions and it was not until sixteen years later, in the Poor Law Act of 1850,[2] that particular provision for the emigration of

[1] *PP*, 1834, XXVIII, p. 330.
[2] 13 & 14 Vict., c. 101, s.4.

children was made. The 'emigration' clause of the 1834 Poor Law Amendment Act had applied to those with settlement, but many children falling into the care of the guardians had no official settlement, and thus could not have been emigrated in any case. The new legislation provided legal authority for guardians to act with regard to such children as were under sixteen years of age:

> And whereas poor Orphans and deserted Children having no Settlement, or whose Settlements are unknown, are frequently chargeable to Parishes, and it is expedient to furnish Means for the Purpose of facilitating the Emigration of such Orphans and deserted Children being so chargeable: Be it therefore enacted that it shall be lawful for the Guardians of any Union or Parish . . . to expend money in and about the Emigration of any poor Orphan or deserted Child under the age of sixteen having no Settlement . . .

There were two provisos to this power of the guardians. First, every application for emigration for each individual child had to be submitted to the Poor Law Board for their approval; second, the child itself had to consent to emigration. No emigration 'of any such Orphan or deserted Child shall take place until such . . . Child shall have consented thereto before the Justices assembled in Petty Sessions . . . and a Certificate of such Consent under the Hands of Two of the Justices present thereat shall have been transmitted to the Poor Law Board'. Experience was to prove how necessary a safeguard for the child this proviso was.

Despite the fact that statutory provision for the emigration of poor orphan children from this country was first made in the 1850 Act, it emerged from a debate in the House of Commons which took place on 28 May of that year that assistance had been given towards girl orphans in Irish workhouses since 1847, and on quite a large scale. Between 1847 and the time of the debate, 4,128 girls aged between fourteen and eighteen had emigrated from Ireland to Australia to meet the shortage of women in general and of domestic servants in particular.[1] In response to requests from New South Wales, a colony particularly in need of more women in its population, the Colonial Land and Emigration Office had inquired of the Poor Law Board in 1848 whether the system of sending out poor orphan girls from

---

[1] Hansard, 3rd series, 1850, vol. CXI, p. 445.

Ireland could be extended to the English workhouses. Apparently, the Board were unwilling to consider the suggestion until proper arrangements for the girls' welfare had been made in the colony, although some of the workhouses themselves were so enthusiastic in their support that they were willing to pay out not only the cost of the necessary outfits of clothes and of their journey to the embarkation port but were prepared also to assist in paying for the girls' passage money.[1] Little further seems to have been done on behalf of the English girls, and the Commons debate two years later arose from a petition presented to the House by a Mr W. Miles, on behalf of the board of guardians of Berwick-on-Tweed, 'praying the House to adopt some measures to promote the emigration of young females to the colonies'. In the course of his speech, Miles referred both to the earlier interest of the Colonial Emigration Commission in the same subject and to the continuing anxiety of the colonies, New South Wales in particular, that girls should be sent out to them to be apprenticed as household servants, since they were unable to get women servants 'at any price'. In conclusion, he moved: 'That it is expedient that the Government with the consent and assistance of the Boards of Guardians throughout England and Wales should take immediate steps to forward the emigration of orphan girls, inmates of the several workhouses, and capable of entering service, to Australia as apprentices.'[2]

Miles' scheme was the subject of a leading article in the following day's *Times*, which commented that it 'will certainly do him more credit than some of his hobbies' and observed that, since there was a shortage of women in the colonies, it was obviously a good idea to arrange for the emigration of 'the inexhaustible supply of orphan girls who have received as good an education as a workhouse can give, and whom we know not what to do with.' *The Times* took strong issue with Miles, however, on the matter of whether such a scheme could be justified on the additional grounds that girls emerged from the workhouse better trained and in better health than boys. The claim came from the reports of the Poor Law Commissioners themselves, especially the reports of Mr Tufnell who had written: 'The girls were generally superior to the boys, that they were

[1] Cf. *PP*, 1847–8, XLVII, pp. 574 and 598.
[2] Hansard, 3rd series, vol. CXI 1850, p. 438.

better grown . . . Confinement and sedentary occupation did not prove so injurious to the female organisation as to the male. The females were employed in needlework, in washing and scouring, in bed-making, in the duties of house maids . . .'[1] On this, *The Times* had some biting observations to make.

> All of this is very encouraging, were there not a fearful weight of testimony, amounting almost to a universal consent, against the results of a workhouse education for girls as well as for boys . . . They may go about in pattens, twirl a mop, and look in all respects like little housewives . . . But they grow up without that deep instinct of filial reverence, those family affections and that self-respect which alone can preserve them in the most trying passage and ordeal of their existence. Even if they leave the workhouse very early, they are too generally found dull, stubborn and intractable . . .

Had the article been intended to attack, rather than approve, the emigration of poor orphan girls, it could hardly have included a more damaging passage. As it happened, the scheme had already foundered after a short debate due to the House being 'counted out' after the departure of all but the handful of its members who were more concerned with the fate of 'many thousands as pitiable objects as society had to deal with' than the outcome of the Derby.

One of those who had remained was Lord Shaftesbury, who had a particular interest in child emigration through his connection with the Ragged School Union, of which he had become president. It was his firm belief that one of the best ways of dealing with slum children was to send them overseas, right away from their depressing and demoralising surroundings and far out of the reach of their parents, often the chief cause of their misery. In 1848, therefore, he had moved in the House of Commons: 'That is it expedient that means be annually provided for the voluntary emigration to some of Her Majesty's colonies of a certain number of young persons of both sexes, who have been educated in the schools, ordinarily called the Ragged Schools, in and about the Metropolis.'[2] Shaftesbury proposed to send out the children to Australia; the boys as shepherds and the girls as domestic servants. He ended his speech by calling for a new attitude to emigration: 'It will be something to have

---

[1] Quoted ibid, pp. 435–6.
[2] Quoted Scholes, op. cit., p. 33.

established a new system of colonization and no longer regarding it merely as the drainage of our gaols or the outlet for the off-scouring of the feeble, the mischievous or the distressed, to hold it up as an object of ambition, the recompense of moral exertion.'[1] The House was sympathetic, but not to the point of carrying the motion. Very largely, this appears to have been because the appeal had only been made on behalf of London children. However, Shaftesbury did succeed in getting Government aid in the following year, and 150 Ragged School boys were very carefully picked for the first experiment. Those chosen had to be able to read and write a little, know the Ten Commandments and the Lord's prayer and have a certificate of attendance at an industrial class for four months or be able to prove their knowledge of a practical skill. These 150 were sent to New South Wales, and were said, both in their behaviour on ship and on their arrival, to have fully justified the trust placed in them. This claim Miles had refuted in the course of his speech on his own motion in 1850, declaring that the boys had not turned out so well as the Parkhurst boys sent to Western Australia. Shaftesbury and other speakers in the debate denied this allegation very strongly, but the fact remains that the Government grant was not renewed that year, and the Ragged Union scheme for emigrating children had to proceed on a voluntary basis.

One of the factors which might well have accounted for a greater success among delinquents emigrated from Parkhurst was the appointment of the Guardian of Juvenile Immigrants, which guaranteed some official supervision of the boys and their employers in the colony. Equally, one of the reasons why, even after the sanction to assisted emigration given by the Poor Law Act of 1850, the numbers of children actually emigrating were relatively few, appears to have been the failure to ensure the appointment of similar guardians in the other colonies. *The Times* leader of 28 May 1850 claimed that 'the public are rightly suspicious of the mass emigration of those tender and helpless creatures for the colonies', and called for the establishment of some body whose responsibility it would be to act as a registry for jobs and employers. It also suggested that the colonies who were so concerned to have the children should appoint their

[1] ibid.

own agents in this country to contact would-be emigrants and make suitable arrangements for their passage.

One group who appear to have been undeterred by the difficulties of emigrating children were the guardians of St. Pancras, London, who were so enthusiastic that they not only anticipated the 1850 Act but failed to meet the requirements of that statute. Hence, in January 1851, the Poor Law Board wrote to the guardians concerning a report that had appeared in the *Morning Chronicle* of a meeting of the neighbouring St Marylebone guardians at which a proposal to emigrate children from the workhouse had been discussed.[1] In the course of this discussion, reference had been made to children having been sent out to the Bermudas by the guardians of St Pancras, under conditions which their neighbours thought 'worse than to transport them'. They thus decided 'not to entertain so absurd and inhuman a proposition, observing that they were legally and morally bound to watch over the interests of the pauper children and not allow them to be jeopardised by so novel a speculation'. As this was the first the Poor Law Board had heard of these activities of the St Pancras guardians, they naturally asked for some explanation. This failed to satisfy the Board, and they sent their inspector, Richard Hall, to make a full investigation. Within the week, Hall reported back, producing minutes of the evidence he had taken from the guardians themselves, as well as copies of letters produced during his investigations which had been written by the children to their friends and relations in this country and to the guardians.[2] Hall's verdict was that the St Pancras emigration scheme was excellent in every way. The children had not been coerced into going, in fact several were said to have cried because they were not taken. No child whose parents or friends refused consent was allowed to go. Those who went, travelled out not as steerage but as 'cabin' passengers, and were each amply supplied with clothes and equipment, including frocks, shifts, petticoats, shoes and stockings, and bonnets for the girls, two complete suits of clothes, shirts, neckcloths, caps and '1 large clasp knife' for the boys. Every boy and girl was issued with a pound of soap, a Bible and a Prayer Book and 2s. 6d. in money. Jobs and good

[1] *PP*, 1851, XL, p. 412.
[2] ibid., p. 414 et seq.

masters, personally vouched for by 'an independent Bermudan gentleman in England' had been secured before the children sailed and every care had been taken by the guardians to ensure the success of the scheme for their children.

From Hall's report, it appears that the guardians had sent out three small parties, each of which included some adults, who were expected to look after the children's welfare on the boat. The first party had sailed in November 1849; the second in June 1850; and the third in October 1850. This represented altogether, twenty-four boys, thirteen girls, nine men and two 'young women'.

The tone of the children's letters clearly showed them to be well and happy. James George, aged thirteen, wrote to the workhouse teacher: 'Dear Sir, I send you my kind love to you and all the boys, Half-a-Loaf, Dabtoe and all the rest . . . please ask Mr Eaton to try to send my aunt to the Bermudas.' George Baron, aged fourteen, wrote to the master of the workhouse: ' . . . I must write you a letter to beg of you to send my sister on here, as I am sure she will be well situated . . . a lady living near us is in want of a girl, and I should be very glad if you would allow her to come. My master and mistress are very kind to me . . .' Even so, time and space can assume formidable proportions when one is small. Martha Dawson, aged eleven, wrote to her sister: 'I am living in a family with Mr. & Mrs. Johnson and four children. I like my place very well; I am very comfortable. I go to chapel twice a week with the family and Sunday school. I was bound for six years, it is a long time to be separated, but if we never meet on earth we must try and meet in heaven.'

From the Inspector's point of view, the problem was not so much whether the children were happy, not even whether the guardians' scheme was properly organised, but whether they had acted legally. Alas! this they had certainly not done. 'In conclusion,' he ends his report to the Board, 'it appears to me that in sending out these children to the Bermudas, the directors did what was for the children's good; that their motive was a regard for their welfare; that the affair was transacted with deliberation; and the children so long as they depended on the directors were amply provided for; but the whole proceeding was illegal.' Certainly they had neither asked the permission of the Poor Law

Board, as the 1850 Act stipulated they should, nor had they even informed the Board that they had sent the children. They had not brought the children before the petty sessions, as the law required, thus there were no magistrates' certificates of the children's agreement to emigrate. They had merely taken verbal agreement as sufficient. None of this did the chairman of the guardians attempt to deny, instead he pleaded ignorance of the law. 'No legal formalities were gone through in sending out these children; no reference made to any Acts of Parliament on the subjects; the directors conceiving they were right, as they procured in every case the consent of the parents or friends of the children who had parents or friends to consult, and sent out none who did not consent, or whose parents or friends objected.'

After studying Hall's report, the Board ultimately wrote a very complimentary letter to the guardians, commending their great care for the welfare of the children in their workhouse at St Pancras, but reminding them that they had broken the law in not seeking permission for their scheme; not providing finances for it in the manner laid down by statute; and not going before the petty sessions with the children. Owing to the highly satisfactory results of the investigation, they declared themselves willing to accept the chairman's explanation that the guardians had acted under a misapprehension but warned that on no account was such a mistake to be repeated.[1]

If a formal investigation ending in an official reprimand – however courteously delivered – seems a harsh reward for efforts so generously conceived and efficiently executed, there can be little doubt that the actions of the Poor Law Board were justified. Ultimately, the Board were legally and morally responsible for the welfare of workhouse children and it was no part of their function to encourage by condoning *ad hoc* local schemes for emigration of whose inauguration and organisation they had neither knowledge nor control. Good intentions had not been sufficient to protect the reputation of the Children's Friend Society: the attempts of the St Pancras guardians to assist their pauper children overseas to a better life than they could expect in their home country had already been labelled by other guardians as 'worse than to transport them'. Understandably, the Board acted with the utmost caution with regard to a policy

[1] ibid., p. 417.

of which the public according to *The Times* were known to be, 'rightly suspicious'.

So much was this the case that state emigration for poor children, though sanctioned years earlier, did not really start on a large scale until the very late sixties when the work of two women, Annie Macpherson and Maria Rye, established two large, charitable emigration societies which at last provided that 'intermediary body' for which *The Times* had called in 1850, the previous want of which had inhibited any marked official encouragement of child emigration. The 1860s was the period of the Evangelical Revival and the beginnings of the work of the religious humanitarians such as Barnardo. The religious drive behind the numerous voluntary emigration societies which sprang up during these and the following years appears to have been the same.

The more striking of these two women was Annie Macpherson, who was a staunch revivalist and who co-operated with Barnardo in the East End where they carried on their main missionary work. A daughter of a Quaker schoolteacher, she was 'converted' at the age of nineteen, when she began her first social work with the temperance movement among agricultural labourers in Cambridgeshire. After a visit to America in 1866, she went to live in the East End of London, where Barnardo had just started his own rescue work among children, and soon immersed herself in work among the 'East End heathen'. Looking around her, Miss Macpherson was to write:[1]

> We can but be thankful that in parts of the East End, four out of every five infants die before they reach their fifth year, because the other side of the picture among the living ones is so black, so awful, so crushing in its dreadful realities . . . While yet in their mother's arms gin is poured down their infant throats and a little later on, as a natural consequence, childish voices beg for coppers to be spent in drink. Alas! no uncommon sight is it to see little girls of ten years old reeling drunk along the streets.

Very soon her interest in the plight of the children widened. Her first introduction to what she called 'the child-slavery of the East End' was when she came across the children employed in match-box making. These children received ¾d. for making a

[1] Quoted Lilian M. Birt, *The Children's Home Finder*, p. 25.

5a. Boys in the exercise yard of Tothill Fields prison (Radio Times Hulton Picture Library)

5b. The Girls' School at Tothill Fields prison (Radio Times Hulton Picture Library)

6a. One of the early parties
of Barnardo's boy emigrants
catching the train to Liverpool

6b. The first party of Barnardo emigrants to make the journey to
Australia by plane

gross of boxes. Appalled by the stress under which the children worked, she both wrote a pamphlet, *The Little Matchbox Makers*, to alert others to their plight, and started a House of Industry in Commercial Street where the children could pursue their employment but also, in the one-and-a-half hours Annie was able to 'buy them off' through the generosity of sympathetic subscribers, could be given food and some education. Before 1869 Annie Macpherson had extended her work still further, and had opened four Revival Homes, named after the *Journal* which had helped start them. Into these she took orphaned and destitute boys and girls, teaching them to read and write, and trained them to do such work as patching and tailoring, shoe mending and housework.

All this, however, only served to convince her more and more strongly that the real hope for the poor of the East End was in America, where she had seen for herself the vast possibilities for hard-working people in a land where labour was as yet still scarce. In 1869, therefore, she and Ellen Logan, another evangelical social worker, put out a circular headed *Emigration, the only remedy for chronic pauperism in the East of London*. As a result a fund was started at the House of Industry to send selected families to Canada, and five hundred people went out that same year. Meanwhile the Revival Homes were overflowing with children who she knew could have little chance of employment. She thus decided to send some of the boys to Canada in the care of the families emigrating through her fund. The following year, 1870, she decided to take out some boys herself and a hundred boys were selected.[1]

> Many are entire orphans, or worse than orphans [she wrote]. We feel it is not enough as Christian workers to cleanse, clothe and pass them away into Strangers' hands. What we wish and hope to do this Spring, the Lord willing, is to establish a branch Home to this Institution in Canada, having a like-minded agent there to care and watch over the welfare of each young boy as he is placed out, saving from his wages, counselling him, and, if sick, caring for him . . .

Among this party of boys, which set out on 1 May, were some of Barnardo's children, and she continued to take a proportion of his boys until he started his own emigration scheme in 1882.

[1] ibid., p. 61.

The pioneer group went to Ontario and were placed in groups of twenty or so in various towns until situations could be got for them. Soon the first Distributing Home was opened in Belleville, Ontario, which was to receive and, as its name suggests, distribute children arriving from England to good Christian homes in which the training begun in the East End could be continued in Canada. Demand for the children soon exceeded the supply. Many who had no children of their own were anxious to take in the orphans of others. 'Send me another', wrote one farmer who had already taken in one boy. 'I can as easily feed a child as a chicken, there's plenty . . . .' Conscious that anxiety to take the children was no guarantee of suitability, Miss Macpherson was anxious that some careful supervision should be maintained over them after they had been placed out. 'It would be easy to set the little emigrant adrift, and, as it were, let him paddle his own canoe on the ocean of life, inquiring no further as to his welfare', she wrote. As far as she herself was concerned, she would prefer to undertake a more restricted work 'and carry out the healthful supervision of employers and employed'.[1] Applicants for children had to have two references as to their character and standing, and a legal contract was signed for each child, stipulating what treatment and what recompense he was to receive.

Despite her concern that the scale of the work should not overtake her ability to ensure that the children were effectively supervised, the numbers emigrated steadily increased, and a second Distributing Home was opened in Galt, Western Ontario, in 1872, followed by yet a third at Knowlton in 1874. In England Miss Macpherson's sister opened a Home at Liverpool as an extension of the work already being done in the East End of London and from here more children were sent to Canada, this time to Nova Scotia.

Meanwhile Maria Rye (previously engaged in the emigration of middle-class women) had also started sending out children, a work in which she had the support and blessing of many, including the then Archbishop of Canterbury. With the support of *The Times*[2] she had raised funds with which she purchased Avenue House, Peckham. Here she collected waifs and strays

[1] ibid., p. 70.
[2] Cf. Scholes, op. cit., p. 40.

and, after giving them an elementary education based on Christian principles, she sailed from Liverpool to Quebec with her first party in the autumn of 1869. There were sixty-five girls and three boys, the forerunners of some 5,000 who followed in the next twenty-five years. The *Niagara Mail* described the arrival of the first party at the society's head-quarters, Our Western Home, in Ontario: 'After prayers and hymns the children retired for the night confident and happy in the knowledge that Miss Rye was with them and that God watched over them all.'

In June of the following year *The Times*[1] advertised a public meeting to be held in the rooms of the Social Science Association, presided over by Lord Shaftesbury,

> to consider the priority of memorialising Mr. Goschen [President of the Poor Law Board] about Miss Rye's proposals to take out and find homes for the pauper children of the workhouses. Miss Rye's suggestion is that she should be allowed to take orphan and deserted pauper girls from seven to twelve, chiefly from the London work-house schools, to Canada. There they will be placed under proper legal protection, till eighteen years of age in respectable families in British North America. In the case of respectable persons living in the United States and applying to that lady for children, she desires to be allowed to use her discretion and place such children with American families.

Two or three London boards of guardians had already availed themselves of Miss Rye's help. What was now being sought was official approval for the use of her services. The Board, presented with what appeared to be practicable means of sending out poor children under such auspices as might allay public suspicion, agreed to give official sanction to their emigration under the care of Miss Rye and also of Miss Macpherson. They thus urged guardians to take advantage of the 'active benevolence' of Miss Rye and Miss Macpherson, and commented on the 'satisfactory arrangements made by these ladies, not only for proper super-intendence during the voyage but also for the support and treatment of the children on their arrival in the colony'. In 1870 146 children, mainly orphans, were sent out in this way to Canada, and 461 in the following year.

Three years later the Local Government Board, which

---

[1] Cf. *The Times*, 17 June 1870.

replaced the Poor Law Board in 1871, decided that, 'having incurred a serious responsibility' by encouraging such emigration, they should send out an inspector to see for himself how the scheme was working out. Mr Andrew Doyle, one of their most experienced inspectors, was thus sent out in 1874. He submitted his forty-page report the following year.[1] It was detailed, very thorough and certainly made astringent reading after the eulogies of the benefits of emigration as set out by Miss Rye and Miss Macpherson.

Doyle's first comments relate to the heterogeneous character of the children sent out by the two women. Not only were they taking out the pauper children from the workhouses but they were also taking out children from the reformatory and industrial schools and 'street arabs' whom they, or some other charitable society, had swept off the streets into one of the many voluntary Homes which had sprung up for the care of children. Here the children were supposed to get a preliminary education and some industrial training before setting sail. In fact many went out after a few weeks, sometimes a few days, whereas the pauper children had usually had some years of training in the workhouse schools. Further, Doyle pointed to the inevitable troubles which ensued from the fact that, unlike children sent out from the workhouses, there were no strict requirements concerning the consent of the street urchins to being sent overseas. More particularly, he pointed to the consequences of mixing the two types of children indiscriminately.

> There is absolutely no distinction made by Miss Rye and Miss Macpherson between the 'arab' and the pauper children. The 'arab' children are often depraved whereas the pauper child has been more carefully brought up. The impression given in Canada is that *all* these children have been picked up, starving from the streets and that therefore the general feeling is that should be grateful for anything they get.

This impression can only have been added to by their appearance on arrival. Doyle travelled with one party across the Atlantic, and deplored the conditions under which they travelled, with insufficient staff to look after the children who consequently

[1] Report by Andrew Doyle Esq. to the President of the Local Government Board on the Emigraion of Pauper Children to Canada, *PP*, 1875, LXIII, pp. 257 and 296.

arrived in Canada dirty, and often their heads crawling with vermin.

Once disembarked, the children were taken to one of the four reception centres which had been established, from where they were supposed to be sent to families and employers within only a few days: thus no attempt was made to provide any industrial training there. To this point, the inspector returned with some force later in his report. His immediate interest was in the fate of the children who were 'placed' from these Homes. The very young children, those less than eight years of age, were usually adopted, and the adoption successful. They were taken into far better homes than they would have known in England and were brought up, literally, as members of such families. The fate of the older children, unfortunately, was not so satisfactory. Sometimes he found them with an employer miles away from any other habitation, poorly paid, and too far from the Societies' Homes to be supervised. Both ladies had started out with the express determination to provide rigorous supervision, the Local Government Board were reminded, supervision both of the home to which the child was to be sent and of the child himself when he had been placed. In fact, Doyle reported, the schemes had all broken down as numbers had grown larger and distances from the Homes greater. Miss Macpherson seems at least to have continued to try in this respect. She apparently had some excellent helpers who did manage to do a little inspecting of the children's conditions, but Miss Rye had come to rely almost entirely on writing to the child's employers to ask how the child was getting along.

It is no surprise, therefore, that Doyle should have come across numerous cases of gross neglect when he himself visited some of the children who had been accepted from the Societies. Some were in a pitiable condition through overwork. Some had not been paid for weeks. To escape from their miserable servitude, many had moved away from their original placement, tempted into the nearest town by rumours, often quite accurate, of the high wages to be earned there but often they were morally ruined into the bargain. Several of the girls had already been left destitute with illegitimate babies by the time they were sixteen or seventeen and, since Canada had nothing resembling our Poor Law at the time, were in a plight more serious than they would have been in England. Miss Rye's own 'principles' apparently prohibited her from offering such girls any assistance herself.

No one, least of all Miss Rye and Miss Macpherson, was under any illusion that many of the older children were taken in 'on account of their future usefulness' as labour. Nor were the children themselves deceived. ' 'Doption, sir, is when folks get a girl to work without wages' one girl told Doyle. Since, in England, many working-class children were still principally valued by their own parents for their labour, that this too should be their main value and attraction for those who took them in Canada was not in itself necessarily objectionable. Doyle contended, however, that the children were being exploited by the Canadians and working under terms of service which were far less favourable than they ought to have been in a country where wages were much higher than in England. In part the low wages that the children earned were an inevitable consequence of their lack of training in any marketable skill, a matter to which Doyle had already addressed himself earlier when talking of the 'street arabs'. It seems, however, that the pauper children were sometimes in no better case.[1]

> No girl or boy of say twelve years or upwards ought to be put out to service in Canada unless after two or three years preliminary industrial training ... To gather children off the streets, or to accept them from the guardians without satisfactory assurance of their fitness for service, and to take them out to take their chance of finding those 'splendid homes' [here he quotes Miss Rye] in Canada that are written about, is to really do serious injury to the children and permanently prejudice a system of emigration that might do infinite good.

A solution to this problem, he suggested, would be to provide some basic industrial training for the children in the Homes to which they were taken in Canada before being placed out. On the other hand, Doyle was also quite convinced that the low wages the children were given were due to the Canadians deliberately exploiting children whose position was too precarious in a foreign land to enable either them or their sponsors to engage in hard bargaining. 'I cannot help feeling', he writes, 'that in a country in which wages are so high, and the cost of

---

[1] ibid., p. 273.

living, for a child in a family at least, so low, the terms of service are less favourable than they ought to be . . . It is easy to understand that Canada, or indeed any other country, can "absorb" any amount of labour upon such terms.'

Doyle ended his report by commenting on the financial arrangements of the two Societies. Since he was unable to extract any details from either Miss Rye or Miss Macpherson, although they were both asked to help him in this matter, the figures he quoted are rough estimates, but they are probably fairly accurate. The cost of the passage across was fixed at £3 5s. per head. The cost of each child's stay in the reception home, where they only remained for a matter of a few days, sometimes only hours, Doyle reckoned to be about £1. The Ontario Government gave a bonus of £1 4s. for every child brought into the Province and, in England, every board of guardians allowed each child £8 8s. plus a complete outfit of clothes. It thus appeared that a profit of about £5 per head was being made on every child taken out to Canada, a profit which was ploughed back into the work of the Societies.

Reviewing all his evidence, Doyle came to the conclusion that if children were to be sent abroad at all, only very young children, preferably under seven or eight years, should be sent out, and then only when great care had been taken to see that there were a sufficient number of good homes to receive them in Canada. This was the policy he commended to the Local Government Board. [1] It is clear that he himself did not relish the idea of any more children at all being taken out in the haphazard manner being practised by Miss Rye and Miss Macpherson, and this reluctance was shared by the Local Government Board after reading Doyle's report. [2]

> The report appears to us to show that if the emigration of children to Canada is to be continued, it should be placed under systematic superintendence and control, not only as regards the arrangements for the voyage to Canada, and for the due care of the children on landing there, but also for securing proper enquiries as to their subsequent destination, and a regular superintendence of them when placed out in service or taken into the homes of the Canadian settlers.

[1] ibid., p. 296.
[2] *PP*, 1875, XXXI, p. xxii.

As with the children sent to the Cape more than thirty years before, so now with the children taken to Canada, the serious problem of supervising their welfare in their new homes had claimed the attention of the government. The resulting caution of the Local Government Board, by whom every emigration application for a pauper child had to be approved, led to an immediate diminution of the pauper children emigrating. In the Board's report for the year following the publication of Doyle's findings, 1876, they noted that in the past year, 'emigration has been on a very small scale',[1] only 108 persons being sent out, most of whom were adults.

In justice to Miss Rye and to Miss Macpherson, it must be remembered that they were both victims of their own success. The basic wisdom of their scheme to take children from a country in which they had little or no hope of any other than a life of penury to where they might reasonably expect to establish themselves in comfort was not to be denied. Their early efforts thus met not only with offers of financial assistance but also with increasing requests from the many charitable organisations working among the poor that they should include among their parties of emigrants destitute children sponsored by such organisations. Not merely did Miss Macpherson take out some of Dr Barnado's children; she also took children from Mr Quarrier's Homes in Scotland; from Mr Leonard Shaw's Boys and Girls Refuges in Manchester; from Dr Thomas Guthrie's Ragged Schools; from Mrs Blaikie's Girls' Home at Edinburgh; and some of Mrs Smyly's children from Dublin. Nor had requests for their services been limited to those from the rescue societies. In the late sixties and in the seventies, the new industrial and reformatory schools revived for another generation of juvenile delinquents the practice of assisting boys, and less frequently girls, to emigrate overseas at the end of their stay in the school. These children then emigrated under the care of the Societies run by Miss Rye and Miss Macpherson. In addition, these ladies were asked to escort children released on licence under an Act passed in 1866, which provided that inmates of reformatories and industrial schools might be so freed after eighteen months' detention on the condition that they were sent to the colonies.

[1] *PP*, 1876, XXXI, p. xxv.

Doyle was himself the first to appreciate these difficulties, and in his report he gave high praise to the vision and the initiative of both. As he saw it, the defects he had observed in their operations had arisen from the fact that neither had been able to recognise that she was no longer able effectively to guide and control an organisation whose size had outstripped the capabilities of its foundress. More than anything else, it seems that it was this slur on her ability to operate on a large scale that rankled most with Miss Rye. Miss Macpherson reacted to Doyle's criticisms by declining to arrange for the emigration of any more poor law children, thus avoiding mixing them with 'street arabs', but nevertheless acting on a good many of his suggestions for the improvement of her work, in particular, arranging for much more systematic supervision than before.[1] Miss Rye, however, apparently carried on in much the same way as before, tracing the fate of the children she placed by means of correspondence and nursing her grievance until, three years after Doyle's report, she wrote him a letter, resisting his criticisms in the strongest terms. People in England, she declared, did not appreciate how good were the homes in which children were placed by her Society, so good, indeed, that 'the inspection of the children is of comparatively small moment'. Further, not for one moment conceding that numbers of her placements had proved disastrous, she claimed the 'enormous' success of her work was due to the lack of the elaborate staff, rules and organisational structure, the very absence of which had so concerned Doyle. Such cases as had been quoted against her she held to have been discussed out of context. The true estimate of her work could be seen in the numbers who now imitated her Society, she informed her detractor, enclosing a long list of such people for him to peruse.[2]

Like so many who resort to pen and paper to rebut what is believed to be a groundless imputation, Miss Rye soon found that Doyle, less inhibited now than in an official report, was only too willing to substantiate every one of his earlier strictures, producing even more damaging evidence to do so. He wrote that her 'evidence' was inaccurate; her case histories misleading; and that she contradicted herself on certain substantial issues.

[1] *PP*, 1877, LXXI, pp. 12–13.
[2] ibid., p. 19.

He repeated that the terms of service which she was prepared to accept for her emigrants were wholly unfair to the children. 'In no other way can one account for the eagerness of Canadian employers to get them, and the unwillingness of the working people in Canada to send their own children into service upon the same terms.' Further, he accused Miss Rye herself of contributing to the Canadian attitude that the children should be grateful for anything they were offered, by deliberately fostering the impression of the squalor and the wretchedness from which the children had been rescued to be brought before the beneficent attention of the Canadian public. 'Nor can Miss Rye be acquitted of having some share in aggravating this evil, notwithstanding her assurance that she is ever "moved by Divine love and compassion for my own little ones".' Not content with this, Doyle moved to a more general attack. 'Miss Macpherson', he observed, 'appears to have placed her system on such a footing as to entitle it to the support of all persons who take an interest in the most helpless of the poor'; whilst Miss Rye's arrogant dismissal of all criticism and her blank refusal to accept the necessity for adequate inspection and supervision only underlined how limited a conception Miss Rye had of her work, and how unfortunate this could be for the children. One cannot help thinking that it gave Doyle some satisfaction to comment yet again on perhaps one of the more curious features of her work: that a Church of England organisation was taking out children supposed to be at least nominally Anglican, to a country where only a tiny fraction of the population were themselves members of the Anglican communion. The result had so far been that 90 % of the children boarded out in Canada lived in Nonconformist households and were obliged to attend Nonconformist chapels.

> Every pauper child that Miss Rye has taken from this country being a member of the Church of England would, if kept at home, be brought up in communion with the Church of England. The law so provides and guardians are careful as a rule to protect that legal right of the child. But under Miss Rye's system the security of the 'Creed Register' is set at nought, and the provision of the law, completely disregarded.

Doyle can scarcely have seriously believed that all the children – paupers, 'street arabs' and juvenile delinquents released on licence – were distinguished for their piety, but this was a shrewd thrust at Miss Rye, who constantly claimed to care for the spiritual well-being of her children.[1]

Despite Doyle's criticisms, Miss Rye still helped some of the children from the workhouses, although the total number had declined drastically after the publication of his report. In 1878, however, the chairman of the board of guardians of St George's, Hanover Square, received a letter from Canada written by Mr J. E. Pell, an official of the Waifs and Strays Society, which threw serious doubt on the wisdom of continuing the emigration of any pauper children at a time when there was, at least temporarily, a surplus of children in Canada's own population.

Sir,

The enclosed item of a printed statement that twenty young girls were to be offered by the Board to Miss Rye to take out to Canada at the end of this month I have cut from the *Toronto Globe* . . . . I beg leave most respectfully to offer you my most solemn protest against the continuance of Miss Rye's work, which is keeping this country overflowing with pauperism. Our Girls and Boys Homes are filled to repletion, because situations cannot be found for the children. There are families upon families in our cities – men, women, boys and girls – in destitution and for want of lack of employment there are hundreds longing to get back to England . . . If Miss Rye is sincere in her work as a philanthropist and Canada is the country she wishes to serve, let her assist us first in disposing of our super-abundant boys and girls; and then, should the need arise, to import some from England. I will be ready again to assist her; in the meantime I most respectfully pray of you not to encourage her in the matter.

How far this additional blow further inhibited the emigration of pauper children it is impossible to say, since precise figures distinguishing children from adults were not published until 1884, but certainly the figures published in the 1896 Mundella Report on Poor Law Schools, which relate to the ten years 1884 to 1894, make it clear that only a very limited use was being made of the statutory powers to assist pauper children to emigrate. Indeed, the Committee who presented this Report was particularly anxious that more use of them should be made in the future 'to the advantage of the children and of the rate-

[1] ibid., pp. 1–14 passim.

payers alike'.[1] The Report records the evidence given on their work by the voluntary societies emigrating children at this time and also an interview with Mr W. Knollys, the Assistant Secretary of the Local Government Board, who gave details of the 'agents', i.e. the voluntary societies, whose services were used by the poor law authorities to emigrate pauper children. He also referred at some length to the regulations that had been in force since 1888 between the Local Government Board and the Canadian Government with regard to the reception and supervision of poor law emigrants. The Canadian Government had agreed to inspect annually all pauper children taken into the country by the voluntary agencies but necessarily required the relevant information about the children to enable them to do so. The Local Government Board thus set out the following rules:

1. The agent was to give a written undertaking to notify the Canadian Department of Agriculture [who were to be responsible for inspection] immediately a child had been placed and also to inform the guardians of the union from which the child had been emigrated.

2. Protestant children were to be placed in Protestant homes, and Roman Catholic children in Roman Catholic homes.

3. The local guardians were to forward a report of a child's placement to the Local Government Board.

4. Before going out to Canada, each child was to have six months' instruction, either at a workhouse, district, or separate school, or paid for by the guardians at a public elementary school.

5. The Medical Officer was to give a written report on the physical and mental health of each child, a copy of which was to be sent to the Local Government Board together with the application to emigrate.

6. The guardians were to have satisfactory evidence that the child had reasonable prospects of a home in Canada.

As a general rule, the Board did not believe in the emigration of girls over ten years of age, and in none except very special cases would they consent to the emigration of girls aged over twelve years.[2]

[1] *PP*, 1896, XLIII, p. 131.
[2] ibid., vol. II, p. 661.

Knolly's comments on the actual operation of these rules over the previous eight years are interesting. In practice, the 'annual' reports promised by the Canadian Department of Agriculture did not mean an annual report on each child emigrant, but merely a general report on all child emigrants. In the earliest of such reports as had been received at the time of his own evidence, it was noted that many children could not be traced owing to wrong addresses having been supplied, but this seems to have been less of a difficulty as the years passed. Later reports had indicated that a more satisfactory system of placements had been achieved, although difficulties still arose from some children of poor health and weak intellect having been accepted for emigration. The fact remained that the emigrant children were still not fully accepted into the community.[1]

> It must however be stated that from expressions constantly recurring in the reports, it must be inferred that the children are as a whole regarded as servants rather than as members of the family in which they are placed, and although they appear to receive kindly treatment in many instances, but little care is taken as regards their education. It further appears the engagements under which certain of the children are placed out have not always provided for their being paid wages on reaching a proper age.

Of all the witnesses to give evidence on behalf of the voluntary societies used by the Local Government Board, the witness who most impressed them as having taken the greatest care to protect the children from bad placement and from exploitation was Dr Barnardo himself. Originally utilising the services of Miss Macpherson's organisation, he in time took over her emigration Home at Liverpool and, in 1882, began his own separate emigration organisation which eventually was to overshadow all others. He devised, as indeed one would expect, the best of all the systems of supervision for children he sent overseas, and in sheer numbers alone his emigration work was a colossal achievement. Between 1870 and 1882 he had sent out 1,000 children. He had sent out 24,346 before the outbreak of the First World War, nearly twice the number taken out by Miss Macpherson over the same period and almost seven times the number emigrated by the Waifs and Strays Society. Not

[1] ibid., p. 662.

only were more Barnardo children sent out than any other group, but they became more sought after by the Canadians themselves, although they had to weather various storms of prejudice first.

Barnardo had several advantages when he started to run his own emigration society. By 1882, his original work had already grown to very large proportions; he had a wide variety of Homes, dealing with various classes and age groups of children. He therefore had a larger number of children from whom he could select emigrants, and he determined to send only the 'flower of the flock'. These he had little difficulty in identifying, since many had lived in his Homes since babyhood and were known to him and to his helpers in a way impossible to the organisers of other types of children's homes. Unlike many of them, he had no need to rely almost entirely on a scanty training in an emigration home just before they embarked. He was already training all his children, and had the necessary buildings and equipment to do so. He had a very efficient health service to select those best equipped physically, and experience of the children over many years in his Homes provided him with the information which enabled him to pick the most 'virtuous' who would earn for themselves and their fellows the most credit in Canada.

All parties of emigrants were accompanied by Barnardo officials and Homes had been opened up in Canada from which the children were placed out on farms. Keenly aware of the necessity for proper inspection of the homes to which his children were taken, he made it 'a fixed principle that every home be inspected before any child be placed, and only exemplary Protestant households be accepted'. Once placed, the children were each visited at least four times a year at irregular intervals. In addition, to give them an added protection, Barnardo constituted himself the children's legal guardian until they reached eighteen years of age, after which he exercised parental guardianship over the boys until they legally came of age and over the girls until their marriage. He also undertook that in case of utter failure in establishing a child in Canada, 'the Colonies shall be safeguarded by their return at our expense wherever possible to England'.

These arrangements would, by themselves, have marked

Barnardo's methods as vastly superior to those adopted by most, if not all, of the other emigration societies, but he adopted two more policies to ensure the safety and the happiness of his children which had become the admiration of many both here and in Canada. First, where Canadian families wanted to adopt one of his children, Barnardo had proper legal documents drawn whereby the prospective parents agreed to enter into a bond to pay the adopted child a certain sum at the age of eighteen. The point of this was to secure the child against 'any possible change of mind during the lifetime of the parent, when they might revoke'. Barnardo's chief agent in Canada was made trustee to such settlements, and he had to satisfy himself personally that the stipulated amount was really paid over into the account the Society held for each of such children who, even though adopted, were still inspected by the Society. The vast majority of children of course, were not adopted, but boarded out with foster parents. For these Barnardo adopted his second and unique policy for paying for the children's keep during their school years, with the result that, like all Canadian children of their age, they were free on holiday and after school to play in the fields, to ride and to learn to skate. Thus the Barnardo child had the opportunity of being fully initiated into his environment. All other emigrant children, not merely the pauper children, were normally expected to 'earn their keep' when they were not attending school. Moreover, Barnardo children above school age had to be paid wages on a carefully graded scale, increasing with age. Barnardo was therefore treating placement of his children in Canada in the same way as he treated boarding out of children in England. He was the only person who did.

Notwithstanding the close supervision that was kept over Barnardo children, by 1894 there were eight applications for every one of the children available. This was itself testimony to the success of his methods. When, that same year, rumours were circulated that this success was more apparent than real, and that numbers of his children had become distinguished more for their criminality than their moral rectitude, Barnardo forthwith set enquiries afoot to see whether the rumours had any substance in fact. The facts he accumulated more than vindicated his boys. Over the ten previous years, the average of convictions among the total number of Barnardo boys in Canada, some 6,000 in all, was 0·136 %; while the average among the Canadian population as a whole was 0·755 %.

If one compares the evidence of his work with that of other voluntary agents or with the work of the Canadian Government itself, it is easy to see why, in their final Report, the Committee should commend Barnardo as the model for all those who wished to help children emigrate to Canada successfully. One of the other agents who had taken out a party of pauper children in 1893, had abandoned them in Montreal and made off with what was left of the money given him by the guardians to expend on their behalf. The system of reporting on the children devised by the Canadian Government compared very unfavourably with reports which resulted from the more frequent and searching inspections carried out by Barnardo's officials, in comparison with which the Government reports appeared very superficial. 'The great importance of close inspection will be readily admitted when it is borne in mind that the scarcity of labour in Canada, whilst rendering it possible for suitable homes to be found for the children, is not unlikely to lead to the adoption of children for the make of the services they can render', commented the Report.[1]

Impressive though Barnardo's work undoubtedly was, it is nevertheless important to notice that, throughout the Report, attention was constantly drawn to the differential success of the emigration of destitute children and of pauper children. Although Barnardo was used as one of the agents for the emigration of pauper children, by far the majority of those whom he sent out were children from his own Homes. In 1894, the total number of children emigrated by Barnardo's organisation was 800, and the total number of children emigrated by the Poor Law authorities was 299. Against pauper children, the Canadians had an even worse prejudice than the English, and the stigma of their workhouse origin, clearly stamped on their immigration papers by order of the Canadian Government, who had stipulated that 'on no account are the two classes to be mixed', made the successful integration of such children very difficult indeed. Even so, the Committee remained convinced that the prospects for workhouse children were markedly better in Canada than they were in England, and they urged a much greater use of emi-

[1] *PP*, 1876, XLIII, p. 133.

gration on the part of the guardians, at the same time calling for a better system of supervision for the emigrants than had proved possible under the existing arrangements with the Canadian Department of Agriculture. They therefore recommended that inspectors should be appointed by the Local Government Board who would live in Canada, report back to the Reception Homes on the welfare of the children placed out from them, and back to London on the prospects for children in any district they visited. Further, they suggested that a new Central Metropolitan Poor Law Authority should be created for London, one of whose duties would be to arrange for the emigration of pauper children, all of whom were to have at least six months' industrial training before they were sent out. More stringent rules were to be followed in the placing of the children and the arrangements with the Canadian Government for the supervision of emigrants should be discontinued, since they had proved far from adequate.[1]

The main effect of these recommendations was felt in Canada. The Canadian authorities continued to inspect the children, but they used rather different methods. In 1895, a special inspector was appointed under the Department of the Interior who was charged with the general supervision of all British immigrant children and of the various Distributing Homes. In addition, the same Department inspected Poor Law children under a special arrangement with the Local Government Board. The children were visited annually, and a report on their condition was sent back to the Board in England. Although the Mundella Committee considered that the guardians had made insufficient use of their powers, by the turn of the century, 7,000 workhouse children had emigrated, mainly to Canada. In the years following, up to the outbreak of the First World War, 5,842 were sent to Canada alone:

Year	Number of children
1901	174
1902	141
1903	398
1904	374
1905	491
1906	441
1907	397

[1] ibid., p. 138.

Year	Number of children
1908	391
1909	422
1910	534
1911	617
1912	492
1913	568
1914	422

The Poor Law Commissioners, reporting in 1909, commended such emigration as a means of separating pauper children from degraded and undesirable relations who otherwise waited until the children were able to go out to work, or reached the age of eighteen and passed from the care of the Poor Law authorities, when they promptly reclaimed them, battening on them for support.

For such children, as well as for those who had no relatives to whose undesirable attentions they might have become prey, emigration continued to be, and remains after the Children Act of 1948, a form of protection afforded by statute. The attendant problems also remained: safeguards and precautions were liable to break down, as evidence to the 1909 Poor Law Commission all too clearly showed. Emigration of the children of the poor has thus never achieved anything like massive proportions, although between the World Wars a steady trickle of them went out to Canada and, increasingly, to Australia.

Schemes for the emigration of children did not always originate with English reformers. One conspicuous exception was the scheme launched in a smoke-filled room in Oxford one dark winter's night in 1909 by a young Rhodes scholar, Kingsley Fairbridge. He proposed not a Barnardo-type boarding out scheme; not scattered home farms like those pioneered in New Brunswick by Mrs Close; nor Colonial Orphanages, such as Sir Charles Kingsley-Cooke had advocated. Fairbridge wanted money to open and equip large farm schools in Canada and Australia, where the children would be housed in cottages, twelve to a cottage, and where there would be both a school for their formal education, and a farm for agricultural training, on the basis of which they would be eligible for regular employment in the major industry of these two countries.

Throughout the First World War, Fairbridge worked at his

scheme, arranging for the emigration of small parties of children, most of whom he escorted to the colonies himself. By the middle of the present century, 2,000 children had gone out to Australia and Canada under the auspices of the Fairbridge Society, the success of whose work is perhaps best testified to by the fact that, in the 1950s, the senior officer of the local authority which still used emigration to any extent, was himself once a field officer of one of the Fairbridge Farm Schools.

Generally speaking, however, the enthusiasm with which child emigration was pursued in the twentieth century was influenced by the changing balance of population in this country, which began to indicate that, instead of emigrating the healthiest and fittest children who were eligible, national policy required that other provision should be made to keep them in their home-country. Under the 1920 Adoption Act, such provision had already been made. Increasing sensitivity to the welfare of the children of even the poorest, together with a revision of public attitudes to the illegitimate, virtually guaranteed that, over the years, adoption would overtake emigration as an acceptable means of caring for 'unwanted' children.

XIX

◇◇

The Illegitimate Child

◇◇

So far, interest has been focused on social policy and practice with regard to children born in wedlock who, for good or ill, were regarded primarily as the responsibility of their lawfully wedded parents. The status and treatment of children born out of wedlock, the illegitimate, had always been and – despite considerable changes both in legislation and social attitudes – still remains, a subject of especial importance. Nowadays, it has been claimed, 'the mores of our society enable us to see children born out of wedlock as deprived of essential love and care, deprived of the normal pattern of family life.'[1] In so far as this is true it reflects very recent modifications in the attitudes to and treatment of large numbers of children who for long have been stigmatised in English society. Obviously attitudes had varied from one age to another and also from one social class to another. Nevertheless, the consistent and ruthlessly enforced policy of the state with regard to this group of children, as revealed in seventeenth- and eighteenth-century legislation, was largely the negative policy of resisting liability for their support. That, in effect, such legislation was only concerned with the illegitimate offspring of the poor does not dispose of, but emphasises, the precariousness of the lives of the children born out of wedlock to the impecunious and the unprivileged; to those who could not,

[1] F. Adler, *The attitude of Society towards the child as an index of its civilization*, 1907.

even if they would, offer 'a cloak of charity' to protect their natural children from the invidious status accorded by English society to its bastards.

To appreciate the real complexities associated with illegitimacy in England, it is important to distinguish between the legal status and the social status of the illegitimate. Under common law a bastard was defined as one conceived and born out of wedlock. Such children the parents had a duty to maintain, and this duty the justices were empowered to enforce wherever possible. Apart from this, the rights of the base born were few,[1]

> being only such as he can acquire, for he can *inherit* nothing, being looked upon as the son of nobody, and sometimes called *filius nullius*, sometimes *filius populi*. Yet he may gain a surname by reputation, though he has none by inheritance . . . The incapacity of a bastard consists principally in this, that he cannot be heir to anyone, neither can he have heirs, but of his own body; for being *nullius filius*, he is therefore kin to nobody, and has no ancestor from whom any inheritable blood can be derived.

Having stated this, however, Blackstone proceeds: 'And really any other distinction, but that of not inheriting, which civil policy renders necessary, would, with regard to the innocent offspring of his parents' crimes, be odious, unjust, and cruel to the last degree . . .' Even at the time he wrote (1758), amongst those very classes where Blackstone's sole distinction between the legitimate and the illegitimate was least relevant, however, civil policy, in the shape of the Poor Law, was intentionally operated in such a way as not only to humiliate the mother but to stigmatise the child. Legislation passed in the first decade of the nineteenth century which limited some of the penalties which might be imposed on the poor woman who gave birth to an illegitimate child did little or nothing to ameliorate the treatment of the mother in practice. Conspicuously attempts to protect the welfare of her child failed altogether.[2]

Whatever their status at law, the bastards of the poor were considered an affront to morality and an undesirable charge either on the rates or on the funds of the voluntary charities. Muller's Orphan Asylum, founded in Bristol in 1836, was for

---

[1] Blackstone, chapter 16, section 3, p. 459.
[2] Cf. vol. I, chapter VIII, pp. 220–1.

children 'lawfully begotten'; the Stockwell Orphanage was restricted to 'fatherless children'; and the London Orphan Asylum, Sir Josiah Mason's Orphanage at Erdington and St Wilfrid's Orphanage at Exeter all specifically excluded the illegitimate, even though such children constituted the largest single class of destitute children. The reason consistently and candidly given was that children begotten in sin would naturally inherit their parents' weakness, and hence they would surely contaminate the minds and morals of the lawfully begotten. Of this attitude, W. Clarke Hall was to write: 'There are few darker blots upon Christianity than the way in which illegitimate children have been sacrified in the name of religion and morality. However strict may be the moral code which it is desired to enforce, there can be neither sense, nor justice, nor policy in punishing the wholly innocent child.'[1] Earlier generations, however, worshipping both God and Mammon in a society in which wealth was exalted and its acquisition possible, found no difficulty in applying the sanctions of orthodox Christianity to the maintenance of what they conceived to be the necessary conditions of economic and social welfare. Illegitimacy was an offence against Christian morality and the institution of marriage; because of the cost which was laid upon the parish and public charity, it was an offence against the well-being of society. The combination of moral failing with lack of financial responsibility was thus a sin from which the righteous might properly recoil.

There is no doubt that concern regarding the rising costs of the Poor Law in the late eighteenth and early nineteenth centuries, due to a variety of causes, had led to particular emphasis being placed on the costs to the parish of maintaining illegitimate children, whose numbers were greatly increasing. Mary Hopkirk, in *Nobody Wanted Sam*, quotes the parish registers of Letheringham, Suffolk.[1] From 1588 to 1600 there were no extra-matrimonial births recorded. From 1600 to 1650 there was one in every 144 registered births. From 1650 to 1700 there was one in 74; from 1700 to 1750 one in 33, and from 1750 to 1800 one in 21. Other studies, notably those of Ashby,

[1] W. Clarke Hall, *The State and the Child*, p. 132.
[2] M. Hopkirk, *Nobody Wanted Sam*, p. 83.

Hampson and Tate, show that the experience of Letheringham was far from unique.[1]

Both Ashby and Hampson ascribe the eighteenth-century increase to a deterioration in economic conditions, but the explanation is a good deal more complicated than this, as Jean Heywood points out:[2]

> The familiar pattern of community life was torn across, the old life of the agricultural pattern changed; in the new towns the social and moral controls of the small intimate parish were absent; in the village it was not so easy for irregular sexual relationships to be followed by marriage. Eden, in his contemporary account of the state of the poor, held that the Settlement Act of 1662 actually promoted illegitimacy, since parish officers often attempted to remove to their last place of settlement young men about to marry, on the ground that their family might become chargeable to the parish. The eighteenth century was a cockpit of social evolution at home and wars abroad, and in such time of unrest, when many people were implicated in political risings, when gaoling and transportation were common punishments, and troops moved about the country to keep the peace or defend the coast many girls lost touch with the fathers before the child was born.

Thus some measure of contemporary responsibility for this increase in illegitimate births must be borne by the troops, regular soldiers, militia men and German mercenaries, who were marched from camp to camp with the inevitable consequences. The Army authorities disclaimed all responsibility for the financial burdens imposed on the villagers in the form of babies. Contemporary Essex workhouse records reveal the presence of many descendants of soldiers brought from other parts of England to defend the east coast. Unable to trace the father or to extract money from him, the village overseer regarded these 'fruits of war' with extreme disapprobation – particularly when he was reluctantly obliged to mark the termination of his enquiries into their paternal origin with the words 'Paid nothing. Ran away'.

Not all fathers were able to abrogate their financial respon-

---

[1] Cf. A. W. Ashby, *One Hundred Years of Poor Law Administration in a Warwickshire Village*, 1912. E. M. Hampson, *The Treatment of Poverty in Cambridgeshire, 1597–1834*, 1934. W. E. Tate, *The Parish Chest. A study of the records of parochial administration in England*, 1946.

[2] *Children in Care*, p. 15.

sibilities so simply. By the law of 1733 the oath of the expectant mother of a bastard child was sufficient to have the putative father arrested on a justices' warrant and committed to prison unless he was able to give some security against his appearance at the next Quarter Sessions, there to enter into a bond to support his illegitimate offspring. In anticipation of repayment, the justices were inclined to order more generous sums to be paid from parish funds for the maintenance of illegitimate children than for legitimate. In Totnes, 1s. 6d. was paid for legitimate and 2s. 6d. for illegitimate children; in Croydon, the widowed mother of a legitimate child was allowed 2s., the unmarried mother of a bastard child, 3s.

Already agitated at the rising costs of poor relief, it is not surprising that local overseers should seek to reduce them with regard to the maintenance of the illegitimate child by attempting to force the putative father to marry the self-declared mother of his child, thus hoping to relieve the parish of the maintenance of the woman and her child. Charles Lacey, Rector of Tring, protested against this kind of compulsory marriage,[1]

> so frequently had recourse to by parish officers to get rid of the chargeability of the female. I have repeatedly known instances of men being apprehended under a bastardy warrant, carried off immediately to a surrogate for a licence, and brought to Church all the same morning, to be married. I have seen the handcuffs removed from the man at the Church door as I approached, and then, with the constable and overseer, as witness to the marriage, I have been compelled in the discharge of my ministerial duty, to pronounce over such a person the words of a Service, which breathes nothing but the spirit of free and sanctified affection . . .

Such marriages were not achieved without some cost to the parish, but although it was claimed that 'not one half of the money paid by the parish to the mothers of bastards is recovered from the putative fathers, and that the portion so recovered is generally recovered at an enormous expense', there is little doubt that the overseers thought such monies well spent; hence the large numbers of entries in parish accounts recording the sums involved. The accounts of the village of Danbury, Essex, for 1832 record two typical entries:[2]

[1] Hopkirk, op. cit., p. 98.
[2] ibid., pp. 97–8.

To the Woodham Constable (the neighbouring parish) for appre-
hending Christopher Appleton: £1 15s. 0d.
Certificate of banns, Christopher Appleton and Elizabeth Smith:
2s. 6d.
Appleton, for marriage portion with Elizabeth Smith: £1.
Marriage fees, ring etc. £1 12s. 0d.

Later in the same year is recorded:

William Collins, marriage portion with Maria Miller, 10s.
Maria Miller's child, 2s. 6d.
Expenses, attending the marriage of Maria Miller, £1 10s. 0d.

Reviewing the operation of the existing Poor Laws as they
related to bastardy, the Poor Law Commissioners of 1832
roundly condemned both forced marriages and the system which
promoted them. They claimed that the early and unsuitable
marriages of young men, lured into marriage by unscrupulous
women who accused them, rightly or wrongly, of fathering their
child could only contribute to the general disadvantage of the
country. Yet such was the inevitable consequence of existing
legislation under which a man so named, unable to pay surety
and unwilling to go to prison, was obliged to marry a mother as
his only remaining 'choice'. A 'choice', as the Commissioners
shrewdly pointed out, which was the more likely to be forced
upon him were he to come from another parish. The Commissioners also made some astringent comments on the higher payments made in some areas for illegitimate as compared with
those made for the legitimate, and on the amounts of money,
expended to secure the removal of pregnant mothers to the
place of their original settlement. By so doing, the overseers
hoped to indemnify the parish not merely from the immediate
expenses connected with the birth of an illegitimate child in their
workhouse but also the long-term liabilities the parish would
have incurred by the child gaining settlement by birth in the
parish.

Summarising their findings on the operation of the Poor Laws
as they affected the illegitimate they wrote:[1]

With respect to the Bastardy laws, the evidence shows that, as a
general rule, they increase the expense which they were intended to
compensate, and offer temptations to the crime which they were

[1] *PP*, 1834, XXXVI, p. 346.

intended to punish, and that their working is frequently accompanied by perjury and extortion, disgrace to the innocent, reward to the shameless and unprincipled, and all the domestic misery and vice which are necessary consequence of premature and ill-assorted marriage. We advise, therefore, their entire abolition.

What we propose in their room is intended to restore things, as far as it is possible, to the state in which they would have been if no such laws had ever existed, and trust to those checks, and to those checks only, which Providence has imposed on licentiousness, under the conviction that all attempts of the legislature to increase their force, or to substitute for them artificial sanctions have tended only to weaken or protect them.

The recommendations which stemmed from this *laissez-faire* philosophy were three in number:

(a) all illegitimate children born after the passing of the Act were to have the settlement of their mother until the age of sixteen or such earlier age as they might gain settlement in their own right;

(b) the mother of an illegitimate child was to be placed on the same footing as a widow in need of relief. Both were under an obligation to try to earn enough to feed and support their children, and only if proved unable to do so, was the mother of an illegitimate child to receive support from the local poor rates;

(c) the mother of an illegitimate child was no longer to be removable from a parish, and no penal sanctions were to be imposed in future on either the father or the mother.

When the Bill incorporating these, as well as the many other proposals for reforming the Poor Laws of England, was presented to Parliament in 1834, however, the idea that the mother alone (or her parents or grandparents, were she unable) should be responsible for the maintenance of her child was vigorously attacked by arguments which might themselves be described as *laissez-faire* in character. Mr Hardy, from his experience at Quarter Sessions, thought it would be wrong to relieve the father of all responsibility, as at present proposed, 'for the father was, at all events in cases of a first child, the criminal and not the woman'.[1] Mr Robinson claimed that the proposal could only have come 'from persons out of touch with the real situation. It would not stop the career of licentious men to inform them that

[1] Hansard, 3rd series, vol. XXIV, col. 536.

they might commit seduction with impunity, and that they might gratify their inclinations at the sole expense of the softer sex.'[1] He further observed that to release the father from his paternal obligations would merely serve to emphasise and possibly increase those of the parish, instead of decreasing them as the Bill purported to do. This theme was taken up by others, and resulted in a clause being inserted in the Act whereby the interests of the local ratepayers were to be protected by giving the guardians, but not the mother, the power to apply to Quarter Sessions for a maintenance order against the putative father of any bastard child under the age of seven who had become chargeable on the rates through the inability of the mother to support it herself. If the order was granted, the guardians could proceed against the father were he to fall into arrears by 'distress' of his goods and chattels, or by 'attaching' his wages.

Appeal to Quarter Sessions, however, was not merely costly but made difficult by the stipulation that no order was to be made 'unless the Evidence of the Mother of such bastard child shall be corroborated in some material particular by other Testimony to the satisfaction of such Court.' In some areas, Poor Law guardians of the new unions thus made little use of their undoubted powers, and the child, and sometimes his mother also, were grudgingly maintained in the workhouses, out-relief allowances for their support having ceased under the new Act. At law the unmarried mother was thus faced with the alternatives of struggling to support her child unaided or, finding herself unequal to the task, relinquishing it to the care of the workhouse. For many the latter was the only practicable solution. Never an easy task for a husbandless woman, the burden of supporting her child was increased for the unmarried mother by the weight of public censure against the conduct which had led to her predicament. It is important to remember that the Poor Law Commissioners were not only sensible of this censure, but were frankly anxious to exploit and increase it for their own purposes. 'We trust that as soon as it has become both burdensome and disgraceful, it will soon become as rare as it is among those classes in this country who are above parish relief, or as it is among all classes in Ireland.'[2] It is interesting to

[1] ibid., col. 541.
[2] *PP*, 1834, XXXVI, p. 351.

reflect that, even as the Commissioners wrote, there was at least one very illustrious exception to this dogma, namely the King's Most Excellent Majesty, who had his nine illegitimate children all living happily *en famille* with him and the Queen at Windsor.[1] The domestic life of the English monarchy had yet to emerge as the pattern for a social ideal of sexual expression restricted to the matrimonial bedroom. For this English society had to await the accession and marriage of a noble Queen to a still nobler Albert. On the other hand, it is quite clear from the tone of some contributions to the debates of the Poor Law Reform Bill in the House of Commons that among less exalted circles, such a social ideal was already thought important and failure among the poor to achieve it deemed worthy of punishment *pour encourager les autres*. Thus Mr Edward Buller believed that though 'the present mode of punishment had little or no effect on the lower classes, it had a considerable effect on the middling classes, and the class just above the lowest, which class was most important as regards the morality of the country at large.'[2]

How far the morality of the richer sections of society could be effectively safeguarded by legislation against promiscuity among the poor was, *pace* Mr Buller, at least debatable. What is significant about this and other comments, both in the Commons and in the Lords, on contemporary sexual morality is the recurring insistence that extra-marital sex was to be condemned and in some way or other should be punished. That the Bill should propose that the woman alone should pay the price of wrongdoing was thought to be unfortunate, even undesirable, but necessary in so far as her guilt at least was evident, and since attempts to operate sanctions against the father had debased the sacrament of marriage, proved ineffective and, worse, expensive. That Parliament should agree to abolish the old, statutory punishments of whipping through the streets at the cart's tail and committing to the House of Correction, might be said to indicate a more humane attitude to the unmarried mother. The more cynical might argue, with some justice, that on the one hand the abolition of the old punishments only underlines the greater importance attached to economic sanctions in an increasingly affluent society, and, on the other, that the strength

---

[1] Hopkirk, op. cit., p. 105.
[2] Hansard, 3rd series, vol. XXIV, col. 528.

of social ostracism as an equally if not more effective, and certainly less expensive, means of enforcing social discipline had been fully appreciated.

As to the truth of this last, the pages of Victorian novels were to prove an eloquent testimony. Written both to entertain and to improve the minds of the thousands of women of the 'middling classes', the treatment of the unmarried mother and her child, where it occurred at all, was brief and condemnatory. In general, the fate of the unmarried mother was shown in their pages to be the workhouse, emigration – or death. When Mrs Gaskell, in *Ruth*, attempted a more sympathetic approach, blaming society itself as the real 'criminal', the novel met with the most hostile criticism purely on this score, and mothers were warned that her book was unfit reading for their daughters – a criticism Mrs Gaskell herself did nothing to challenge by declining to allow her own daughters to read it. Such a climate of opinion amongst those most likely to be their employers, made the prospects of an unmarried mother being able to support her illegitimate child extremely doubtful. If in domestic service, she would almost certainly be dismissed at once; if employed elsewhere, everything would depend on how reliable a worker she remained, both before and after the birth of her child, and the attitude of her employer, if and when he discovered her condition. In these circumstances, to lay the responsibility of supporting her child solely on the mother was to lay a very heavy burden on her indeed.

Not until 1844 was the mother herself empowered to apply to the justices of Petty Sessions in her own right for a maintenance order against the putative father of her child.[1] Such an order could allow her £1 a week towards its maintenance for the first six weeks after birth and 2s. 6d. a week thereafter until the child was thirteen years of age. The order could be enforced by the court by 'distress' or commitment to prison. But it could only be granted, as had been the case in proceedings brought by the guardians, if the mother herself was able to bring corroborative evidence of the child's paternity. Moreover, the power to apply to the justices now granted to the mother was by the same Act withdrawn from the guardians. Not merely were the guardians prohibited from taking action themselves but they could in fact

[1] 7 & 8 Vict., c. 101. An Act for the Further Amendment of the Laws relating to the Poor in England.

be fined 40s. for interfering in any way in the obtainment of such an order. One guardian was to protest that they could be fined 'merely for recommending that these young persons should seek out their seducers'. This was indeed the case, and may at first sight seem unreasonable until one recognises that the children with whom this Act was immediately concerned were not, at least at the time of the application for a maintenance order, necessarily a charge on the rates.

One of the clear intentions of the 1834 Act had been to de-limit the responsibilities of the Poor Law and its local officers who, in the north of England for example, had involved them-selves not merely in safeguarding the interests of their parish but in protecting the interests of deserted mothers, not all of whom were paupers. In evidence to the Committee which reported to Parliament in 1838 on the operation of the Act passed four years previously, the Assistant Poor Law Commis-sioner for Lancashire and the West Riding described such activities 'as a system not of administering relief, but of pro-moting redress for the woman under the grievance sustained . . . and not as an indemnity to the parish, for a number of these cases were brought before the parish which were not cases of destitution, the parish being applied to by the woman to set her right as regards the contribution on the part of the man to the maintenance of the child'.[1] The Committee, like the Poor Law Commissioners before them, took the view that it was in principle desirable 'that relief to the poor should be mixed up as little as possible with matters which seem to be more properly and directly concerned with the administration of justice; and that relief to the mothers of bastard children, and to the children themselves, should be granted or refused on con-sideration arising out of their necessities, and not on any other grounds, or with a view to other objects . . .'. They therefore argued for some statutory provision, such as was in fact made by the 1844 Act, whereby a woman could herself make an appeal 'to some easily accessible and inexpensive tribunal . . . for redress in cases of seduction or of breach of promise of marriage. This would be free from some of the objections to which all parochial interference in these questions is liable.'[2] One parti-

[1] ibid., p. 34.
[2] *PP*, 1838, XVIII pt I, p. 362.

cular objection to parochial interference, that it could and did lead to forced marriages, had been raised time and again in discussion of the old bastardy laws. Under the 1844 Act a Poor Law officer who procured a forced marriage of a mother of a bastard child was guilty of a misdemeanour, and could be punished. Only if, after the mother died, or remarried, the child became chargeable on the rates through the default on an order made against him by the magistrates, could the Poor Law guardians now intervene and themselves apply to the justices for the enforcement of the order. In these circumstances, the payments were then to be made to the approved guardians of the child, on the condition that he would then cease to receive support from the parish or union.

Not surprisingly this drastic curtailment of their power to institute proceedings provoked protests from the guardians who regarded themselves and the ratepayers as the main sufferers of a system which imposed on the unmarried mother the sole financial responsibility for maintaining her child and the sole legal right to attempt to obtain some contribution from its father. Poor, friendless, often illiterate, many mothers were reluctant to institute proceedings, and were frequently unable to produce adequate corroborative evidence if they did. Nobody could force a woman to take action; if she failed to do so and could not support the child herself, its support inevitably fell on the parish. Not all the protests were motivated merely by the self-interest of those on whom the cost fell. Many people had disliked the idea that the father should be allowed to get away 'scot-free', and despite the view that the administration of the Poor Law should be distinct and disentangled from the adminis- tration of justice, some guardians still felt that they ought to be allowed the power to assist those who could not easily help themselves 'because we have seen some of the cases where the hardships they have gone through have been so apparent that, if we had had the power to do so, we should have gone to any expense to prosecute the men'.[1]

The Poor Law Amendment Act of 1868[2] eventually restored the guardians' powers of instituting proceedings against the

---

[1] Second Report of the Select Committee on Poor Relief, *PP*, 1861, IX, p. 53. Evidence of Mr H. Potter of St James's Westminster Board of Guardians.
[2] 31 & 32 Vict., c. 19.

putative father at Petty Sessions, although the law still required corroborative evidence to be given in person by the mother, thus leaving the onus of proof with her, and, in the event of her death before the action was brought, making it impossible for the guardians to proceed at all.

Four years later, in 1872, the Bastardy Laws Amendment Act[1] consolidated previous legislation with respect to the custody and maintenance of the illegitimate child, and remained the 'Principal Act', with only minor amendments, up to and beyond the Children Act of 1948. The Act provided that a 'single' woman might apply for a maintenance order in respect of her illegitimate child; it allowed the guardians the powers already granted to them under the 1868 Act to institute proceedings themselves. It also retained the principle of corroboration (an unusual legal requirement in civil proceedings) with the result that, if no corroborative witness was forthcoming, a case had to be dismissed without the putative father being heard. Yet in many cases without his evidence the full facts could never be known. Strict limits were still imposed on the orders which could be made. At first the courts were unable to make an order for more than 5s. a week, a limit subsequently raised to 10s., and, by 1948, to £1 – sums which indicate not merely a continuing interest in protecting the local rates but also the fact that, far into the twentieth century, illegitimate children who were not likely to become a burden on the rates, because of the more fortunate financial circumstances of their parents, did not receive the attention of Parliament, and hence might be the victims of considerable financial injustice. All orders were to cease when the child was thirteen years of age – although the courts in certain cases had powers to make orders effective until the child was sixteen.

One may well ask, however, whether in practice the 1872 Act, any more than the Acts it consolidated, effectively protected the interests of those with whom it was principally concerned. When introducing the original Bill in the House of Commons, Mr Charley, who had also introduced the Infant Life Protection Bill two months previously, quoted the evidence of a Mrs Main, who ran a home for deserted mothers and children. In the 1,000 cases she had dealt with only 3 per cent of the women had

[1] 35 & 36 Vict., c. 65.

7. A girl street-vendor of a hundred years ago

8. Board-school children
playing 'Nuts in May', 1903

been able to obtain anything from the fathers. Seventeen years later the Kensington guardians reported almost exactly the same level of success with regard to proceedings they had instituted.[1] In both cases the principal obstacle had been the same: the lack of corroborative evidence. Recognising the fact that only a very small proportion of women legally entitled to seek the protection of the courts actually did so (some years after the Act became operative, the proportion was calculated to be not more than one woman in ten) the irrelevance of such legislation to the lives of both mother and child becomes all too apparent.

Earlier it was shown that, at law, the only alternative solution for an unmarried mother unable to support her child herself was to allow it to be supported from the rates, which in effect meant the child entering the workhouse, the hated 'Bastilles' of the reformed Poor Law. It is a fact that by far the largest single category of children in the workhouses in the nineteenth century was illegitimate. It is also a fact that other women, the number of whom it is impossible to calculate accurately, took other steps to relieve themselves of what, both for social and economic reasons, proved for them to be an insupportable burden. For many years, it had been known that the prevailing infant death-rate, that is to say the death-rate of children under one year of age, was considerably higher among illegitimate children than among legitimate. Equally, it had long been known that among the several explanations of this, infanticide and desertion were to be numbered.

During the Napoleonic wars the newspapers were filled with reports of abandoned innocents. For example, in 1806, Catherine Hardy, a young woman nineteen years of age, was charged at Marlborough Street by the parish officers of St Giles with placing her infant daughter in the street a few hours after dark. At the trial Sarah Hempstead deposed that, when returning home between the hours of eleven and twelve o'clock she heard the cries of a child, and discovered a newly-born infant lying in the middle of the street, quite naked, 'and in such a situation that a vehicle could not have passed without going over it'. On the same day 'as a person was passing through some fields near Grindleford Bridge, he found a child only a few weeks old, laid in a box stating that its name was Mary Ann Wakefield and that

---

[1] Cf. Report of the 1889 Poor Law Conference, p. 292.

it would be called for in a year from the time when it had been left . . .'.[1] Both these illustrations are taken from London where, in the previous century, Coram had been so disturbed by the numbers of children left exposed on the street, often to die there, that he had raised the money to open the Foundling Hospital into whose charitable care scores of abandoned illegitimate children were accepted. But neither the Foundling Hospital nor the other similar charitable institutions established for the same purpose in London and elsewhere were capable of admitting the numberless children left to their fate in the streets and alleys, in the lanes and the hedgerows.

In all too many cases the distinction between desertion and destruction was narrowly drawn; even the most distracted mother must have been aware of the hazard to her child's life when left in the middle of the highway. Other cases which attracted widespread attention in the contemporary press show that some unmarried mothers knowingly and deliberately destroyed the issue of their illicit unions. In March 1810 'an inquest was taken at Salperton on the body of a newly-born male infant found in the Thames and Severn Canal where its mother Jane Jones had placed it . . . The Jury returned a verdict of wilful murder.' In August, 'Betty Amplett, convicted at Gloucester Assizes on the preceding Friday for the wilful murder of her bastard child, was executed in front of the County Goal, and her body delivered for dissection. She conducted herself with dignity and decorum, acknowledging the justice of the sentence.'[2] From the security of the twentieth century, it is possible to wonder at a society which could report such events with such composure.

It was a composure far from being undisturbed, however. Charitable enterprise outside Parliament and expression of opinion within it show that at least a minority were considerably perturbed by the evidence of the deliberate destruction of the lives of illegitimate children whose mothers would not or could not for shame support them. Constantly, in the 1834 debates on the proposal to make the mother solely responsible for the maintenance of her illegitimate child, the fear was expressed that the consequence would be to increase the rate of infanticide,

[1] Hopkirk, op. cit., p. 86.
[2] ibid., p. 87.

an offence which was 'already too rife among us'. One Member went so far as to urge that: 'if they believed that a single child would be put to death in consequence of the passing of that law, they should not pass it'.[1] Nevertheless the law was passed and the predicted consequences did follow. Speaking in the debates on the 1872 Act, Mr Henley argued that 'the present bastardy laws have very much to do with the fearful increase in infanticide . . . since the enactment of the existing law . . . though the births of illegitimate children had decreased the crime of infanticide had increased in far greater proportion.'[2] It was an argument which Sir John Simon's reports to the Medical Committee of the Privy Council, the revelations of the Registrar General, and the evidence collected in support of the Infant Life Protection Bill, very fully corroborated.

The Infant Life Protection Bill itself was primarily concerned to protect the lives of children fostered out or placed in baby-farms. Prominent amongst those so 'cared' for were illegitimate children whose mothers, with deliberate knowledge, would pay the baby-farmer a lump sum totally inadequate for the child's long-term maintenance, with the result that it very soon languished and died through starvation and general neglect. Even after the Bill was enacted in 1872, its requirements that baby-farmers be registered and licensed by the local authority, and that the death of infants had to be reported and a doctor's certificate produced, otherwise an inquest must follow automatically, were widely evaded. In 1896 a Mrs Dyer of Reading was caught disposing of babies entrusted to her care by strangling them and throwing them into the Thames. She was found guilty and executed, and figured in the ditty: *Mrs. Dyer the Baby Farmer*, with its refrain:

> The old baby farmer 'as been executed,
> It's quite time she was put out of the way,
> She was a bad woman, it isn't disputed,
> Not a word in her favour can anyone say.

As has been seen, subsequent modifications of the law had given the unmarried mother the undoubted right to petition the courts for an affiliation order. Even in the minority of cases

---

[1] Hansard, 3rd series, vol. XXIV, col. 530.
[2] Hansard, 3rd series, vol. CCLXXV, col. 1486.

where that right had been exercised – and the even smaller minority where the petition had been successful – the amounts granted had been made subject to strict controls imposed by Parliament. In the debates on the introduction of the Bastardy Laws Amendment Act, 1872, it was represented that these limitations were themselves a cause of infanticide. Thus Mr Charley[1] explained that

> the chief object of the Bill was to enlarge the discretion of the magistrates with regard to the granting of bastardy orders . . . 2s. 6d. had been shown by medical witnesses to be quite insufficient to keep a child alive . . . The mother had this alternative placed before her – either to maintain her child or to destroy it, for otherwise she could not possibly go to service. She could not maintain her child, and so she destroyed it.

From time to time prosecutions reported in the national press of our own day startle the public into the awareness that the deliberate destruction of the lives of illegitimate children has not been entirely eliminated from English society, even though the earlier socio-economic pressures which lay at the root of nineteenth-century infanticide have been radically reduced over the intervening years. The sensationalism attached to these reports, however, is itself an indication of the fact, easily validated from more reliable sources, that infanticide has long ceased to be a significant factor in infant mortality in this country, especially infant mortality among the illegitimate. Nevertheless, infant mortality among this particular group of children still requires special explanation since it continues to compare very unfavourably with mortality among the legitimate. In 1948, the year of the Children Act, 42 children died out of every 1,000 legitimately born. Amongst the illegitimate, 60 children died in every 1,000 born. Thirty years earlier, in 1918, the comparable figures had been 91 and 186, a disparity which was then explained, as later disparities were to be explained, as being largely due to the fact that illegitimate children had to be artificially fed 'almost from birth' because of the difficulties experienced by their mothers in making a home and keeping their children with them. Of recent years the quality of baby foods has vastly improved and the difficulties of an unmarried

[1] ibid., col. 1494.

mother in making a home for herself and her child have been in some ways reduced. The continuing disparity between the infant death-rates of the legitimate and the illegitimate still indicate how much more difficult it is for a woman to rear a child single handed.

Even had the physical difficulties of child-rearing been more speedily and effectively remedied, the illegitimate child would still have laboured under a formidable burden of social disadvantage. The doctrine of *filius nullius* continued to be upheld throughout the nineteenth century. The Births and Deaths Registration Act, 1874, permitted, but did not require, the registration of an illegitimate child in the name of his father, provided the father's consent had first been obtained. It requires no particular effort of the imagination to understand why the Act was so little used. In 1893 a Bill was introduced in the House of Commons 'to alter and amend the Law by Legitimating Children born before Marriage on the subsequent Marriage of their Parents', thus assimilating the law of England to that of Scotland where this inducement to marriage had long existed. The Bill was dropped, however, without a second reading.

By the beginning of the present century, the accumulating medical evidence of the disastrous consequences of being born, and of remaining, illegitimate in English society prompted renewed attempts to make legitimation possible. One Member of Parliament, Joseph King, introduced a Bill to this effect each session after his election. The correspondence and communications he received 'from all sorts and conditions of men and women', due to press notices of his Bills, indicated very clearly that outside Parliament there was a body of public opinion sensitive to the plight of the illegitimate and sympathetic to the introduction of legislative reform with reference to them. Equally clearly, general public opinion was neither sufficiently formed nor informed on the matter for King to believe that Parliament would accept such legislation unless the Government itself took it up. This it was hardly likely to do until the Home Secretary was made aware that he could not safely disregard the demand for it. In his pamphlet *Filius Nullius*, published in 1913, King therefore urged all those anxious for legislation to write to their M.P. Very interestingly, he also suggested that boards of guardians, many of whom by now had special ladies committees to deal with the peculiar problems relating to the unmarried mother and her child, should pass resolutions to the effect that 'the laws affecting illegitimates are the cause of numerous injustices, and ought to be amended by a Government measure' and send these resolutions to the Local Government Board.

Although King's efforts proved of no avail, they indicate how attitudes were changing on the subject of illegitimacy. In 1917, W. Clarke Hall's *The State and the Child* contained similar indications:[1]

> The cruel doctrine that an illegitimate child is *filius nullius* – a doctrine invented by men to shield them from the consequences of their misdeeds – is still the law of the land. The obvious natural law that every child born into the world has a right to fatherhood, as well as to motherhood, has not yet been recognised. If, in the nature of things, it is impossible, in practice, to insist upon this right, has not the State a very special duty towards one who is 'the child of no father'?

In answer to his own question, Clarke Hall suggested that there were two alternatives and one possible compromise.[2]

> Either the State must itself take over the care of these children or it must enforce on *all* those who are responsible for the lives of such children the duty of properly caring for them. The former alternative is Socialism in its must advanced form, and would destroy all individual responsibility for parenthood; the latter would be difficult, if not impossible, to enforce in practice.

With 'great diffidence and after much careful thought', Clarke Hall thus suggested a policy of compromise.

First, he proposed that the registration of an illegitimate child in the name of its father, only permissible under the 1874 Act, should now be made obligatory, subject to certain safeguards for the alleged father. Second, he argued that the courts should be enabled to grant right of access to the father.

> The existing law discourages in every way all interest by the putative father in his child. It gives him no authority over the child and refuses him all right to see it. All he is asked or permitted to do is to pay money, for the spending of which no account is given to

---

[1] p. 133.
[2] ibid., p. 134.

him. His child may be starved or neglected or ill-treated, but he has no right to interfere. It may be dying, but he must not see it. Much is said of the injustice of the law to the mother, but to the father whose natural instincts of parenthood are not dead it is also unjust.

Third and last, Clarke Hall suggested that all illegitimate children should become the wards of the Court of Summary Jurisdiction in whose area they resided.[1]

> What is required is not merely control over the money (i.e. the affiliation order) but a control over the child, such as the Courts of Chancery exercise over their own wards. The cost of such control would involve comparatively little cost, while it would effectively protect illegitimate children from starvation, ill-treatment and neglect to which they are now so often subjected.

By 1917 far more radical proposals regarding the rights of the illegitimate child, giving equal rights with the legitimate, had been made and accepted in Norway where, as in so many other countries, the law had long been modified in their favour. In England, a country deeply involved in a war the costs of which, both in men and money, had already far exceeded expectations, Clarke Hall's own proposal passed virtually unnoticed by a distracted legislature.

The unsettled conditions of war were themselves to be reflected in an increased illegitimate birth-rate. In 1916 the Registrar-General drew public attention to the increasing number of such children born and to the increasing proportion of them who died – over 200 in every 1,000 live births, more than double the number of deaths among children born in wedlock. A large number of these deaths happened a few days or weeks after the child's birth, and indicated society's lack of concern for the child born out of wedlock, and its condemnation of, and failure to care for, the mother.

Shocked by this rejection of the unmarried mother, which was reflected in so scandalous a mortality among illegitimate children, a group of prominent and socially responsible women and men, under the leadership of Mrs Lettice Fisher, wife of the distinguished historian, founded on Valentine's Day 1918, the National Council for the Unmarried Mother and her Child. The founders were attached to no particular religion, ethical

[1] ibid., pp. 137–8 passim.

view or political persuasion. The Council's strength lay in the fact that it drew on the support not only of the religious organisations, but of people of no particular creed. It worked closely with, and won the strong support it still has, of the ministers and local authorities concerned with the problem of the unmarried mother and her child. Over more than half a century, the Council has laboured, both at the local and the national level, to produce a more sympathetic social attitude to a group of women and children towards whom little compassion had been shown. It was the chief agency of attempts to promote legislation to protect the unmarried mother in a society only recently made aware of the need to secure the rights of her married sisters. To the unmarried mothers themselves, they gave advice, comfort and support, helping them in the early years when it was thought best that, wherever possible, mother and child should be kept together, to find suitable work and lodgings and later, when adoption had become an accepted practice, assisting those who wished to arrange for an adoption of their offspring.

From the first the Council believed that the best way of helping the child was to help the mother, because their welfare was indivisible. One of their first actions was to sponsor a Bill to include the provision that money granted under affiliation orders should be 'in proportion to the circumstances of both parents', an aim not in fact achieved until 1968, the year of the Council's Golden Jubilee. But they also took an active part in initiating and supporting attempts to provide legal protection for the child itself, for example by providing a means whereby such a child could be legitimated and also legislation to give all children parity under the law.

A Bill providing for the legitimation of children was introduced in Parliament in 1923, but shelved at the Committee stage. The following year a second Bill was introduced in the Lords which, like its predecessor, proposed the legitimation of children by the subsequent marriage of their parents. It also included a highly controversial new clause, proposing that the illegitimate offspring of adulterous unions might subsequently be legitimated by their parents' marriage. Introducing the Bill, Lord Buckmaster argued in its support that such far-reaching legislation was necessary to remove the stigma from every illegitimate child, 'who suffers for wrongdoing for which he is in no way responsible'. Majority opinion was against him however. The new clause was vigorously attacked in the interests of maintaining domestic happiness; on such practical grounds as the problem of deciding whether the illegitimate child of an adulterous union should, on legitimation, take priority over the eldest born child of the first marriage; and on the ground that it was not allowed 'in any other civilised country, or in the Colonies, except Southern Australia'. Above all, the clause was attacked as being certain to weaken the 'backbone' of society, marriage and the family, since it must encourage adultery and divorce.

Though Parliament rejected this particular clause, debate on the rest of the Bill revealed that the principle of legitimation had powerful supporters, among them Archbishop Davidson. Unencumbered now by the proposal that, however indirectly, adultery should be connived at or condoned, the amended Bill went forward to receive the Royal Assent in 1926 as the Legitimacy Act: an Act to amend the law relating to children born out of wedlock.[1] Under English law, unless either parent was married to a third party at the time of birth, illegitimate children could now be legitimated by the subsequent marriage of their parents, and were granted rights of inheritance similar to those actually born in wedlock save for the proviso that they might not inherit titles or estates attached to titles. The bastard at long last need not always be a bastard; a child with no name, no parents, no kin, and no right of inheritance.

Immensely important as the Legitimacy Act was, it was only relevant in cases where the natural parents were anxious to provide a normal family background for a child or for children born to them. A solution to the problem of providing such a background for the illegitimate child whose natural parents were either unable or unwilling to do so was offered in the Adoption Act[2] passed by Parliament in the same year.

The unwanted child had for generations been a familiar figure to local overseers and philanthropists. Most were illegitimate, born to both rich and poor parents, but many were the legitimate children of the poor, who were either unable to support them on account of poverty or the death of the breadwinner, or because

[1] 16 & 17 Geo. V, c. 60.
[2] 16 & 17 Geo. V, c. 29.

of the shifting habits of their lives, or, quite simply, because they did not choose to accept the responsibility of parenthood. Some such children were taken in by relatives or friends – not always with very happy results. Legal adoption, however, was impossible. At common law the transfer of parental rights and liabilities was unknown and the father's rights over his children were regarded as so sacred that, until 1866, the courts regarded any voluntary relinquishment of them, for example in a deed of separation, as void. Inevitably this attitude to parental rights expressed itself in a very strong reluctance to proceed to legal adoption, which recognises the relinquishment of parental powers and responsibilities. So strong, in fact, that by the nineteen-twenties Britain was the only English speaking country and one of the few western countries without adoption laws.

The historical background of the acceptance of the principle of legal adoption in this country in 1926 was very much that of the acceptance of the principle of legitimation in the same year. William Farr's statistical analysis of infant death-rates, which had drawn especial attention to the differential mortality of the illegitimate had also revealed the appalling consequences of the unregulated traffic in unwanted children in general. The evidence of the Select Committee on the Protection of Infant Life, appointed in 1871, with its vivid descriptions of the lives and deaths of unwanted children, both legitimate and illegitimate, placed out with baby-farmers, underlined Farr's own findings and so powerfully operated on public and Parliamentary opinion as to produce the improvement of the Bastardy Laws in 1872 and the Child Life Protection Act of the following year. Both these Acts were symptomatic of an increasing sensitivity to the needs of the unwanted child and a heightened awareness that the state had more positive responsibilities to such children than previous generations had been willing to concede. The operation of the Acts was itself to increase this sensitivity and awareness. The social consequences of the First World War were to make further legislation well-nigh inevitable. The publicity given to the unhappy lot of war orphans on the one hand and of unwanted 'war babies' on the other prompted an increased concern regarding the dangers of unregulated, *de facto* adoptions and to demands for the institution of legal adoption as practised in other countries. From 1919 onwards a number of private and charitable adoption societies had been established in an endeavour to provide satisfactory homes for unwanted children. All of them had been inundated with applications for children from those who had lost sons in the war; and from unmarried mothers who were anxious to part with their children. Their experience made the societies increasingly aware of the dangers and drawbacks of unorganised adoption, and the desirability of some form of public control. Hence, in 1920, the first Conference of Associated Societies for the Care and Maintenance of Infants was convened to discuss common problems and to attempt to form a common mind on their solution. In the event, discussion revealed highly divergent opinions on particular aspects of adoption, but a general conviction that it was the responsibility of the Societies to inform and guide public opinion on the complex problem associated with it.

The Conference's deliberations reveal the problems then envisaged. It was argued that whilst legal adoption might be beneficial in certain cases – so as to avoid the stigma of illegitimacy, for example – it was in general undesirable to break the natural ties between parent and child if this could rightly be avoided. Because they believed this to be true, many of the great voluntary societies only used *de facto* adoption as a last resort, usually for orphans or deserted children, preferring to foster children or to give support of various kinds to assist the unmarried mother to keep her child. Fears were also expressed that adoption societies were undesirable institutions, because their activities would inevitably encourage parents to part lightly with their children. The adoption societies themselves argued that the problem of the unwanted child had now reached new dimensions with the urgent additional need to relieve the moral and economic distress of post-war unmarried mothers. To reject a mother's application for them to arrange the adoption of her child might, they believed, prove highly dangerous for the child since the mother could become prey 'to unscrupulous persons offering to arrange the adoption with evil intentions', one of which was the intention to procure girls for prostitution. On these grounds, the Societies urged that adoption, instead of being discouraged, should be promoted but, knowing from their own experience how serious were the dangers and drawbacks of *de facto* adoption, they also urged the Conference to support a policy of State regulation of any adoption scheme. Even where a child was placed happily with *de facto* adoptive parents, it was made very clear that his happiness might well prove to rest on uncertain foundations. He was not, after all, legally a member of the family in which he had grown up; he could not obtain a birth certificate in the name in which he was known. The position of the adoptive parents was insecure, since the natural parents retained at law the right to reclaim their child at any time; on the other hand, the natural mother's position was no less insecure since the adoptive parents had the reciprocal right to demand that she resume responsibility for her child whenever it suited their purpose. Persuaded that the Societies' arguments were substantially correct, the Conference sent a deputation to the Home Secretary, urging an official enquiry into the question of adoption and making the case for some form of legal control with regard to it.

The Government responded by appointing the Hopkinson Committee whose terms of reference were to consider two specific questions: was it desirable to make legal provision for the adoption of children in this country and, if so, what form should such provision take? One year later, in 1921, the Committee presented its Report, with a clear recommendation in favour of making such legal provision but no clear recommendation as regards the form it should take, with the result that in the course of the next three years, 1922–4, six different Bills were introduced into Parliament, each making different proposals and none getting as far as a third reading. In an attempt to reconcile divergent opinions, a further Committee was appointed in 1924, the Tomlin Committee, which produced two Reports the following year, in the second of which was produced a draft Bill which later formed the basis of the Adoption Act of 1926.

The Reports of the two Committees and the debates which ensued in Parliament showed very clearly that both Houses were agreed on the dangers of *de facto* adoption and the need for some system of control. Thus the Hopkinson Committee stated:[1]

> We believe that the absence of proper control over the adoption of children . . . results in an undesirable traffic in child life . . . Children

[1] Cmd 1254, paras 61 and 64.

may be handed from one person to another with or without payment, advertised for disposal, and even sent out of the country without any record being kept; intermediaries may accept children for 'adoption' and dispose of them as and when they choose . . . The time has now come when the State should at least have cognizance of all such transactions and a record of all such 'adoptions'.

Again, while many *de facto* adoptions were found to be beneficial for the child, there still remained many cases in which proof had been given of definite acts of cruelty, of gross neglect, and of exposure of the child to grave moral dangers. Some witnesses had drawn special attention to the not uncommon practice of parents demanding their child back as soon as it was old enough to go out to work. Others again had spoken of children being adopted by wealthy people, brought up in luxury, then, when the adoptive parents grew tired of them, being sent to the workhouse.

Where opinion sharply divided, however, was on the critical issue of how far the State should seek to legislate against the dangers of *de facto* adoption and to control adoption in this country. There were those who advocated control of all adoption, thus prohibiting *de facto* adoption altogether, but this, as the Tomlin Committee pointed out, was clearly impracticable. Parents could not be compelled to relinquish their parental rights simply because they handed their children over to others to rear. The remedy lay rather in strengthening the Children Act of 1908.

Sensibly enough the Tomlin Committee itself approached the problem of drafting legislative proposals by asking themselves just what evils was legal adoption supposed to remedy? Their draft Bill indicated that these were perceived as being the unrestricted power of the natural parents to reclaim their child; the inability of *de facto* adoption to establish legally recognised relationships between the child and his adoptive family and thus secure for the child a form of guardianship; and the failure of the existing system to protect the welfare of the child.

The Adoption Act which stemmed from the Tomlin Committee's deliberations applied only to England and Wales and was intended as a cautious and experimental measure. Its provisions mainly related to the conditions in which adoption orders could be granted, including the consent required; the jurisdiction of the courts; and the appointment of a guardian of the infant *ad litem*. The effects of an adoption order granted under the Act were broadly to deprive the natural parents of their rights and duties in regard to future custody, maintenance and education, and to vest them in the adopting parents, and to enable the adopted person to obtain a birth certificate in the name by which he was known.

One effect the Act certainly did not have was to make the adoptive parents 'parents' in the full legal sense of the word. On this matter, the Committee expressed the view that in introducing a system of legal adoption into English Law, 'it would be well to proceed with a measure of caution and at any rate in the first instance not to interfere with the law of succession . . . The adopting parent will only hold the position of a special guardian', that is to say that he would be a parent only in relation to the future custody, maintenance and education of the child. Distinction was thus made between the natural and adopted child in relation to rights of succession. An adopted child could inherit from his natural family and they from him, but unless special testamentary provision was made, an adopted child was incapable of inheriting from his adoptive parents until as recently as 1949.

The legislation of adoption encouraged its practice, but *de facto* adoptions were still very numerous, partly through ignorance of new procedures, partly through the inertia of the adoptive parents, and continued to give rise to anxiety for the welfare of the children involved. To this continuing anxiety was added an anxiety regarding the methods – some of them very questionable – used by the numerous adoption agencies which had sprung into existence. There was in addition a very grave concern regarding the number of individuals who were making a profession of arranging private adoptions, advertising children as 'available for adoption' in a way all too reminiscent of baby-farming.

Prompted by such anxieties, a delegation of representatives of the child welfare societies waited upon the Home Secretary, asking for an enquiry into 'the evils associated with unregulated and unsupervised adoption' with the result that a Departmental Committee (the Horsbrough Committee) was appointed in 1936 to 'inquire into the methods pursued by adoption societies and other agencies engaged in arranging for the adoption of children, and to report any, and if so what, measures should be taken in the public interest to supervise or control their activities'.

The Committee in fact found no evidence of widespread traffic in children, but was concerned by evidence of a number of undesirable cases, especially among those arranged by private individuals, where the welfare of the child had clearly not been considered as of paramount importance. On the other hand, it was shown that many adoption societies made inadequate investigation of the adoptive parents before placing children with them. None of the chief adoption societies appeared to have appropriately trained social workers on their staffs to make such investigations feasible.

The chief recommendations of the Horsbrough Committee were embodied in the Adoption of Children (Regulation) Act, 1939[1] which came into operation in 1943. It provided for the registration of adoption societies and for the regulations as to their conduct; and for the supervision by local authorities of children under the age of nine years placed through a third party for legal or *de facto* adoption, thus offering to such children the same supervision as that provided for in the Child Life Protection Acts.

Legal adoption was, of course, no substitute for legitimation. It established guardianship, guaranteed protection, and gave the right to claim a name. But it did not, as first instituted, fully integrate the illegitimate child into the family of his adoptive parents, although later legislation has gone a great way towards this. It also did not provide a conclusive answer to the question of such fundamental importance to any individual in human society: 'Who am I?' Even with the substantial modifications in the laws of adoption in this country which have taken place in more recent years, this question remains unresolved both in the minds of the adopted and in the minds of social workers. Indeed, the constant emphasis on the 'right' of an adopted child to know 'who he really is' and on the moral obligation of the adoptive parents to make clear at the earliest possible moment to any child whom they adopt that

---

[1] 2 & 3 Geo. VI, c. 27.

they are not 'really' his mother and father, only serves to draw attention to this dilemma and to underline the ambiguous status of the child not fortunate enough to have been born into a normally constituted family.

XX

The Prevention of Cruelty
and Neglect

In some respects the redefinition of social policies and attitudes to the illegitimate child is one particular example of the growing concern in England over the past hundred years for the protection of all children from abuse either by their parents or by those who *de facto* acted as their parents. Today public concern for the prevention of neglect and cruelty to children expresses itself in frequent letters in the Press and in vigorous debates in Parliament. Prosecutions for neglect and cruelty, of which there are still far too many, are given great prominence in the national press where reports are not infrequently accompanied by editorial comment, criticising the light sentences handed down by the courts. By contrast, until late in the nineteenth century, both Parliament and the national press were largely unconcerned with the way in which parents treated their children, regarding even the most barbarous cruelty as beyond comment and beyond public intervention since children were not then regarded as citizens in their own right. In our own day a child has rights against its parents; it can give testimony against them in the courts; and this testimony can be, and often is, corroborated by the witness of an officer of the National Society for the Prevention of Cruelty to Children. A hundred years ago a child had no such rights and the National Society was not yet in existence.

Those who were personally involved in the process of securing at law the rights and protection of children were themselves sensible not merely of the fundamental changes in social attitudes towards children which such legislation required, but of the relatively short period of time during which these attitudes had developed. In the course of the debates on the second reading of the Children Bill of 1908, neither the first nor the last piece of legislation to be hailed as a 'Children's Charter', the Lord Advocate declared that:[1]

> There was a time in the history of this House when a Bill of this kind would have been treated as a most revolutionary measure; and, half a century ago, if such a measure had been introduced it would have been said that the British Constitution was being undermined. Now a Bill of this kind finds itself in smooth water from the outset. This measure is not the development of the political ideas of one party, but the gradual development of a quickened sense on the part of the community at large of the duty it owes to the Children.

What were the origins of this 'quickened sense of duty . . .'? Many would date its beginnings as far back as the eighteenth century with the work of Fielding and of Hanway for the abandoned and the destitute, the uncared for and the unloved. Others would associate it with the humanitarianism which characterised a good deal of late eighteenth-century intellectual development in Europe. But the influence both of the philanthropists and the philosophers was slow to make any impression on general social policy, and tended to express itself in the following century in local, rather than national, experiments in child welfare, and in piecemeal legislation, regulating the hours and conditions of work of children in particular industries rather than in industry as a whole, and which in practice was largely ineffective till the mid-nineteenth century. Not until the second half of the last century does one sense a general awakening, a 'quickening' of social, rather than individual, conscience over neglect and physical cruelty of all kinds – the evils associated with baby-farming, with the exposure of young children to drunkenness, immorality, with the hazards attached to the employment of children in certain occupations, and the exploitation of children by indolent parents.

As in so many other fields of social reform, concerted action

[1] Hansard, 1908 vol. CLXXXVI, col. 1251.

was impossible in the absence of convincing information, and even when such information had been collected, some particularly sensational piece of evidence was often needed to rally a wavering public to the cause of the reformers. An instance of this was the way in which the Infant Life Protection Act found its way on to the Statute Book. About the beginning of May in the year 1870 the bodies of sixteen young babies were found in Brixton and Peckham, some in the streets and some in other open spaces. It was not unusual to find dead babies in such places in London at that time. In 1870 the number so found was no less than 276, the majority being under one week old. But it was unusual to find so many within a few weeks in so small an area, and a capable police officer, Sergeant Relf, was selected to investigate the matter. His preliminary enquiries led him to think that a private lying-in home in Camberwell Road might provide a clue to the mysterious deaths, and taking in an assumed name a furnished room opposite the home, he kept it under observation. On 28 May 1870 he saw a cab drive up; a woman got out, entered the home and returned with a delicate looking young lady who, he said, 'appeared to have been recently confined'. He followed the cab to a house in Loughborough Road, Brixton, where he interviewed the father of the young lady, Mr C.

Miss C., who was seventeen years of age, had been brutally assaulted by the husband of a friend with whom she had been staying and had been confined at the lying-in home in Camberwell Road a fortnight before she had been seen by Sergeant Relf. For some time previously, her father had been pondering the problem of how to provide a suitable home for the expected baby, and on 1 May, in a weekly newspaper he noticed the following advertisement:

'Adoption. A good home, with a mother's love and care, is offered to any respectable person wishing her child to be entirely adopted. Premium £5, which includes everything. Apply, by letter only, to Mrs. Oliver, Post Office, Grove Place, Brixton.'

He answered the advertisement and on 17 May 'Mrs Oliver' called and arranged to take the child, who was given her that night by Mr C. at Walworth railway station. Three days later 'Mrs Oliver' called for the baby's clothes, but at first refused to take any money for the care of the baby, saying that Mr C. had already been put to enough expense. She consented, however, to accept £4; Mr C. gave her £2, and though she said she would call for the balance later, she did not return.

This story naturally interested Sergeant Relf, at whose request Mr C. wrote to 'Mrs Oliver' at Brixton Post Office, suggesting another interview, but the letter was returned through the post undelivered.

In the meantime Sergeant Relf, who had become an assiduous reader of newspaper advertisements, noticed that on 5 June 'Mrs Oliver' had reinserted her advertisement in the popular weekly journal, and he wrote to her saying that he wished to find a home for a little boy. He received a reply in which 'Mrs Oliver' assured him that it would give her great pleasure to adopt the little boy as her own, adding, 'Should you entrust your little one to my care you may rely upon his receiving the love and care of a mother.' He made an appointment to meet her at Camberwell New Road railway station, and arranged that Mr C. should be an unobserved witness of the interview. At the station, he was met by a woman who wore the same dress as the 'Mrs Oliver' to whom Mr C. had entrusted his grandson, but she was not the same woman. After the interview Sergeant Relf shadowed her to her home at Frederick Terrace, Brixton.

On the following morning, 11 June, he called at the house and saw the woman he had met on the previous evening, whose real name was Sarah Ellis. He asked to see the child of Miss C. and was informed that there were no children in the house. On his insisting, she called 'Margaret', and the tenant of the house, her sister, Margaret Waters, appeared, who took him into the kitchen where five young babies were lying on the sofa asleep. In the background were five more babies also asleep. He left the house and returned with Mr C. and Dr Puckle, the Medical Officer of Health for Lambeth.

Mr C. identified one of the babies as his grandson who, when he last saw him was a fine healthy boy, but now was extremely emaciated, very dirty and saturated with wet, and, according to Dr Puckle, under the influence of a narcotic. 'The children', said the doctor in his evidence at the trial that ensued, 'were all very quiet, and that struck me afterwards as a very remarkable thing. I was in the house half an hour, and there was no crying or movement by any of them.' The explanation of this tragic silence was not far to seek; a half-empty bottle of laudanum was found in the house. The police also found pawn tickets relating to various sums, amounting to £14 advanced on baby clothing.

The two women were taken into custody and charged at the police court with cruelty to infants by not providing them with sufficient food. Mr C. took away his grandson, and the nine other infants were taken to Lambeth workhouse. Three were claimed and removed; two were restored to health; and four died. The child of Miss C. never recovered but died on 24 June; and on 26 July Margaret Waters and her sister, Sarah Ellis, were committed for trial on four charges: wilful murder, manslaughter, conspiracy, and obtaining money under false pretences.

The prisoners were tried at the Old Bailey in September 1870 and the charges related solely to the child of Miss C. Sarah Ellis was acquitted of murder and manslaughter, but sentenced to eighteen months' imprisonment for conspiring to obtain money under false pretences. The charge of murder was, however, pressed against Margaret Waters. For the defence, it was urged that in ordinary circumstances the mortality of hand-fed children was very high – one of the medical witnesses for the prosecution in cross-examination estimated it was about 33 per cent, adding that great skill and care were required to bring up a child by hand. It was proved that Mrs Walters had called in a local doctor to see a child who was suffering from diarrhoea, but he made only one attendance.

The Lord Chief Justice in summing up put two points to the jury: 'Did the prisoner know or believe that the treatment adopted and the line of conduct pursued toward the child would probably accomplish or accelerate its death, or, still more, did she intend by that course of treatment and line of conduct to shorten its life?' If they were satisfied on either or both these points, he added, then it was their duty to find her guilty of murder. She was found guilty, and executed on 11 October in her thirty-sixth year.[1]

The case of Margaret Waters, which created an immense sensation, was followed by that of Mary Hall, another notorious baby-farmer. One of the most remarkable features of both these cases was that advertisements by both women were inserted in

[1] G. F. McCleary, *The Maternity and Child Welfare Movement*, p. 88.

newspapers that had then, as some of them have still, a wide circulation and a reputation for respectability; one was a popular religious journal.[1] Even after the execution of Margaret Waters such advertisements, though they became much less frequent, did not wholly cease to appear.

The disclosures in these cases came as no surprise to the medical men and social workers who were interested in the protection of infant life. Largely at the instigation of its honorary secretary, Dr J. D. Curgenven, the Harveian Society had already appointed a committee to investigate the subject of baby-farming, and formulated a series of recommendations which they laid before the Home Secretary at an interview in January 1867, but owing to the preoccupation of the Government with the franchise question, no action was taken. In the following year, Dr Ernest Hart published a series of articles on baby-farming in the *British Medical Journal*, which attracted attention to the subject, and Lord Shaftesbury in the House of Lords endeavoured to move the Government to do something about it. The Lord President of the Council, however, although he agreed that it was 'unfortunately too true that a system of baby-farming existed under which the grossest crimes could be committed', was unable to do more than say that the Government would 'turn their attention to the matter during the recess', and that he hoped 'that they would be able to discover means which, embodied in a Bill, would obviate the abuses to which attention had been directed'. These dignified utterances were but a prelude to an official policy of inactivity.

Meanwhile, Dr Curgenven persevered with his campaign to rouse public interest in the evils of baby-farming. In 1867 and 1869, he read papers to the Health Section of the Annual Conference of the National Association for the Promotion of Social Science in which he described the methods of baby-farmers and their disastrous results. On both occasions resolutions were passed calling for the registration, as being of suitable character, of women who undertook the care of young children in the absence of their mother. The earlier of these motions applied only to women who accepted payment for the care of illegitimate children, usually for periods much longer than a single day. The later resolutions, however, applied to all nurses, including those

[1] ibid., p. 90.

who undertook the daily care of legitimate children of women employed in factories.

Encouraged by the support of his own society and that of the National Association, Curgenven now devoted his energies to establishing a society of those anxious for the statutory supervision of baby-farming, which could act as an effective pressure group on a lethargic legislature. As a result the Infant Life Protection Society was formed in July 1870,

> to prevent the destruction of Infant Life, and the moral and physical injury, caused by the present system of Baby Farming; and with this in view to promote a Bill in Parliament requiring that any person taking charge of an infant or young child for gain shall be certified as of good character and be registered; and that every child so placed out shall be subject to proper supervision.

In its *Prospectus*, issued early in 1871, the Society made special reference to the trials of both Margaret Waters and Mary Hall; the sensational publicity given to which had enabled it both to recruit members and to gain influential support for their Infant Life Protection Bill when it was introduced into the Commons that February by Mr Charley, the Member for Salford, and sponsored, *inter alia*, by Lyon Playfair, the much respected public health reformer. The Bill provided that no person could receive a child under six years of age for reward without an annual licence from a magistrate; that in no circumstances could more than two children be received; and that all premises in which children were so received should be inspected monthly by the local Poor Law medical officer, who should report to the Poor Law Board. Although the primary intention of the Bill was to protect the lives of illegitimate children put out to nurse, it also contained a clause so framed that, if enacted, the registration and supervision of nurses in the manufacturing districts who took children for the day only would have been required. Of this, the promoters of the Bill were well aware, and, indeed, such had been their intention, but within and without the House of Commons, an immediate storm of protest arose. The National Society for Women's Suffrage published a *Memorial* in which they claimed the provisions of the Bill 'would interfere in the most mischievous and oppressive way with domestic arrangements . . . and would be costly and tyrannical in the case of poor women who take charge of infants for hire without sinister motives, while they would be ineffective to prevent the destruction of illegitimate children.' Others saw the Bill as an infringement of the liberties of the parent. 'It is not against the licensing of women as nurses that we protest – a Bill empowering suitable authorities to grant certificates of fitness to all nurses who desire to possess them, and can show they merit such distinction, would command our support – it is to the compulsion to be put on parents to employ none but those holding such licences that we object,' declared the Committee for Amending the Law in Points where it is Injurious to Women.[1]

> The responsibility for the child in infancy as in later life, lies with them, and we emphatically deny that the State has any right to dictate to them the way it shall be fulfilled. We hold that its functions ought to be confined to the imposing of penalties for the culpable neglect of this, as of any other department of parental duty. If, through indifference, ignorance, or wilful malice, parents place their infants in untrustworthy hands, and the child suffers in the consequence, the law should punish them equally with the nurse. Let self-interest and a wholesome fear of penalties be thrown, by all means, into the same scale with natural affection but beyond such precautions against their exercising their right to choose a nurse, carelessly and wickedly, the State should forbear to limit their perfect freedom in this, as in all matters connected with the rearing and maintaining of their families.

In the House itself similar objections, fatal alike to any hopes that the Government might itself adopt the Bill or that in its proposed form it might carry as a Private Member's Bill, led to its withdrawal on the understanding that the whole issue of the licensing and inspection of nurses should be investigated by a Select Committee of the House of Commons. In July of the following year, 1872, the Committee issued its Report which was to form the basis of the legislation subsequently enacted. The evidence given to the Committee showed that the worst forms of baby-farming were practised on a large scale and that the mortality of babies was enormous – the Society for the Protection of Infant Life estimated it at 60–90 per cent. The Committee, however, did not condemn the practice of boarding out when suitable arrangements were made. On the contrary,

[1] Cf. Margaret Hewitt, *Wives and Mothers in Victorian Industry*, p. 172.

they found that the children boarded out by the Poor Law authorities under the regulations of the Poor Law Board were 'generally well and properly cared for', and they received authoritative evidence to the effect that young children developed more satisfactorily in body and mind when placed with suitable foster parents than in an institution. This was the conclusion reached after many years' experience by the Foundling Hospital, as the Committee heard from Mr G. B. Gregory, Treasurer of the Hospital and a Member of Parliament. How best and how far it was possible to legislate against the conditions in which thousands of children were far from well and properly cared for presented a number of problems, among them the vexed problem of whether or not such legislation should cover women who only took children for the day, and of whose harmful effects the Committee had received a good deal of evidence. Since even those witnesses who had drawn attention to the deleterious effects of day-nursing in the manufacturing districts were themselves divided as to the advisability of enforcing registration and inspection of such nurses, and in view of the outcry that had greeted the proposal of the original Infant Life Protection Bill to do so, the Committee elected to confine its recommendations to the protection of those children who were boarded out for longer than twenty-four hours, the majority of whom their evidence showed to be illegitimate.[1]

> We are of the opinion that it would be reasonable and expedient to register persons, who, for payment, take charge at the same time of two or more infants under one year of age for longer periods than one day ... Such limited registration would not interfere to any inconvenient extent with the habits of those persons in the manufacturing districts who are accustomed to put their children under the charge of a caretaker for the day, or for the hours of work.

This was the recommendation which was embodied in the Infant Life Protection Act[2] which received the Royal Assent in 1872. The Act required all persons receiving for reward two or more children under one year of age for more than twenty-four hours to register their homes with the local authority, and local authorities were empowered both to refuse registration in any

[1] ibid., p. 173.
[2] 35 & 36 Vict., c. 38.

case in which they were not satisfied that the home was suitable, and the person of good character and able to maintain the child, and to remove unsuitable homes from the register. The Act also required a person so registered to inform the Coroner within twenty-four hours of the death of any infant taken for reward, and the Coroner was required to hold an inquest unless he received a death certificate from a doctor.

At the same time, the Act tried to avoid a system of too stringent registration. Not only were the day-nurses excluded from its provisions, but so also were relatives and guardians; institutions, such as the Foundling Hospital, 'established for the protection and care of infants'; and those who fostered children under the provisions of the Poor Laws.

Though an important landmark in the progress of statutory protection for the child, the Act was all too easily evaded; hence the many attempts made by the London County Council, which took over the administration of the Act in London from the Metropolitan Board of Works in 1889, to secure amending legislation. Once more, reform waited upon the discovery, trial and execution of another notorious baby-farmer, Mrs Dyer, in 1896 (see page 597). The following year the Council achieved the passing of their amended Infant Life Protection Act,[1] which raised the age limit of children subject to protection from one to five years, and laid a duty on local authorities to institute enquiries in their areas as to whether there were persons fostering for reward. The inspectors of the local authority were given powers to apply for authority to enter a house where they were refused entry and had reason to believe that an infant was being nursed, and to remove the child to a place of safety. Improper care was defined in the new Act as a state when an infant was:

(a) Kept in any house or premises which are so unfit or so over-crowded as to endanger its health;
   or
(b) retained or received by any person who, by reason of negligence, ignorance or other cause, is so unfit to have its care and maintenance as to endanger its health.

In fact, child life protection legislation had begun to progress from the single purpose of protecting a vulnerable group of

[1] 60 & 61 Vict., c. 57.

children from criminal neglect to a larger concern for their general physical welfare, although it did not link up with the administration of public health until 1929. In the meantime, the Children Act of 1908 consolidated the earlier infant life protection legislation, extended its application to the fostering for reward of only one child, raised the age under which children were to be protected from five to seven years (subsequently raised to nine years by the Children and Young Persons Act, 1932) and laid down much more stringent provisions for the administration of the law, including the appointment of infant life protection officers.

The 1908 Act, however, was concerned with much more than the protection of life among a restricted group of children. Its second section was intended to strengthen the law protecting all children from cruelty and abuse not merely from strangers, but, no less important, from their own parents. Concern on this score had been mounting over the previous half-century and, as in the case of infant life protection, was expressed both by individuals, and the creation of voluntary societies whose aim was to educate both public and Parliamentary opinion. As early as 1868,[1] boards of guardians had been authorised to prosecute parents who wilfully neglected to provide for their children so that their health was endangered, but this legislation, though it could be described as preventive of injury and cruelty in that the likelihood of injury and not the fact alone was made a punishable offence, was limited to children with whom the Poor Law was directly concerned. Its chief object was to prevent pauperism arising from the conditions of neglect. There was no effective method of discovering and repressing cruelty until the formation of the voluntary societies for this purpose.

The movement towards the prevention of cruelty to children took shape from the example of pioneer work in New York, Boston and other great American cities, which had been observed by Thomas Agnew, a Liverpool merchant and banker, while visiting that country in 1881. On his return to Liverpool the following year he discussed the experiments with his Member of Parliament, Mr Samuel Smith. The result of the Member's support was that a few weeks later, at a meeting organised by the Society for the Prevention of Cruelty to Animals, an appeal

[1] Poor Law Amendment Act, 31 & 32 Vict., c. 122.

for a Dog's Home became extended into an appeal for the protection of children. That societies to protect animals from cruelty were established before societies to protect children is one of the better known, bizarre features of English social history. Less well known, perhaps, is that Parliament itself intervened to protect animals from abuse more than three-quarters of a century before it thought it proper to extend statutory protection to the young child. As in the case of infant life protection, so here, reluctance to legislate was rooted in the contemporary view that it was both improper and, indeed, unsafe to invade the privacy of the home. Thus Lord Shaftesbury, replying in 1871 to a letter canvassing his support for legislation to protect children from parental cruelty wrote: 'The evils you state are enormous and indisputable, but they are of so private, internal and domestic a character as to be beyond the reach of legislation, and the subject, indeed, would not, I think, be entertained in either House of Parliament.'

The reformers however, like Shaftesbury himself in the sphere of factory reform, believed that social attitudes were not immutable, but susceptible of change through private effort and public pressure stemming from unequivocal information. So, in 1883, the Liverpool Society for the Prevention of Cruelty to Children was formed. Similar societies were formed in most of the large towns; Bristol and Birmingham each founded a society in 1883, and London, Glasgow and Hull founded societies two years later. In London, Benjamin Waugh, a Congregational Minister of dynamic personality, was made honorary secretary of the Society, and it was largely due to his untiring efforts that the impact of the regional associations became united and coherent. Benjamin Waugh's experience in Greenwich had convinced him that, whatever other protection existing law offered to young children outside their own homes, 'the worse sufferings of little children arose through the instrumentality of vicious and degraded parents, and were practised in the privacy of the home', against which children had no protection at law. This situation Waugh set himself to remedy, well aware that many of his contemporaries, like Shaftesbury, were profoundly convinced that it was both unnecessary and possibly dangerous to meddle in domestic affairs: 'The cruelties he warned against were unseen, and therefore unrecognised; and public feeling resented any invasion of what was considered the sanctity of the home. To change this feeling it was necessary to show how little of the sacredness of family life existed among the more depraved, and the manner in which a man exercised his right to do what he would with his own.'[1]

By 1889, thirty-one cities and towns had formed organisations to protect children from cruelty, and many of them were making separate representations to Parliament for legislation to protect the unguarded child. In May of that year, therefore, through Waugh's initiative, the London Society amalgamated with some of the branches in the provinces and thus formed the National Society for the Prevention of Cruelty to Children, which was able to co-ordinate efforts to promote legislation in Parliament. There can be no doubt of the importance of the contribution of the National Society in facilitating the passage through Parliament in 1889 of what was bound to be a highly contentious Bill. Lord Herschell, for example, was one of those who had been seriously concerned by the report specially prepared by the Society. 'I confess,' he told the House of Lords, 'the more I have looked at this matter, the more I have been astonished and alarmed at the amount of cruelty practised in this country.'[2] The Bill in support of which he was speaking represented a thorough-going and wide-ranging attempt to deal with this situation. It intended action to be taken before actual injury occurred, and also attempted to be a deterrent measure by making cruelty a punishable offence:

> Any person over sixteen years of age, who, having the custody of a child, being a boy under the age of fourteen years or being a girl under the age of sixteen years, wilfully ill-treats, neglects, abandons, or exposes such a child or causes or procures such a child to be ill-treated, neglected, abandoned, or exposed, in a manner likely to cause such child unnecessary suffering, or injury to its health, shall be guilty of a misdemeanour

and thus liable to a fine of up to £100 or imprisonment up to two years. Punishment, it will be noticed, was to be confined to acts of wilful cruelty, that is, to acts of criminal intention, and not to cases of neglect due to ignorance, poverty, or any of the

[1] Gertrude Tuckwell, *The State and Its Children*, p. 127.
[2] Hansard, 1889, CCCXXXVII, col. 951.

other prevailing evils of the time. Subsequent provisions of the Bill underlined the special need to protect young children from ill-treatment and neglect in certain types of employment not covered by existing factory legislation, a need to which, once again, the work of Benjamin Waugh and the National Society had drawn attention. Hence it was now proposed that the employment of children in the street 'for the purpose of begging or receiving alms', or 'for the purpose of singing, playing or performing for profit, or offering anything for sale, between 10 p.m. and 5 a.m.' should be carefully restricted. Radical legal changes were incorporated in the Bill to enable necessary evidence to be brought before the courts. A spouse was to be a competent, but not compellable, witness against the other spouse, and the evidence of a child of tender years, though not given upon oath, could be received by the court. Two important powers of a new kind were envisaged. First, the magistrates, on the sworn evidence of any person having reasonable cause to believe a child was being ill-treated or neglected, could issue a warrant to be executed by a police officer to enter a house and search for the child and take him and detain him in a place of safety until he could be dealt with by the court. Second, the courts were to be given power to take a child out of the care of a parent convicted of neglect and ill-treatment, and to commit him to the charge of a relative or other fit person. The term 'fit person' was to cover industrial schools and charitable institutions. When the child has been committed, the court might still order the parent to contribute towards his maintenance – a measure intended to emphasise the parental responsibility which the committal order procedure might otherwise seem to destroy.

In Parliament, it soon became clear that some Members were disposed to attack the Bill as a piece of fussy legislation, pointing to the pride with which children made their modest contribution to the family income and to the enviable position of child performers who, it was claimed, were so well fed and cared for that, according to one doctor, 'the little fairies and goblins had a better chance of recovering than their less cared for neighbours'.

More dangerous opposition, however, came from those who, whilst not denying the necessity for some sort of legislation to protect young children from cruelty and neglect, disliked those clauses of the proposed Bill which constituted a substantial modification of the common law rights of parents. Thus Sir Richard Webster, the Attorney General, assenting to the second reading, urged that the Committee stage be postponed 'on the ground that in some respect, the measure goes too far'. When the Committee stage was reached, the Attorney General took an early opportunity of expanding his earlier statement in the course of introducing a Government amendment to clause I, which reduced the age up to which boys were to be protected from 16 to 14 years.[1]

> I need hardly say that not only I, but Her Majesty's Government, sympathise most warmly with any proposals for legislation which will put a stop to, and punish people for, inflicting any acts of cruelty upon children. In so far as this Bill does propose to deal with acts of cruelty committed upon children, we most warmly support the measure. At the same time, we have to be most careful that we do not interfere with the legitimate conduct of parents and guardians with regard to children. I am sure the Right Honourable Gentleman [Mr. Mundella, who had introduced the Bill into the House of Commons on behalf of the National Society] who takes so much interest in the Bill, would be very sorry indeed, under cover of any Bill of this kind, to interfere with the proper and legitimate control of the parent over the child, and certainly to interfere with anything like the reasonable earnings of children assisting their parents.

Mundella declined the smoothly worded invitation to protect the rights of parents rather than the interests of the child. 'Children have very few rights in England,' he replied, 'and by this Bill I am really only anxious that we should give them the same protection that we give under the Cruelty to Animals Act and the Contagious Diseases Act for Domestic Animals.' The Attorney General's argument illustrated very clearly the dilemma of those who, in conscience, could not reject legislation to protect the child, but, nevertheless, from conviction, were loth to undermine what they believed to be the legitimate rights of parents. This particular amendment was accepted by the Committee. A later proposal, that not until injury to the child had actually been proved were the offending parents to be brought to court, was not so successful. Predictably, Mundella resisted this amendment 'because this Bill is one to prevent cruelty to children, whereas according to this amendment the

[1] Cf. Hansard, 1889, CCCXXXVII, cols 227 and 229.

Act need not come into operation until the act of cruelty had been done'.[1]

Later, when the Committee considered clause 5 of the Bill, which stated that 'Husband and wife respectively shall be competent and admissible witnesses, and in some cases compellable witnesses', Mr Pickersgill moved that the clause be withdrawn since it represented a substantial departure from common law. 'Common Law should not be changed piecemeal in this fashion by such legislation', he declared. Again, concern for traditional structures confused discussion of the changes in the law essential to the effective operation of the proposed Bill. It fell to Mr Channing to point out to the Committee that, 'My honourable Friend, in moving this amendment, has forgotten that in any of the worst cases with which the Society for the Prevention of Cruelty to Children have had to deal, practically cases of manslaughter by the father and mother together, conviction would be impossible without the evidence of one or the other.' Interestingly enough, Pickersgill's conservatism on the issue of a wife giving evidence against her husband did not prevent him from moving – this time successfully – an amendment of considerable importance regarding the admissibility of evidence of children. The original clause 6 of the Bill had already proposed that judges might accept evidence from the child itself, even though it was conceded that children might not understand the nature of the oath normally administered in the courts. Pickersgill was anxious that this particular recommendation be strengthened by admitting the depositions from children who had in fact died in the period between the committal and trial of those accused of abusing him.[2]

> In a recent case, where an important witness dies between the committal for trial and the trial itself, the learned judge who presided at the trial ruled that the depositions could not be put in evidence. It is therefore clear, as the matter stands, that in the most serious cases of all, the offender might escape owing to the fact that the evidence of the principal witness would not be admissible at the trial.

He therefore proposed an amendment to the clause: 'And the

[1] ibid., col. 233.
[2] ibid., cols 1365 and 1371.

evidence of such child, though not given on oath or affirmation, but otherwise taken and reduced in writing . . . shall be deemed to be a deposition . . .'

Both the acceptance of Pickersgill's proposal and the success of the amended Bill in the late summer of 1889 were a tribute to the careful preparation and patient propaganda of Waugh and the National Society. The powers of protection for the inarticulate child conveyed by the Act for the Prevention of Cruelty to, and better Protection of, Children were new in English social history and the legislation was referred to in Parliament as the 'Children's Charter'. Those whose life-work it was to protect those weaker than themselves well knew, however, that this particular victory only marked the end of the first phase of their battle:[1]

> The traditions and customs of law, fought and conquered in Parliament, had still to be fought and conquered in the legal mind and institutions of the country before the legislative rights of the children could be realised in their lives. The National mind thought as if the right of the child to be fed, clothed, and properly housed and treated by its parents had originated in 1889 in England by an Act of its Parliament. Administrative authorities were disposed to resent as an outrage on 'the liberty of man' the liability of 'neglect to provide' to imprisonment with hard labour. The Act was regarded as 'grandmotherly legislation'. 'I dismiss the case, the woman did not know the law' was constantly heard in Courts. Whilst some simpler authorities had an instinctive sense of the duty of a mother to give drink to the thirst of her baby as a law of Nature, others regarded the requirement as arbitrary and un-English . . . It was nothing less than a National education which was undertaken . . . It was a crusade primarily to the intellect of the Nation, preaching the existence and the magnitude of the work to be done for needlessly suffering children.

Certainly it was not a crusade exclusively to the poor. In 1892 Mrs Montague, 'a lady of position', was convicted of manslaughter and sentenced to twelve months' imprisonment for having tied up her little daughter in a locked cupboard for five hours, as a result of which the child had died. In her defence it was argued that a parent had a right to chastise his child in a

---

[1] *The Power for the Children, being the Report for 1895–6 of the N.S.P.C.C.,* pp. 39–40.

K

reasonable manner, and that this right had been expressly protected by the Prevention of Cruelty to Children Act. This particular case was reported in *The Times*. The *Children's Guardian*, which had become the official journal of the National Society, regularly recorded other cases of the appalling brutality to children which its officers met in the normal course of their work:[1]

> Punishing a child by putting pins into its nostrils; putting lighted matches up them; biting a child's wrist till a wound was made, and then burning the wound with lighted matches; burning the hands of a boy of six with matches; biting them till they bled the limbs of a seven months old baby; forcing the bone ring of a feeding bottle up and down the throat of a three months old baby till it bled; throwing a little girl of two years, ill of bronchitis, out of its bedroom window, breaking its bones and ending its life; . . . leaving a baby unlifted out of its cradle for weeks, till toadstools grew around the child out of its own rottenness; . . . keeping the stumps of little amputated legs sore, to have the child with its little face puckered up in pain, to excite pity; tying a rope round a boy of six, dipping him in the canal, leaving him immersed till exhausted, bringing him up, recovering him, and putting him in again, repeating misery time after time; . . . keeping a child always in a cool celler till its flesh became green . . .

In the five years following the passing of the first Prevention of Cruelty to Children Act, 5,792 persons were prosecuted for cruelty, and 5,460, or more than 94 per cent, of them convicted. In addition, 47,000 complaints were investigated by the Society. At the end of that time, new legislation was passed.[2] The age limit at which ill-treatment to boys was a punishable offence was raised to sixteen years. Cruelty was widened to include assault and the terms 'suffering' and 'injury' were more clearly defined. In dealing with offenders, the Act made some significant alterations. In the first place, it underlined the deterrent nature of the legislation by extending the length of maximum imprisonment, but it provided some new powers to deal with offenders who were habitual drunkards. Experience had shown that the majority of cases were committed when the adult was drunk and

---

[1] Tuckwell, op. cit., pp. 132–3.
[2] Prevention of Cruelty to Children (Amendment) Act, 57 & 58 Vict., c. 27. Prevention of Cruelty to Children Act, 57 & 58 Vict., c. 41.

uncontrolled and the magistrates were now given powers to send such offenders not to prison but to an inebriate's home, where constructive treatment could be given without the branding of a prison sentence. The offender's consent was required before such an order could be made. This marks a positive step forward in constructive work towards the prevention of further cruelty. Other clauses in the Act controlled the employment of children in places of public entertainment or in occupations of risk of danger to them, such as those of acrobat or contortionist. Factory Inspectors were authorised to inspect and examine premises where children performed, and courts were enabled to issue licences before they performed, after satisfying themselves of the health and kind treatment of the children.

That within so short a space of time the provisions of the original Prevention of Cruelty to Children Act should be not merely strengthened but amplified, was a notable tribute to Waugh and the National Society. Speaking to the 1894 Bill in the House of Lords, Lord Herschell commented:[1]

> Your Lordships will, I am sure, agree that if ever the necessity for legislation such as Parliament passed in 1889 has been exhibited it has been in the present case. No doubt the powers which were then entrusted to various persons in reference to the protection of children were considerable, and there were not a few who at that time entertained some apprehensions with regard to entrusting powers so large – fears were expressed lest it might involve so much interference with parental control as to lead to dangerous results. Happily, those who have been chiefly instrumental in putting this Act into operation have exhibited a care, discretion, and tact which has prevented those consequences which might well have resulted if less care and tact had been shown, and proves, I think, that your Lordships may well enable powers in addition to those already exercised to be put into operation . . .

The contribution of the National Society for the Prevention of Cruelty to Children, to which the Lord Chancellor paid such eloquent testimony in the House of Lords, found Royal recognition the following year. 'Being desirous of promoting the Society and the welfare of Her youthful subjects', Her Majesty, by Royal Charter dated 28 May 1895, incorporated the Society and assigned it 'the following specific duties':

[1] Hansard, 1894, XXIV, col. 1609.

(1) To prevent the public and private wrongs of her children, and the corruption of their morals.
(2) To take action for the enforcement of the laws for their protection.
(3) To provide and maintain an organisation for the above objects
(4) To do all other such lawful things as are incidental or conducive to the attainment of the above objects.

For over three-quarters of a century, during which the law for the prevention of cruelty to children has been amended extended and clarified, the National Society has conscientiously worked to fulfil these duties. Over the years, the total number of cases dealt with has steadily decreased and those which actually reach the courts are now far exceeded by those successfully dealt with by warning and advice from the Society's inspectors. This is not to say that cruelty and neglect show signs of being eliminated: immediately before the passing of the 1948 Children Act, the number of children assisted by the Society was something in the order of 100,000 a year. But that these children can be assisted effectively – if need be by the prosecution of their parents – is very largely attributable to the efforts of Benjamin Waugh and the National Society 'everywhere and in all cases whether in street or in home . . . to raise in the mind of the Nation the idea of the civil rights of every child to an endurable life, and to give universal effect to it in the lot of children'.

There are, of course, numbers of ways by which a child's life might be made 'unendurable'. The legislation which the National Society for the Prevention of Cruelty to Children promoted and continues to help put into effect was concerned with wilful neglect and cruelty, to acts of criminal intention. Early in the present century, a very large number of cases investigated by the NSPCC were cases of deliberate starvation in which the actual poverty of the parents could not be argued as a mitigating circumstance. At the same time, the no less alarming fact that very much larger numbers of children were grossly underfed by their parents not from criminal intent but through economic circumstances, was becoming a matter of urgent public concern. Fears for national efficiency and changing attitudes to poverty and national welfare were prompting demands that adequate standards of nutrition, health and moral training, should be provided for a far wider group of children than those affected by he criminal intentions of their own parents.

Once again, agitation was the consequence of specific information. Before the 1880s, remarkably little was known about he physical conditions of the majority of children in this country. Such evidence as did exist was largely contained in the various Reports of the Children's Employment Commission, and this was largely related to the effects of certain trades and occupations on children's health and physique and thus not applicable to the conditions of children in general. Apart from Blue Books, there are some descriptions given by philanthropists such as Dr J. C. Lettsom, a Quaker physician who worked among the poor in East London; and brief references in reports of Poor Law officials and in the minutes of boards of guardians; but there was no exact information until the end of the nineteenth century. The importance of adequate nutrition for the children of the poor was, however, emphasised by those confronted by the appearance of pauper children massed in the large poor law district schools after 1867. Not altogether surprisingly, one of the first to comment was himself a doctor, Dr Edward Smith, Medical Officer of the Poor Law Board, who submitted in 1867 a Report on the Inferiority of Workhouse Dietaries in the course of which he pointed out the very special obligation of the authorities to provide better food for pauper children. 'It is not, perhaps, well appreciated', he wrote, 'that up to adult life each period is devoted to a particular part of growth, and if for any cause, the growth does not occur, the evil is irremediable. Hence the great responsibility of those who have the power to withhold or to supply food in childhood and youth.'[1] Some few years later, in 1874, Mrs Nassau Senior urged the Poor Law Board to consider improving the dietary standards for pauper children as a means of ensuring that they would have the health and strength to support themselves in later life, and thus not return to the workhouse and the support of the rates:[2]

Unless we strengthen and develop the bodies of these children by

[1] 'Report on the Inferiority of Workhouse Dietaries' – 20th Annual Report of the Poor Law Board, *PP*, 1867-8, XXXIII, p. 59.
[2] 'Report on the Education of Girls in Pauper Schools', 1874 published in Third Annual Report of the Local Government Board, *PP*, XXV, p. 322.

every possible means, we shall endeavour in vain to raise them in the social scale. If they go out to the fight of life with weakly bodies, they cannot long be self-supporting. They will be sickly and helpless children ... I do not think that those who have given attention to the physical state of pauper children, will say that I make any mistake in speaking thus strongly of the importance of using every means of strengthening their bodies and invigorating their health and spirits, were it only with a view to their success in after life.

The district schools only provided information regarding the physical condition of a particular category of children. The Education Acts of 1870 and 1876 swept in to the new board schools children from all ranks of the working classes. Lord Shaftesbury's 'crooked alphabet' had come to learn to spell. Now, for the first time, could be seen, *en masse*, the results of the urbanisation of England expressed in terms of child health, physical and mental. Now it became clear that the great hope of elementary education, that it would assist the prosperity of the nation by raising the ability of the working classes, could not be realised if children came to their lessons too undernourished in body to be alert in mind. Amongst those interested in the education of the poor, the association between a full belly and an alert intelligence had long been recognised. The charity schools had frequently raised additional funds to provide meals for their pupils, and so had the industrial schools and the ragged schools. But what had hitherto been the local experience of unconnected groups of philanthropists now became recognised as a serious, country-wide problem. Prompted by concern expressed by the London School Board, the National Association for the Promotion of Social Science held a special discussion on the feeding of the necessitous schoolchild at its annual conference in 1871. Up and down the country charitable associations were formed to meet this particular need.

The local education authorities themselves proved very slow to take any direct action. Twenty-one years after the subject had first been discussed by the National Association, the London School Board held its first full-scale enquiry into the question of underfeeding. It revealed that there were 'six principal supply associations ready to provide funds when applied to, besides which there were no less than 287 local agencies said to exist which made provision for either one school or all the schools in one parish, or in the vicinity of one chapel'.[1] As a result, the London Schools Dinner Association was formed to co-ordinate the efforts of these voluntary organisations and to ensure that their work was carried out with the maximum economy and efficiency. Two more enquiries were to follow before the London County Council assumed the responsibilities of the London School Board, each of which underlined the desperate need for cheap or free meals for many of the children gathered in the authority's schools, and each commended more effective ways of co-ordinating voluntary efforts to meet a need so clearly revealed in the schools to which the working-class child was now compelled to go.

To the evidence of the condition of working-class children being accumulated by local authorities was added the results of special enquiries made by medically qualified investigators. For more than a generation, sanitary reformers and medical practitioners had been interested in the effects of industrial urbanism on the physical condition of specific populations. The concentration of children of the urban working class in a nationwide complex of elementary schools now made it possible to replace *ad hoc*, empirical observation, by systematic, comparative study. In 1889, Dr Francis Warner was commissioned by a joint committee of the British Medical Association and the Charity Organisation Society to conduct an enquiry 'for the purpose of collecting evidence by scientific methods as to the conditions existing among children'. Between 1889 and 1906, five investigations were made into the physical condition of schoolchildren in London. All revealed the same disturbing facts of stunted growth, weakly bodies, and chronic malnutrition.

Important as these reports were to those already aware of poor physique of the children of the working classes, the evidence which thoroughly awakened the nation at large to the perils of neglecting the health of the young was the very high proportion of recruits rejected as physically unfit to serve in the Boer War. Many years earlier, Herbert Spencer had written that 'to be a nation of good animals is the first condition of national prosperity', pointing out that the physique of individual soldiers could be decisive in times of war. 'Hence, it is becoming of special importance that the training of children should be carried

[1] The Joint Committee on Underfed Children. First Report, 1904–5, p. 2.

on, as not only to fit them mentally for the struggle before them, but also to make them physically fit to bear its excessive wear and tear.'[1] The Report made in 1902 by the Inspector General of Recruiting on the Rejection of Recruits for the Boer War showed all too clearly that England, far from being a nation of 'good animals', was a nation which contained large numbers of men physically unfit to bear arms, a revelation which the hastily appointed Interdepartmental Committee on Physical Deterioration confirmed in its own Report published two years later. Equally clearly, both these Reports indicated that this state of affairs could only be remedied if serious attention were paid to the health of the nation's children. 'We must begin with the children' became the recurring theme of the increasing number of people only recently made aware of the importance of maintaining the health of even the most lowly of the population.

It was already evident that voluntary efforts to feed the undernourished were not adequate. In some circles, however, there remained considerable reluctance to accept the feeding of the necessitous schoolchild as a public responsibility since to do so might undermine the proper discharge of parental responsibility. Thus charitable feeding had itself been criticised by the Charity Organisation Society not on the grounds that children were sufficiently well nourished, but because they believed that such schemes must inevitably breed that habit of 'injurious dependence' against which the Society had so firmly set its face, and tempt mothers to neglect their natural duties to their children in the knowledge that others would discharge them. The studies of Charles Booth and Seebohm Rowntree had, of course, already shown conclusively that in many cases the inability to support a family adequately was due to causes beyond the individual parent's control. The problem to be resolved, therefore, was how to give help to the needy without subsidising the negligent. An immediate remedy was the Relief (School Children) Order issued by the Poor Law authorities in 1905. The Order empowered boards of guardians to grant relief to a child living with its father who was destitute, by providing him with free meals, on application to the local education authority or its officers. As a protection against the unscrupulous, the parent was to be pauperised by this relief, although he was not required

[1] *Education*, N.Y., 1868, pp. 222, 223.

to enter the workhouse or undertake some form of prescribed labour. If, none the less, a parent was found on investigation to be neglectful rather than destitute, the guardians were to recover the cost of the child's meals, if necessary by a court order.

The Relief Order was not a success. Parents refused to allow their children to accept relief on such conditions. The local guardians, anxious to keep down the poor rates, often disallowed that a child needed feeding; the local education authorities on the whole did not make much use of their powers under the Order, as many felt that they themselves, and not the boards of guardians were the proper authorities to deal with the feeding of schoolchildren. At the same time, many voluntary feeding associations, believing that their functions had been taken over, now began to turn their attention to other aspects of child welfare, thereby forcing local education authorities to take the initiative in co-ordinating such charitable resources as remained within their area. In the big cities, some education authorities found that to meet the local needs of their schoolchildren, they had no alternative but to supply the fuel, premises, staff and equipment necessary to produce meals, and had to rely on other sources for the actual materials, which they had no power to provide from the education rate.

A solution to this dilemma was offered by the Education (Provision of Meals) Act, 1906,[1] which made the local education authorities responsible for the feeding of schoolchildren and empowered them, if there were no local voluntary funds available, to levy a rate not exceeding one halfpenny to meet the cost of food. It was not a power that the local authorities seized with much enthusiasm. In London the education authorities battled for two years to avoid imposing such a levy and appeals were made for voluntary subscriptions to meet what was freely admitted to be an urgent need. Even when a thorough investigation conducted in the year 1907–8 had revealed that at least 38,612 children out of an elementary school population of 600,000 were underfed, rather than finance their provision from the rates, an appeal was launched through the columns of *The Times* for voluntary subscriptions to meet the cost of school meals. Only when the public failed to subscribe voluntarily to a service which could legitimately be financed compulsorily, was the

[1] 6 Edw. VII, c. 57.

Education Committee of the London County Council forced, in 1909, to resort to the rates to meet the cost of the materials for the meals so desperately needed by thousands of young children attending its schools.

The reluctance with which the London County Council adopted the practice of subsidising school meals from the local rates was shared by a good many other local authorities. According to the Minority Report of the 1905–9 Poor Law Commission, 'what eventually forced them to do so was the absurdity of wasting costly education on hungry and starving children'.[1] Whilst there was a good deal of truth in this, it was far from the whole truth. Without doubt, the institution of a national system of elementary education had been largely justified in many minds as a capital investment necessary to improve the quality of the adult labour force. Accumulating evidence from many sources regarding the health of children in the schools had indicated that the investment would be unproductive if the minds of the pupils were unreceptive through the malnutrition of their bodies. As we have already seen, however, evidence of quite another kind, relating to the health of the adult population, was rousing the public to a recognition of the importance of maintaining the health and strength of those who could not so maintain themselves. To the fear that money spent on educating the underfed was money wasted, there was added another and more profound fear that to neglect the physical welfare of the young was to undermine and positively endanger the political and economic security of the nation – a fear that consciousness of a diminishing birth-rate and continuing high infant mortality rate only increased. It was this latter concern which weighed so heavily on the public mind and which led to the acceptance of a basic theory of prevention; that the state as a whole was responsible for, as it benefited from, the health and efficiency of each of its members and not least its weakest and most helpless members, children. It was this concern, above all, which in the early twentieth century, prompted the provision of social services to reduce the amount of sickness and neglect.[2] Among these measures were the permissive power of the local education authorities to feed children at school, granted in 1906,

[1] p. 837.
[2] Cf. McCleary, op. cit., pp. 4–5.

and the duty laid upon them the following year to provide for the medical inspection of all children attending public elementary schools, while the preservation of infant life and health was safeguarded by requiring the notification of all births to the local Medical Officer of Health, in addition to their registration, in order that the skilled advice and help of the health visitor might be available at the earliest and most crucial period. It was this concern also which made possible the extensive improvements for the health and benefit of children maintained in public institutions under the auspices of the Poor Law authorities, the prison authorities and authorities such as the Metropolitan Asylum Board.

This piecemeal but constructive legislation, early and tentative as it was, laid the foundation of the present welfare state. In so far as it affected children, it marked the re-emergence of a general social concern for children long lost in English society. It was a concern which, as in Tudor times, represented a blend of humanitarianism and self-interest. Between sixteenth- and twentieth-century provision for the child, however, there were fundamental, qualitative differences. The range of legislation discussed in this chapter reflects a growing understanding and appreciation of the necessary conditions for human life, health and happiness based on scientific knowledge denied to our forbears. But, even more important, it also represents a belief, incomprehensible to earlier generations, that children are citizens who have social rights independent of their parents, rights which the State has a duty to protect. It is the public emphasis placed on these rights by the 1908 Children Act which makes it so very different from sixteenth-century legislation and justifies its description, the 'Children's Charter'.

XXI

❖◇❖◇❖◇❖◇❖◇❖◇❖◇❖◇❖◇❖◇❖◇❖◇❖◇❖◇❖◇❖◇❖◇❖◇❖◇❖

'Children of the State'

❖◇❖◇❖◇❖◇❖◇❖◇❖◇❖◇❖◇❖◇❖◇❖◇❖◇❖◇❖◇❖◇❖◇❖◇❖◇❖

THE experience of the generation between the passing of the 'Children's Charter' of 1908 and the Children Act of 1948 was to underline certain deficiencies in the one which called for remedy in the other. Even as the earlier statute was being drafted, it was already being argued that the welfare and protection of the child was not fully guaranteed by a system of administration in which it was not only possible for the work of one government department to overlap the work of another, but actually to duplicate it.[1] Further, some years of operating a system of boarding out had already prompted the Local Government Board and its inspectors to call attention to the fact that not even a technically coherent administration could operate effectively without adequate and properly trained staff to support, maintain and supervise it.[2] Strongly though these issues were being pressed in the early years of the present century, and urgently as the Minority Report of the 1905–9 Poor Law Commission advocated both the need for a rationalisation of children's services, and the recruitment and training of adequate personnel to staff them, little if anything was done until appalling evidence produced by Lady Allen of Hurtwood in 1944, and the tragic death of a young boy, in 1945, roused widespread public concern

---

[1] Cf. above chapter XVII, p. 496.
[2] Cf. above, p. 532.

that, in the mid-twentieth century, children in public 'care' could still be at considerable risk.

It is important to look once more at the report of the committee set up as a consequence, the Curtis Committee, since its findings brought new emphasis to the urgency of finding some practical solution to the defects inherent in the piecemeal provision of public care for children, which had been inherited from the nineteenth century.

Early in their Report, the Committee drew attention to the almost unbelievably complicated administrative and statutory arrangements for the care of deprived children in this country:[1]

> Responsibility for providing or supervising the substitute home for the deprived child may be taken by the State, by local authorities, by voluntary organisations, or by private persons. The State through the Ministry of Health supervises the work of local authorities in caring for destitute children under the Poor Law. Such children may, however, be accepted by voluntary Homes independent of any public authority, in which case, if the voluntary organisations concerned receive subscriptions from the public, the State, through the Home Office, brings them under inspection; or it may do so through the Ministry of Health if that Department 'certifies' the Homes as suitable for Poor Law children or if Poor Law children are received in them. If the voluntary organisations receive no public subscriptions, and do not take in Poor Law children, their Homes may, if they take children under 9 years of age 'for reward', be visited by the welfare authority's child protection visitors; otherwise they come under no public supervision at all. Children under 9 years of age 'fostered' for reward, or placed by private persons (not the parents or guardians) for adoption, are supervised by local authorities under the direction of the Ministry of Health through the child life protection service. Those over 9 received for reward and those for whose maintenance no reward is given are not the care of any public authority. Children removed from their homes by order of a Juvenile Court may, if 'committed to', and accepted by the local authority as a 'fit person', be entitled to full parental care and guardianship from the authority; normally this responsibility is exercised by boarding the children out under the rules laid down by the Home Office, but if there is difficulty in finding a foster home the child may be left in a public assistance institution, in which case the Ministry of Health is concerned. Other children removed from

[1] Paras 98 & 99.

their homes by Court order may be in approved schools for remedial training or in remand homes awaiting the decision of the Court, in which case, though the local authority (or voluntary organisation) may provide the institution, the Home Office is directly and closely concerned with its management . . . The groups of children we have enumerated are assumed to be physically and mentally normal. Then there are the mentally disordered, or mentally defective and ineducable, who should be in local authority or voluntary institutions inspected by the Board of Control; the retarded and educationally handicapped, and the physically defective, also divided between local authority and voluntary establishments, and inspected by the Ministry of Education.

It will be observed that not only does the responsible department vary, but so does the closeness of State direction and control. In some cases, e.g. the 'fostered' children, it is remote. At the other end of the scale there are the war orphans, in whose case it is immediate. Between the two there are several shades of difference. With local authorities, too, the degree of responsibility may vary. The care of destitute children under the Poor Law is laid upon them clearly by statute; but when children are removed from their homes as in need of care or protection it is open to the authority to refuse to accept the charge of them. There are reasons, historical and other, for these differences, and some of them are good, and correspond to a genuine difference in circumstances. But it would not be difficult to find children similar in type and circumstance whose treatment has been quite different merely because they have been dealt with by different departments under different statutes.

To read this analysis of administrative confusion is to be reminded of the strikingly similar analysis of the administrative arrangements for the care of children forty years earlier, contained in the Minority Report of the Poor Law Commission. Equally startling to those familiar with the Majority Report of this Commission, is the description given by the Curtis Committee of the nursery of one of the public assistance institutions ('workhouses') they visited. In feeling and detail it is a description almost identical with the description of a workhouse nursery[1] given by one of the Poor Law Commission's own investigators:[2]

In one workhouse the Matron had made a valiant attempt to gather

[1] Cf. above chapter XVII, pp. 536-7.
[2] Report of the Care of Children Committee, para. 143.

the children together in the most difficult circumstances. She had to use the institution kitchen as a dining room for the toddlers. We saw them just after the tables had been cleared at dinner time. Most of them had folded their arms on the table and were asleep, with their heads on their hands, while their feet swung aimlessly from a too high wooden bench. The kitchen fire provided warmth and comfort; compared with the cheerless and bare day room they were better off in the warm kitchen. They had large chipped enamel mugs to drink from, such as were familiar at one time in casual wards; we were told that casual wards are now supplied with crockery. At this institution the 'mother' in charge of the children was a harassed looking woman doing her best in difficult circumstances.

It was as well that the Curtis Committee were able to report that such nursery conditions were not typical, since they found the standard of institutional care of older children 'much below the nursery standard'. In particular, they drew attention to the continued presence in the workhouses, sometimes for periods far longer than the six weeks laid down in the Poor Law Institution Order of 1913, of children of over three years of age. In some badly bombed areas, this had been made necessary through lack of more suitable, alternative accommodation. But in others it had become necessary through local inertia, both official and unofficial:[1]

> It was clear that . . . the workhouse served as a dumping ground for children who could not readily be disposed of elsewhere, and . . . in some districts . . . where children's Homes provided insufficient accommodation, or boarding out had not been well developed, older children, for whom there had never been properly planned accommodation, were looked after in the workhouse for a considerable length of time.

Since for many years successive central Poor Law authorities had declared the workhouse a wholly unsuitable place in which to provide indoor relief for healthy children except for the briefest time, the fact that some local authorities had failed to pursue an active policy of ensuring that this could only happen in the rarest of cases was very properly held by the Curtis Committee to be in itself lamentable. To many who read and commented on their Report, however, the conditions and the quality of care provided in the workhouses were even more

[1] ibid., para. 138.

lamentable. More than a century after poor law inspectors and private philanthropists had started to rouse the public conscience regarding the deplorable conditions of child care in the workhouses of their own day, a hitherto largely complacent public now read in the national press of instances where the declared policy of the 1834 Poor Law Act, of providing workhouse accommodation in which children could be segregated from the adult and infirm inmates, had not been fulfilled: and of cases where, because of shortage of suitable staff, 'children were being minded by aged inmates and cleaners, or were simply placed in a ward with senile old men or women to be looked after by the nurse on duty'.[1]

In no uncertain terms, the Curtis Report drew out the consequences of administrative chaos combined with public chaos:[2]

Many of the institutions served not only for 'reception' (i.e. cleansing and emergency care), and for hospital treatment for children over the age of 3, but also provided for healthy children received under 'place of safety' orders, as defective, or simply on the order of the relieving officer as destitute. They were sometimes admitted as children in need of care or protection, pending their appearance in Court, or awaiting placement after their committal to the care of the local authority as a 'fit person'; some of them were awaiting board-out or placement in a children's Home, or they had been brought back from either place for a change of plan when for some reason the arrangement made for them had broken down.

An example of this kind of motley collection was found in one century-old Poor Law institution providing accommodation for 170 adults, including ordinary workhouse accommodation, an infirmary for senile old people and a few men and women certified as either mentally defective or mentally disordered. In this institution there are twenty-seven children, aged six months to fifteen years. Twelve infants up to the age of eighteen months were the children of women in the institution, about half of them still being nursed by their mothers. In the same room in which these children were being cared for was a Mongol idiot, aged four, of gross appearance, for whom there was apparently no accommodation elsewhere. A family of five normal children, aged about six to fifteen, who had been admitted on a relieving officer's order, had been in the institution for ten weeks. This family, including a boy of ten and a girl of fifteen, were

[1] ibid.
[2] ibid., paras 139–40.

sleeping in the same room as a three year old hydrocephalic idiot, of very unsightly type, whose bed was screened off in the corner. The fifteen year old girl had been employed in the day-time dusting the women's infirmary ward. These children had been admitted in the middle of the night when their mother had left them under a hedge after eviction from their house. No plan appeared to have been made for them. Another family of three children, aged eight to twelve, were sleeping with the toddlers in the 'nursery' part of the building. They had been brought into the institution on a 'place of safety' order. We were told in the education and public assistance offices that their case was shortly to be considered with a view to further action, but they had already been in the workhouse for four months. We were told in another county that in some of the institutions of this area there was nowhere to put the older children to sleep except in the adult wards. Children had occasionally been sent back to the homes in which they had been neglected because it was thought better for them than the conditions under which they would have had to be cared for in the workhouse.

Comparison with the voluntary Homes, which provided for a large proportion of the children with whom the Committee were concerned, was not invariably to the advantage of the latter except that they, unlike the workhouses, had been specifically opened to receive only children.[1]

In type the Homes were of much the same kinds as are described under Public Assistance Homes. There were a large number of institutional Homes of the 'barrack' variety often with imposing buildings, built as a symbol of Victorian philanthropy and intended to catch the eye and to impress the passer by. In these Homes the rooms were often bare and comfortless, and so large that it was usually impossible to set aside any place for quiet occupations or hobbies. As voluntary effort became allied with modern ideas on child care more Homes were built in the style of Grouped Cottage Homes. While the cottages are not as small in size as the more enlightened societies would like, they do represent in their smaller groups and individual houses and grounds a very great advance upon the institutional home. Probably the bulk of the voluntary Homes visited fell into the Single Home group. These may be Homes established by a large organisation with central administration or Homes run by local committees, and they varied in size from Homes for 50 to Homes for 8. We came across no examples of voluntary Homes equivalent to Local Authority 'Scattered Homes', though in

[1] ibid., para. 230.

L

a number of cases small single Homes in a row of houses of the same size and type were seen. Finally one or two of the large organisations had instituted a system of boarding out, in some cases only for babies, in others for the whole period of childhood.

For the voluntary organisations, almost as much as for the public institutions, the fundamental difficulty of providing accommodation for the children in which they could be brought up in groups small enough to allow personal attention to their individual needs was the inadequacy of finance. 'Much as many would like to move or build, their chances of getting rid of premises are slight and funds do not allow the purchase of more modern buildings.'[1] On the other hand, simply because they were privately financed, the considerable funds donated to some, usually the larger, societies, had enabled them to acquire or build Homes for the children in their care of a standard far superior to any workhouse. A description of one of the voluntary Homes visited by members of the Committee illustrates this very clearly:[2]

This is a large private dwelling, the oldest part of which is about 200 years old. There is a large garden, with beautiful trees, and the farm, at present let off, is part of the estate. In spite of the scale of the house, it has proved unusually adaptable for its purpose. The living rooms provide three good play-rooms – one used for toddlers (with lavatory and wash-basin adjoining, and good large low cupboards and shelves), one for boys, if they want to play separately, and one large pleasant room which can be used by all the older children. This room with wide windows over-looking the garden, has one wall lined with ample glass fronted book-cases and individual curtain-covered shelves below. There is plenty of room here for round games or for dancing. The few older girls also have a low ceilinged store room kept entirely for dolls play, surrounded by cupboards, decorated with toy tea sets, and full of dolls and prams and all the material for family play. This room is regarded as strictly their one and grown-ups only come in by invitation. In addition there is a squash court in the grounds which provides excellent space for romping play and for dramatics which can be watched from a little gallery. The sleeping rooms divide up well for different age groups, the largest containing about twelve beds, being used for older boys, and the three others, containing about

[1] ibid., para. 233.
[2] ibid., para. 235 (2).

eight beds, for girls and toddlers. The dining room has French windows opening on to a verandah. The children sit at tables for about six, the staff scattered round with them. The tables are attractively arranged with bright American cloth and flowers.

American cloth and flowers, as the Committee were well aware, do not by themselves make an institution a 'home' in the full sense of that word, and whatever their strictures on standards of building and accommodation, their final judgment on the adequacy of residential accommodation provided for the deprived child rested on the quality of the personal care and attention that was given in them. It was the poverty of this, far more than the poverty of the material surroundings in which so many children were being brought up, that so much disturbed them:[1]

By far the greater number of Homes were, within the limits of their staffing, accommodation and administrative arrangements, reasonably well run from the standpoint of physical care, and in other ways the child has more material advantages than could have been given to him in the average poor family. Where establishments fell below a satisfactory standard, the defects were not of harshness, but rather of dirt and dreariness, drabness and over-regimentation. We found no child being cruelly used in the ordinary sense, but that was perhaps not a probable discovery on a casual visit. We did find many establishments under both local authority and voluntary management in which children were being brought up by unimaginative methods, without opportunity for developing their full capabilities and with very little brightness or interest in their surroundings. We found in fact many places where the standard of child care was no better, except in respect of disciplinary methods, than that of say 30 years ago; and we found a widespread and deplorable shortage of the right kind of staff, personally qualified and trained to provide the child with a substitute for a home background. The result in many Homes was a lack of personal interest in and affection for the children which we found shocking. The child in these Homes was not recognised as an individual with his own rights and possessions, his own life to live and his own contribution to offer. He was merely one of a large crowd, eating, playing and sleeping with the rest, without any place or possession of his own or any quiet room to which he could retreat. Still more important, he was without the feeling that there was anyone to whom he could turn who was vitally interested in his welfare or who cared for him as a person. The effect

[1] ibid., para. 418.

of this on the smaller children was reflected in their behaviour towards visitors, which took the form of an almost pathological clamouring for attention and petting. In the older children the effect appeared more in slowness, backwardness and lack of response, and in habits of destructiveness and want of concentration. Where individual love and care had been given, the behaviour of the children was quite different. They showed no undue interest in visitors and were easily and happily engaged in their own occupations and games.

Given the inherited buildings which made housing in family-size groups virtually impossible; the inadequacy of either public or private finance to provide more suitable accommodation; given the lack of staff adequate both in numbers and in qualification to the task of compensating deprived children for the lack of normal home care, it was inevitable that the Committee should express a preference for those two methods of provision – adoption and boarding out – which offered homes, not Homes, to such children. Regarding both, they had reservations, but they believed that with closer supervision under an integrated system of administration for all child care, either system offered a child a better substitute for his own home than most of the existing residential establishments. 'We found in the children in the foster homes almost complete freedom from the sense of deprivation we have described among children in the Homes. ... On the whole our judgment is that there is probably a greater risk of acute unhappiness in a foster home, but that a foster home is happier than life as generally lived in a large community.'[1]

So urgent had they felt the need for attention to be paid to the recruitment and training of staff, that the Interdepartmental Committee had issued an interim report in March 1946 in which they recommended the formation of a Central Training Council in Child Care, and the provision of special courses in training.[2] In September of the same year, they published their final report in which they proposed radical revision of the administrative organisation of services for the deprived child. The Committee was convinced that the divided responsibility at local and central levels was bedevilling existing administration, and called for a

[1] ibid., para. 422.
[2] Cmd 6760.

sureness and clarity of direction and insight impossible within the muddled framework of inherited legislation. They thus aimed at recasting the whole machinery of administration and care. At the central government level, the relevant powers under the Poor Law Act, Children and Young Persons Act, Public Health Acts, and Adoption of Children Act were to be concentrated in one department, which would be responsible for the care of deprived children, defining and maintaining standards by direction, inspection and acting as a clearing house for progressive ideas. The actual provision for the deprived child should lie with the voluntary organisations and the local authority, aided by exchequer grants, the local authorities having immediate responsibility and working through a single *ad hoc* committee with specialist executives to be known as Children's Officers.

The publication of the Curtis Report received a great deal of publicity in which, although they themselves had been careful in no way to exaggerate, the conditions in some of the worst children's homes became the focus of a number of dramatic articles and anxious letters to the press from all quarters. So much was this the case that, within a very short space of time, there was a call for a more balanced approach to the evidence and a clearer appreciation of the fundamental importance of the apparently less sensational, yet nevertheless radical, proposals made by the Committee regarding staffing and reorganisation. 'The truth is that there is a great deal of unnecessary agitation about the Curtis Report,' commented *The Economist* tartly. 'The Committee found a few very black spots. It also found and gave equal prominence to some very good examples of children's homes, which commentators on the report have tended to ignore.'[1] The fact remains, however, that it had taken a public scandal to prompt the Government to appoint a committee of enquiry into the operation of child care in this country, and the public 'agitation' which the publication of its Report aroused made it impossible for that Government not to act on its recommendations. The post-war society of the mid-twentieth century to which Miss Curtis addressed herself, unlike the pre-First World War England which Mrs Webb had tried to arouse, had become sensitive to the emotional needs of children; to their

[1] 'Commonsense on Curtis', *The Economist*, vol. CLI, p. 866.

right to the care and protection of a normal home; and to the responsibility of society to secure, by one means or another, the proper conditions under which these needs and rights might be met. That society had failed in its responsibilities to however few of its weakest members became a political issue of major importance. An article on 'Helpless Children', published in the *Spectator* a month after the Curtis Report had been circulated, illustrates this point very well:[1]

> The Report of the Child Care Committee, presided over by Miss Myra Curtis, is almost as valuable for the light it casts on the deplorable conditions under which homeless children are maintained in some public institutions as for the specific proposals it makes for remedying evils that stand urgently in need of remedy. It must not be supposed that all institutions are as bad as some of those described in detail in this Report, but the manifestly and uncontestably bad are obviously numerous enough to raise a very pointed question. Why did the thousands of persons who must have been thoroughly familiar with these conditions and could perfectly easily have called public attention to them never do so? Now the Curtis Committee has let in the light of day and sweeping changes must inevitably result.

What resulted was the Children Act of 1948,[2] which provided for a unified system of child care, under the authority of one ministry and staffed by trained social workers. 'For the first time in our history, men and women with theoretical qualifications in social science and practical experience in social case-work were appointed, as a national policy, to key positions in the social services.'[3]

When the Curtis Committee recommended that the central authority for deprived children should be vested in a single government department, they did not suggest which one this should be. In fact, the practical choice lay between the Ministry of Health, the Ministry of Education and the Home Office. The Ministry of Health, however, was heavily burdened by the post-war housing programme and the administration of the recently inaugurated National Health Service. The Ministry of Education, although *prima facie* the more appropriate of the

---

[1] *Spectator*, 18 October 1946.
[2] 11 & 12 Geo. VI, c. 43.
[3] Heywood, *Children in Care*, p. 154.

other two possible choices since it was the one Ministry concerned exclusively with children, was already engaged in the administration of the 1944 Education Act. Moreover, the *Spectator* argued:

> It is completely wrong to think of a child's life as a whole. The child lives in two worlds, the world of home and the world of school. One is a complement to the other, and it is most important that they be kept separate. Home is a background and a shelter, a place to which school troubles can be taken and in which a completely different atmosphere from the school atmosphere prevails. There is really everything to be said for making the Home Office responsible for the substitute homelife which is the best the deprived child can hope for, and for letting it go from that to the local school, where the Ministry of Education is, of course, through the local authority, supreme.

It was the further argument advanced by the *Spectator* which eventually determined that the Home Office, not the Ministry of Education, should be the central authority responsible for the new children's services. 'Ever since Lord Samuel's Act of 1908 was passed into law, the Home Office had had a Children's Branch conspicuous for its humanity and sympathy, dealing not (as is commonly supposed) with delinquents only, but with large numbers removed for no fault in themselves, from bad homes and neglectful parents.'[1]

Under the supervision of the Home Office, local authorities now had an inescapable duty to receive into care, as a voluntary measure, children whose parents were temporarily or permanently unfit or unable to care for them, and to carry out the duties laid on the local authority by earlier child protection measures which were not repealed. Thus they had to supervise, under child-life protection provisions, children maintained for reward; to register adoption societies and supervise direct third party placings for adoption; to provide the magistrates with information about the background of children appearing before the courts, and to be responsible for the care of children sent to remand homes or committed by the courts to the local authorities as fit persons, or to approved schools.

At the immediate level of impact with the child, the responsibility for reception and care was laid squarely on the local

[1] 'The Government and the Child', *Spectator*, 22 November 1946.

authorities, the councils of counties or county boroughs with their specially constituted Children's Committees and specialist Children's Officers. For the first time, voluntary organisations became properly integrated into the field of child care. Every voluntary home had now to be registered at the Home Office and a new and stricter control was imposed. Grants could now be made by the Home Secretary towards making improvements in the premises and equipment of voluntary homes, and to assist with the provision of better qualified staff. Local authorities, too, were enabled to make contributions to any voluntary organisations whose object was to promote the welfare of children. Working under the same central control and subject to the Home Office, the voluntary organisations continued to play an important part in child welfare, and had the power, based on independent income, to go beyond the statutory legal provisions and, where they found a need unsatisfied, devise a means of care.

By these means, the alliance of local and voluntary initiative and statutory organisation and support, introduced in England in the sixteenth century, was revived in the twentieth. The old central supervision which the Privy Council had once exercised over the limited area of the relief of the poor child was now assumed by perhaps the strongest and most powerful of the central departments of Parliamentary government, whose area of responsibility was extended to the care of all children in need, irrespective of their parents' wealth. It was a responsibility the better exercised by the recognition of the need to train and develop special skills relevant to the task.

The Children Act of 1948 was not, of course, the old Poor Law for children re-interpreted. Nor was it an isolated piece of legislation in which the whole of contemporary concern for the welfare of children was expressed in the provisions of a single statute. It was the last in a series of post-war statutes – of which the Education Act of 1944 was the first – whose purpose was to guarantee the necessary social and economic conditions in which young and old alike might find fulfilment in the society of their birth, irrespective of rank, privilege, or wealth. The aim of the Education Act was to secure the principle of equality of educational opportunity for everyone. The Family Allowances Act, the National Insurance Act, the National Health Service Act and the National Assistance Act, all passed within the next four years, were conceived as means of supporting and strengthening not merely the individual, but the individual within his own family. Indeed, taken together, they represented a 'family charter', which strengthened and supported the family as never before.

It was a type of family in which children, once a financial asset, had become a liability. Factory legislation, dating from the early nineteenth century and becoming progressively more extensive and effective after the 1850s, had protected children from exploitation, but had not been associated with any schemes to enable their parents to make up for the loss of their wages. Hence some of the opposition and evasion by working-class parents to which factory inspectors time and again refer. After 1870 compulsory education – even when it became free – made an even greater impact on the working-class family by requiring the complete dependence of children for an increasing number of years. The Education Act of 1944 raised the school-leaving age to fifteen without exception. Only a hundred years earlier, children of half that age, and less, were regularly employed for twelve hours a day, contributing their earnings to the family purse. In effect, nineteenth-century legislation gradually imposed on the working-class family a pattern of child-dependence which the middle and upper classes had developed several generations before. Unfortunately, it was a luxury which not all could afford. Seebohm Rowntree, in his investigation of the causes of poverty at the opening of the present century, showed that, in the families of lower paid wage groups, young children were a very significant cause of poverty. The welfare legislation of the 1940s was a determined attempt to prevent them being so.

In the meanwhile working-class parents had increasingly adopted the techniques of family limitation to which the middle and upper classes had already resorted as a means of controlling family expenditure. For, if working-class parents found their financial resources depleted by restriction on their children's employment, the upper classes had become well aware of the demands on their own incomes made by the need, on the one hand, to educate and train their sons to enter occupations increasingly recruited by examination and merit, and on the other to maintain their daughters in that state of idleness which testified to the affluence of their parents. The result has been a considerable decrease in the effective size of the family in this country over a considerable number of years. The average number of children in the family in mid-Victorian times was between five and seven. In the mid-twentieth century it was just over two.[1]

As has been shown, both the decline in the birth-rate and the diminution of family size prompted a greater concern for the protection of the lives of those born than had been known in previous generations.[2] At the same time a concern, stemming from fears for the national economy rather than advanced ideas of social democracy, was growing in other quarters regarding a rather different kind of neglect – the neglect of the basic education of the majority of children in this country. Pre-industrial England had relied on the inculcation and application of long-established, largely unvarying, techniques of production. The newly factorised industries, competing now for world, not regional, markets, required a different type of labour force in which the intelligent use of rapidly changing industrial techniques was a *sine qua non*. Just as, in the sixteenth century, Burghley had perceived the need for mental rather than physical agility among those born to rule, so then, in the nineteenth century, men like Forster appreciated the necessity of cultivating intelligence among the labouring classes, rather than acquiescing in their continuing illiteracy. The difficulty which some, including reformers like Shaftesbury, quite rightly saw in such a policy was how to educate for work without encouraging to rule.

The tale of how a third-class system of education was devised for those considered third-class citizens has been well described elsewhere. Surely and inexorably, a gradually better educated working-class pressed for a system of education which was national in something more than name. A system whereby, in a society in which, more than at any other time of our history, knowledge was indeed becoming power, they themselves might have a significant role. Two world wars, in which barriers of class were lowered by the need for national defence, precipitated discussions of social equality and opportunity, and so habituated

---

[1] Cf. the *Registrar General's Statistical Review*, 1961, part III, commentary, table XLIII, p. 70.

[2] Cf. above, chapters XVIII and XIX.

men's minds to the possibility of their attainment that, by the end of the second war, political differences were differences of means rather than ends. In the field of education, what had traditionally been the privilege of the few now became the right of the masses. Of course it is true that the 1944 Education Act failed to secure for working-class children the proportion of places in grammar schools and universities which their numbers in the population would, on political grounds at least, have justified. On the other hand, only the most cynical would maintain that the greater proportion of middle-class children in either was a result of political intrigue, not sociological pressure.

In fact, far from being a superbly disguised manoeuvre to maintain a distinction between the working and middle classes, the Education Act and the other welfare legislation of the 1940s were together to impose middle-class values on the working class and thereby reinforce the tendency for class differences of family structure to diminish. Writing some years ago, Professor Titmuss queried whether this was as socially desirable as it had become politically expedient.[1] Yet, even without the growing egalitarianism of the present century it is difficult to see how things could have been otherwise. The social reformers of the nineteenth-century were predominantly middle-class men and women who judged working-class conditions by their own, middle-class standards. The reforms they devised were a cautious attempt within the limits of their political outlook – rarely egalitarian – to make it possible for the working-class family to adopt a pattern, though not a standard, of life not so offensively different from their own. The introduction of professionalism and professional standards into the social services which later

---

[1] Cf. 'The Family as a Social Institution', published in the *Report of the British National Conference on Social Work*, 1953, p. 9:

Conflicts between mothers' ways and one's own self-made ways, conflicts between the experts' ways and one's own self-willed ways, conflicts between behavioural norms of another social class imposed by the authority of the expert and the norms permitted by one's own environment; all these may disturb a mother's trust in her self . . .

The critical problem for all those who come into contact with families is that intervention to make parenthood a more self-conscious affair invokes the risk of undermining the natural self-confidence of mothers and fathers. In a community still highly stratified, still saturated by class thinking, these risks are considerable. In the pursuit of what is called 'higher standards of child care', there is the danger of assuming that the norms of one social class are relevant to the needs of another.

developed from their work resulted in even the standard becoming approximated, since it is the nature of professional ethics that men and women should be advised irrespective of class or creed.

It has been fashionable to assert that the development of social services, originally conceived as supporting the family, have in fact enfeebled it as a social institution. Of this, a number of things might be said. First, such sociological and socio-anthropological studies as have been made of working-class families, precisely those families which the social services are intended most to assist in their functions of socialisation and support, have all demonstrated their continuing and extraordinary effectiveness as social units.[1] Second, by increasing the period of child dependence and requiring universally higher standards of child care than have previously been known in this country, the family has actually had increased burdens and responsibilities thrust upon it. Third, far from readily assuming the functions of the family and relieving it of its responsibilities, the new legislation insists that only in extreme cases should the agencies of the state act as a substitute for a child's natural family. Unlike Tudor legislation, which permitted and indeed encouraged a disregard for family ties in its provision for the poor child, twentieth-century statute laid on the local authorities a duty to restore those received into care to their own natural homes. Section I (3) of the Children Act, 1948, stipulates:

> Nothing in this section shall authorise a local authority to keep a child in their care under this section if any parent or guardian desires to take over the care of the child, and the local authority shall in all cases where it appears to them consistent with the welfare of the child so to do, endeavour to secure that the care of the child is taken over either –
> (a) by a parent or guardian of his, or
> (b) by a relative of his, being, wherever possible, a person of the same religious persuasion.

Regard for individual conscience had never been a characteristic of Tudor practice, but the importance which they attached

---

[1] Cf. E. Bott, *Family and Social Network*, 1957; R. Firth, *Family and Kinship in Industrial Society*, Sociological Review Monograph no. 8, October 1964; M. Kerr, *The People of Ship Street*, 1958; P. Marris, *Widows and Their Families*, 1958; P. Townsend, *The Family Life of Old People*, 1958.

to religious and moral education continued, uninterrupted, through successive generations and found its expression in the 1944 Education Act which, for the first time since the introduction of compulsory education in this country, made religious instruction and a regular act of worship a compulsory provision in all State schools. Here again, however, individual conscience was protected by the so-called 'withdrawal' clause which gave parents the right to decline to allow their children to attend either religious instruction or the daily act of worship. The motives for including the 'religious clause' in the 1944 Act varied a good deal among its supporters. Certainly the terms of the Act, by requiring a daily act of worship but, with certain exceptions largely referring to Church schools, forbidding that it should take place in a church, was meant to convey the difference which Parliament saw between religious instruction and religious indoctrination. If, however, unlike Lord Burghley, Lord Butler declined to limit the religious instruction of the young to instruction in the tenets of one Church, the Church of England, there is little doubt that his reason for including a compulsory religious clause in his Act was a firm conviction that it was the business of schools to teach concepts of right behaviour, and that these were best conveyed in the traditional context of religious instruction.

If the new Education Act incorporated an idea of moral education with which the Tudors would not have been unfamiliar, so too it reinstated a concept of education 'according to aptitude and ability' on which some Tudor institutions, such as Christ's Hospital, had been founded. Albeit on a far smaller scale than in the mid-twentieth century, Tudor England was not without an 'educational ladder' up which the poor child might climb to the highest offices of Church and State.

So also, in their own idiom, had Tudor legislators constructed a form of 'children's service' in which it was laid down as a social duty that children in need had to be offered not merely shelter, but a training which would enable them to become self-supporting and self-respecting members of the commonweal. It is sometimes said that men can learn little from history. Certainly, the constant repetition of similar situations of crisis and tragedy in successive generations which this study traced enforces the idea that men often do learn little from history. It can only be hoped that, by studies such as this, modern students of social development will be disabused of the idea that earlier generations contributed nothing from which we ourselves might learn if we choose.

Bibliography

Official publications and reports

Select Committee on the State of Mendicity in the Metropolis, First Report, *PP*, 1814–15, III; Second Report, *PP*, 1816, V.

Report of the House of Lords on Transportation, *PP*, 1826, IV.

Report of the Select Committee on Criminal Commitments and Convictions, *PP*, 1828, VI.

Report from the Select Committee on the Police of the Metropolis, *PP*, 1928, VI.

Report from the Commissioners on the Administration and Practical Operation of the Poor Laws, *PP*, 1834, XXXVI.

First Annual Report of the Poor Law Commission, *PP*, 1835, XXXV.

Second Annual Report of the Poor Law Commission, *PP*, 1836, XXIX.

Third Annual Report of the Poor Law Commission, *PP*, 1837, XXXI.

Third Report from the Commissioners on Criminal Law, *PP*, 1837, XXXI.

Fourth Annual Report of the Poor Law Commission, *PP*, 1838, XXVIII.

Fifth Annual Report of the Poor Law Commission, *PP*, 1839, XX.

Report from the Governor of the Cape of Good Hope to the Secretary of the Colonies relative to the Condition and Treatment of Children sent out by the Children's Friend Society, *PP*, 1840, XXXIII.

Half-yearly Reports of Factory Inspectors, *PP*, 1840, XXIV and *PP*, 1864, XXII.

Sixth Annual Report of the Poor Law Commission, *PP*, 1841, XI.

Second Report from the Select Committee of the House of Lords appointed to inquire into the Execution of the Criminal Law, especially respecting Juvenile Offenders and Transportation, *PP*, 1847, VII.

General Board of Health, Report on Quarantine, *PP*, 1849, XXIV.

Second Report of the Inspector of Reformatory Schools, *PP*, 1859, XIII, pt II.

Second Report of the Select Committee on Poor Relief, *PP*, 1861, IX.

Fourth Report of the Medical Officer of the Privy Council, *PP*, 1862, XXII.

Third Annual Report of the Local Government Board, *PP*, 1874, XXV.

Fourth Annual Report of the Local Government Board, *PP*, 1875, XXXI.

Report of Andrew Doyle to the President of the Local Government Board on the Emigration of Pauper Children to Canada, *PP*, 1875, LXIII.

Report of the Reformatory and Industrial Schools Commission, *PP*, 1884, XLV.

Eighteenth Annual Report of the Local Government Board, *PP*, 1889, XXXV.

Report of the Departmental Committee on the Education and Maintenance of Pauper Children in the Metropolis, *PP*, 1896, XLIII, pt I.

Report of the Royal Commission on the Poor Laws and the Relief of Distress. Majority Report, *PP*, 1909, XXXVIII, pt I; Minority Report, *PP*, 1909, XXXVIII, pt II.

Report of the Child Adoption Committee, Cmd 1254. 1921.

Report of the Departmental Committee on Adoption Societies and Agencies, Cmd 5499. 1936–7.

Annual Report of the Ministry of Health, *PP*, 1937–8, XI.

Report of the Interdepartmental Committee on the Care of Children, Cmd 6922. 1945–6.

Registrar General's Statistical Review, 1961, pt III.

Publications and reports of societies

First Report of the Philanthropic Society, 1789.

Second Report of the Philanthropic Society, 1789.

An Address to the Public from the Philanthropic Society, 1790.

Reports of the Society for bettering the condition of the poor, 1802, I and III; 1803, IV.

Report of the Committee of the Society for Investigating the Causes of the Alarming Increase of Juvenile Delinquency in the Metropolis, 1816.

Report of the Committee of the Society for the Improvement of Prison Discipline and for the Reformation of Juvenile Offenders, 1818.

The Society for the Suppression of Juvenile Vagrancy. Report of the Hackney Wick School Sub-Committee, 1833.

Fifty Years Record of Child Saving and Reformatory Work (1856–1906), being the Jubilee Report of the Reformatory and Refuge Union.

CARLETON TUFNELL, 'The Education of Pauper Children', *Transactions of the National Association for the Promotion of Social Science [TNAPSS]*, 1862.

Report of the Conference of Managers of Reformatory and Industrial Institutions, 1869.

R. W. COOKE TAYLOR, 'What influence has the Employment of Mothers . . . on Infant Mortality?', *TNAPSS*, 1874.

Report of the Conference of Managers of Reformatory and Industrial Institutions, 1881.

Report of the Fifth Conference of the National Association of Certified and Industrial Schools, 1891.

The Power for the Children, being the Report for 1895–96 of the N.S.P.C.C.

Annual Reports of the Howard Association, 1896, 1897 and 1899.

Hansard debates – third series

1814, vol. XXVII, cols 929, 931.

1834, vol. XXIV, cols 528, 530, 536, 541.

1837–8, vol. XXXIX, cols 1083–5.

1838, vol. XLIV, cols 760, 766–7.

1839, vol. XLVIII, cols 159, 161, 549.

1839, vol. XLIX, col. 492.

1850, vol. CXI, cols. 433, 445, 452, 457.

1872, vol. CCLXXV, cols 1486, 1494.

1874, vol. CCLXXXVI, col. 813.

1886, vol. CCCVI, col. 3.

1889, vol. CCCXXXVII, cols 227, 229, 233, 951, 1365, 1371.

1893, vol. CCXV, col. 41.

1894, vol. XXIV, col. 1609.

1908, vol. CLXXXVI, col. 1251.

Nineteenth-century publications

An account of the Origin and Progress of the Society for the Promotion of Industry, in the Hundreds of Ongar and Harlow, and the Half Hundred of Waltham, in the County of Essex. 1797.

ARCHER HANNAH, *A Scheme for Befriending Orphan Pauper Girls.* 1861.

BOUYER R. G., *An Account of the Origin, Proceedings, and Intentions of the Society for the Promotion of Industry, in the Southern District of the Parts of Lindsey, in the County of Lincoln* (3rd ed.). 1789.

BRENTON E. P., *Observations on the Training and Education of the Children of Great Britain.* 1824.

BRENTON E. P., *The Bible and the Spade.* 1837.

BRENTON JAHLED, *Memoir of Captain Edward Pelham Brenton by his brother, Vice Admiral Sir Jahled Brenton, Bart.* 1842.

A Brief Exposure of the Most Immoral and Dangerous Tendency of a Bill affecting the Rights of Parents now under Consideration of Parliament, or, Summary of Reasons why this Bill, entitled 'Custody of Infants Bill', should not be allowed to become the Law of the Land. 1838.

BROWN JOHN, *A Memoir of Robert Blincoe.* 1832.

CAPPE CATHERINE, *An Account of Two Charity Schools for the Education of Girls.* 1800.

CARPENTER MARY, *Reformatory Schools for the Children of the Perishing and Dangerous Classes and for Juvenile Offenders.* 1851.

CLARKE HALL WILLIAM, *The Queen's Reign for Children.* 1897.

COBBETT WILLIAM, *Weekly Political Register.* 18 May 1816.

DAVENPORT HILL FLORENCE, *Children of the State.* 1868.

DAVENPORT HILL R. and F., *The Recorder of Birmingham: A Memoir of Matthew Davenport Hill.* 1878.

EDEN SIR FREDERICK MORTON, *The State of the Poor.* 1797.

FAWCETT HENRY, *Pauperism: Its Causes and Remedies.* 1871.

FRENCH, *Life of Crompton* (3rd ed.).

KAY-SHUTTLEWORTH SIR JAMES, *Four Periods of Public Education.* 1862.

NORTON CAROLINE, *English Law for Women, in the Nineteenth Century.* 1854.

NORTON CAROLINE, *The Natural Claim of a Mother to the Custody of her Child as Affected by the Common Law Rights of the Father and Illustrated by Cases of Peculiar Hardship.* 1837.

Separation of the Mother and Child by the Law of Custody of Infants Considered. 1837.

SHERWOOD MRS M. M. B., *The History of the Fairchild Family,* published in three parts from 1818 to 1847.

TALLACK WILLIAM, *Peter Bedford, the Spitalfields Philanthropist.* 1865.

TRIMMER SARAH, *The Oeconomy of Charity.* 1801.

TUCKWELL GERTRUDE, *The State and Its Children.* 1894.

WAUGH BENJAMIN, *The Gaol Cradle – Who Rocks It?* 1875.

Twentieth-century publications

ABBOTT G., *The State and the Child,* vols I and II. 1938.

BARNETT M. C., *Young Delinquents, A Study of Reformatory and Industrial Schools.* 1913.

BAYNE-POWELL R., *The English Child in the Eighteenth Century.* 1939.

BECK WILLIAM, *Peter Bedford, the Spitalfields Philanthropist.* 1903.

BIRT LILIAN M., *The Children's Home Finder.* 1913.

BOTT E., *Family and Social Network.* 1957.

CADBURY J., *Young Offenders.* 1938.

CARLEBACH J., *Caring for Children in Trouble.* 1970.

CLARKE HALL W., *The State and the Child.* 1917.

COHEN E., *English Social Services.* 1949.

FIRTH R., 'Family and Kinship in Industrial Society', *Sociological Review Monograph No. 8.* 1964.

FISHER LETTICE, *Twenty-one Years and After. The Story of the Council for the Unmarried Mother and her Child.* 1937.

FLETCHER R., *The Family and Marriage in Britain.* 1966.

GEORGE D., *England in Transition.* 1953.

GRAVESON R. H. and CRANE F. R., *A Century of Family Law.* 1957.

HEWITT MARGARET, *Wives and Mothers in Victorian Industry.* 1957.

HEYWOOD JEAN, *Children in Care.* 1959.

HOLMES H. T., *Reform of the Reformatories*, Fabian Tract no. III. 1906.

HOPKIRK M., *Nobody Wanted Sam.* 1949.

KERR M., *The People of Ship Street.* 1958.

LYND S., *English Children.* 1942.

MARRIS P., *Widows and Their Families.* 1958.

MCCLEARY G. F., *The Maternity and Child Welfare Movement.* 1935.

PINCHBECK IVY, *Women Workers and the Industrial Revolution 1750–1850.* 1930.

PINCHBECK IVY and HEWITT MARGARET, *Children in English Society*, vol I. 1969.

PLUMB J. H., *England in the Eighteenth Century (1714–1815).* 1950.

RATHBONE HERBERT (ed.), *Memoir of Kitty Wilkinson of Liverpool.* 1927.

RUSSELL C. E. B. and RIGBY L. M., *The Making of the Criminal.* 1906.

SCHOLES A. G., *Education for Empire Settlement.* 1932.

SPEILMAN M. A., *The Romance of Child Reformation: London Reformatory and Refuge Union.* 1921.

STRACHEY RAY, *The Cause.* 1928.

TOWNSEND P., *The Family Life of Old People.* 1958.

WEBB SIDNEY and BEATRICE, *English Poor Law Policy.* 1910.

Index

STUDIES IN SOCIAL HISTORY

Editor: *HAROLD PERKIN*

Professor of Social History, University of Lancaster

Assistant Editor: *ERIC J. EVANS*

Lecturer in History, University of Lancaster

◇◇